Witches, Werewolves, and Fairies

Witches, Werewolves, and fairies

Shapeshifters and Astral Doublers in the Middle Ages

Claude Lecouteux

Translated by Clare Frock

Inner Traditions
Rochester, Vermont

Inner Traditions
One Park Street
Rochester, Vermont 05767
www.InnerTraditions.com

First U.S. edition published by Inner Traditions in 2003
Originally published in French under the title *Fées, Sorcières et Loups-garous* by
Éditions Imago

Library of Congress Cataloging-in-Publication Data
Lecouteux, Claude.
Fées, sorcières et loups-garous au Moyen Age. English]
Witches, werewolves, and fairies : shapeshifters and astral doublers in the middle ages /
Claude Lecouteux ; translated by Clare Frock.— 1st U.S. ed.
    p. cm.
Includes bibliographical references and index.
  ISBN 0-89281-096-3 (pbk.)
1. Double (Parapsychology) 2. Werewolves. 3. Wizards. 4. Fairies.
I. Title.
  BF1045.D67L4313 2003
  133.1'4—dc21
                                    2003009563

Printed and bound in the United States at Lake Book Manufacturing, Inc.

10 9 8 7 6 5 4 3 2 1

Text design and layout by Mary Anne Hurhula
This book was typeset in Times with Sabon and Democratica as the display typefaces

Inner Traditions wishes to express its appreciation for assistance given by the government
of France through the Ministère de la Culture in the preparation of this translation.

Nous tenons à exprimer nos plus vifs remerciements au government de la France et le ministère de la Culture pour leur aide dans le préparation de cette traduction.

Contents

Foreword

I open my remarks with the paradoxical conclusion that, along with this remarkable study, we need to start reading the trilogy whose first two parts are called *Fantômes et Revenants au Moyen Âge* (Imago, 1986) and *Les Nains et les Elfes au Moyen Âge* (Imago, 1988). Claude Lecouteux spares no effort to show that our ancestors did not regard our concept of death with—as our distressing ultramodern notions would have it—such finality. In fact, if we go back to our culture's true sources, this notion is squarely refuted by all manner of ancient and medieval testimonies.

After decades of constant contact with ancient Scandinavian texts, I am still struck by the inanity of modern categories, dichotomies, and exclusions. This is not to say I give the brilliant comparative texts offered us by Claude Lecouteux (which are his peerless trademark) the power to veto opposing opinion, but they provide sufficient grounds to verify that this is a matter of something far different from simply the legacy of a unique culture. I will concede, given that we are told this repeatedly in this book, that our Old Norse sources, as Christianized as they may be, remain closer to a fundamental truth that has been slighted over the course of the centuries. This, of course, is what makes these testimonies valuable, as long as they are properly understood. Yet what clearly emerges out of their study is that their authors were simply incapable of drawing a clear line between this world and the hereafter, between "life" and "death."

This does not imply that they were indifferent to what must be called a change in condition or status, or that they did not conform to what is an obviated observation, that is, the *dauxi*, the "dead person," does not have the same type of reality as the *lifandi*, the "living person." But the distinction does not lead to a dramatic change in our ideas of *nothingness* or *non-being*, words for which Old Norse simply does not have adequate terms! There is a mentality in which a dead person can come along at any moment and adopt the shape of the living, the living can animate the deceased, and a surprising (for us) movement is established between the two realms. This is taken to such an extreme that we often cannot know, when we are reading a certain saga or text from the *Eddas*, in just which realm we are wandering. Is the Poetic Edda *Baldr's Dreams (Baldrsdraumar)* to be added deliberately to the purely oneiric category, as their title could suggest, or is it necessary, instead, to view this level as the only admissible one, and to see clearly that an ontology is captured here at its very source? For this poem's argument is not immaterial to the subject at hand: It is Odin himself who creates a woman seer so that she can tell him what happened to his son Baldur, who has recently died.

On the opposite end, we may ask if the impressive parade of ghosts in *Eyrbyggja saga (The Saga of Snorri the Godi)* is a gripping fabrication of a distant conventional theme that was taken from Latin hagiography (but then how did it happen that this was precisely the imagery that was retained?), or if it might go back to some homeless, nomadic archetype that takes us to the sources of the human condition.

For, as Claude Lecouteux repeatedly shows us, there is something derisory about our current pragmatism, realism, and materialism. There is something distressing in this absurd renunciation of what has been for so long the very material of our mental foundations. Let's be serious: Who among us, to paraphrase a quotation by André Malraux, would really accept nothingness and be happy with that? Who dares deny, in good anthropology and even in orthodox phenomenology, this life force (*livskraf, asu,* as it was said in Sanskrit, again something the Aesir, the Gods of the North, would borrow and turn to their own benefit) that justifies both our presence and the essential aspects of our behaviors? The utterly banal findings that each of us can make, *hic* and *nunc,* are absolutely counterproductive. What Teilhard de Chardin put so eloquently and substantially is that humanity is perfectly incapable of just going through the motions and sitting around idly when faced with the prospects of redemption that await it. And there is something precisely suicidal in the rages of negation that possess our technocratic millennium. It is still easy for us to find consolation by telling ourselves that the afore-mentioned furor affects only a fraction of humanity. For, as a Scandinavian—a modern one this time—has proclaimed, life goes on; in truth, Knut Hamsun says, "Life lives," *men livet lever!* This is certainly the point of view retained in Lecouteux's book, without anyone feeling the express need to say it. It is that self-evident. We are only a phase, a moment in the great momentum that drives us, and there is nothing gra-tuitous about the race: It is situated on a trajectory that has existed for-ever, and whose end point, thank God, we cannot see and will not see. There is nothing axiomatic or naive about this declaration. For we have points of reference at our disposal, and this is where this book comes along to remarkably fulfill an expectation, to answer one of these crucial questions that exhaust us.

Out of these testimonies, Claude Lecouteux has chosen to emphasize one theme, which is certainly, truth be told, the most significant, the most clear, the most familiar overall, if we agree to become aware of it. It is the theme of the Double. There! He could just as well have discussed the *androgyne* or the *dioscuri,* which would have come back to the same thing (as he suggests this in passing, we are given hope that he may one day return to it). Furthermore, it is quite remarkable that his preferred cul-tural area for his examples is the same one where I believe investigations into the androgyne will be taken the furthest (Swedenborg, Almquist, Stagnelius—all Swedish). The same is true for a study of twins and their images, from *Freyr/Freyja* to *Fjörgyn/Fjörgynn* by way of that "couple" in which, as Tacitus pointed out, the "man," Njödr, has a woman's name (Nerthus) and the "woman" a masculine name (Skadi).

The prevailing, well-researched idea here—and not only in the Germanic sources, I must note—is that each of us has a Double that is not only spiritual, but also (and this is where references to Old Scandinavian work wonders) potentially physical. It is a Double that has our "form" *(hamr),* "accompanies" us *(fylgja),* and "gives us form" *(hugr),* therefore annihilating all interruptions between any ambiguous occult world and the "real." The demonstration of proof seems to me to be brilliantly carried out, and I leave to the reader the pleasure of following the author's argument. Let me clarify as well and thus broaden the debate a little: One can go beyond the context that the author, scrupulous scholar that he is, has set for himself. For it clearly seems to me that we are dealing here with one of the invariables of our human identity. I truly wish that the Church, in its determination to eradicate "paganism" by banishing into demonology all that too obviously escaped from its magisterium, had struggled against those representations that did not exactly coincide with its own concepts, though it also professed a kind of belief in a Double— precisely spiritual, this one: that guardian angel whom, very logically, Old Norse will call *fylgjuengill, fylgja,* "angel." In fact, to take the reasoning in another direction, has there ever existed a culture that, except in self-denial, has objected to this prodigious image/reality?

Let us venture strictly into the field of religious history. Whatever religion is according to the etymology that we seek to retain from the word *religion* (which "links" our world to the supernatural one, or which "reorganizes" our "real" realm in a way that conforms more to that irresistible need for the absolute or perfect that we carry within us, *re-ligere* or *re-leger*)—suppose that every religion was started, perhaps, by worship of the great natural forces or (but I believe this comes back to that in truth) worship of the great ancestors, consequently, of the dead, who ordinarily take responsibility for the attributes of the forces in question, on the physical level as much as in their intellectual or spiritual sense. Everywhere we still find the phenomena of reincarnations, metempsychoses, transmigrations, which make what we believe, hope, and love return infallibly to these great archetypes or prototypes. Consequently, continuity from what was to what will be—passing through what is—is assured.

And here is one of the teachings of this important book: Our idea of temporality, which plagues us so much, is not well founded. There is a Double who precedes us, escorts us, and follows us (the fylgja allows for all these connotations), who leaves us or reenters us almost at will (hamr supports this interpretation very well) through the means of catalepsy or levitations, abolishing all the representations of necrosis surrounding us and enlightening us on demand, so to speak (this is the role of the hugr, *anima mundi,* or *mana,* if you like). In short, there exists the alter ego, of which we are a captivating part, most assuredly, but only momentarily or spatially, for it does not truly participate in space-time categories. The Swede Strindberg, writing only a century ago, directs these words to one of his characters: "Whoever sees his Double is going to die." This is very precisely what the author of the *Hallfredar Saga* professes six hundred years earlier, and I am sure that Strindberg never knew this saga. This continuity of an irrational certainty reveals that we are very much at the heart of a worldview.

In this regard, all the cultures that Claude Lecouteux discusses, even if he favors the Germanic culture in its various incarnations, agree with a consensus that stuns the skeptic. I repeat this from book to book: The power of the author does not lie in advancing preconceived theories that he will then make every effort to verify through texts. There are too many researchers who fall into this trap, including some of the experts. Lecouteux is not one of this number. In a surprising effort of erudition and eclecticism he allows these texts to say plainly what they have intended to say unconsciously. To wit: There is no "death"; nothingness is only a perverse and personal mind game; and within each of us is a precisely immortal life principle that manifests itself in diverse ways depending on the era, cultural status, and place we have in mind, but that is never absent from our texts. Ghosts are limited incarnations and messengers from the other world; dwarves and elves represent the unveiled mysteries of the other world through their agency—in this book it is the Double who summarizes and glorifies all this imagery.

In sum, this is a very lovely, extremely instructive book that is even more convincing because it remains tapped into not exactly the idea of life but, appropriately, the "over life." And nothing could please us more.

RÉGIS BOYER,

FORMER DIRECTOR OF THE INSTITUTE OF

SCANDINAVIAN LITERATURE AND LANGUAGE AT THE SORBONNE

Acknowledgments

This book would not have seen the light of day without the help of my friends and colleagues Christoph Gerhardt (Trèves), Sieglinde Hartmann (Frankfurt), and Harald Kleinschmidt (Stuttgart, now in Tsubuka, Japan), who provided me with documents that were inaccessible to me in France. May they be warmly thanked!

Preface to the 2001 Edition

Research never stops, and, once published, each study risks becoming outmoded. It is necessary, then, when you have completed your own analyses, to be aware of the results of any works published since that time. Other scholars, as a matter of fact, can have access to sources of which you are unaware, especially when texts are written in languages that you have not mastered or when they are from places very far away. Fortunately, however, if you are researching a subject, the great fraternity of researchers enables those who are interested in it to appear and bring you up to date with their discoveries. Thanks to this, I can update this third edition and in this way facilitate the research of anyone else who desires to form his or her own opinion. Let me say this first off: My results have never been questioned—on the contrary, the works and articles that I have received have brought grist to my mill and confirmed my beliefs and their implications with regard to witchcraft, the fairy world, and enchantment.

Since the second edition of this book, Eva Pócs, a member of the Academy of Science in Budapest, sent me the book *Fairies and Witches at the Boundary of South-Eastern and Central Europe,*[1] in which she analyzes the relationships among fairies, nature spirits, weather demons, guardian spirits, and witches, as well as the links between the two worlds— our world and the other world, which includes a focus on mediators. Her study meets mine in large part. She treats werewolves and vampires in passing (on pages 22, 28, 40, and 82, and in note 237), and the idea of the Double is omnipresent. Even if it is not evoked expressly, it certainly emerges in the relationships Pócs establishes between the objects of her study and shamanism.

Dr. Philippe Wallon, psychiatrist and researcher at the Institut National Français du Recherche Médicale (INSERM) has devoted a long chapter to the Double in his book on the paranormal. One of the focuses of this work is the similarity between contemporary testimonies and those of long ago. Dr. Wallon concludes: "The Double still remains a dreamlike product of the imagination. The emanation of an underlying mental effort, it lasts only as long as this effort. One can therefore expect it to be eminently changeable, on a moment to moment basis, in its consistency and even in its physical acts."[2]

On the fringes of these literary and historical testimonies, the reader will find examples concerning "reality" in the book that Ernest Bozzano has devoted to phenomena related to haunting. For example: One night, Miss Clara Griffing sees her maid taking down the laundry hanging on the line in the yard. The next morning, she mentions this to the maid, who is surprised because she knows she did nothing of the kind, yet she admits that before falling asleep she stayed awake until one o'clock in the morning, tormented by the thought that she should have gone out to bring in the laundry. Her Double thus carried out what was consuming her thoughts. Another example from Bozzano's book corresponds exactly to what I have said about the *vardøjer:* A young man falls asleep at his club, but his father sees him returning home well before he actually arrives.[3]

In perusing the book that Jean-Marie Ertlé devoted to witches both male and female, I have discovered the same testimonies as those from Germany, though some would appear very brief and cryptic to anyone not familiar with the concept of the Double. For example, in Sologne, some claim that asps are witches; they have the tongue of the devil and all the venom of hell. To kill one of them is to destroy evil. A man once crushed one, and an old village woman likewise died in her bed, her kidneys crushed.[4] Most research has largely focused on the werewolf. I received a highly researched study from Leszek Pawel Slupecki, accompanied by striking illustrations, in which he shows that the wolf represents only one form of metamorphosis.[5] His real goal, however, is to show that were-wolves originally made up a brotherhood of masked warriors.

Chiwaka Shinoda devoted a book to a similar subject,[6] but we can also find valuable information in his work on the metamorphosis of fairies, a comparative study of French and Far Eastern traditions that includes some excellent information on the werewolf.[7] This researcher emphasizes the different types of metamorphosis: clothing, celestial, and alchemical.

A team of Franco-Japanese researchers translated and published some Chinese texts on tiger men and tiger women, which are the equivalent of our European wolf men and thereby reveal a similarity of belief across a variety of cultures.[8] The focus of these studies rests on, among other things, their age, given that they range from the fourth to the thirteenth centuries. With metamorphosis being effected through a tiger skin in these instances, the central issue seems to be that of the persistence of a human spirit in animal form. I've observed in these texts that enchant-ment is the result of an illness, punishment for the transgression of a taboo, or the result of an attack by a soul tiger who throws a skin on his victim, causing the person to become and behave as an animal. This pun-ishment is not definitive; there does seem to be progressive redemption, with the head being the last part of the body to experience metamorpho-sis in reverse. Sometimes the tiger skin does not adhere completely to the human body, which means it can be torn off, leaving the victim chafed.

In pursuing my exploration of the alter ego, I ultimately discovered that it had become incorporated into the writing of science fiction novel-ists. In A. van Vogt's *The Book of Ptath* (1947), the protagonists, in a state of lethargy, leave their bodies and go elsewhere to possess the bodies of others, either living or dead. Their possession of the dead brings the corpses back to life. In *Ortog et les Ténèbres* (1975), K. Steiner borrows from the legend of Orpheus to tell of a Double's voyage in search of the woman he has lost. Thanks to a marvelous machine invented by some monks, the hero is able to double himself and reach the other world to search for his beloved, but he fails in his undertaking.

The cinema has not been idle in incorporating the alter ego, given that the underlying schema of *The Matrix* (1999)[9] is certainly that of the Double. Here again, it is thanks to a machine that the alter ego can fulfill its mission. One of the most telling scenes of the film is when we see the body of one of the protagonists in a state of lethargy, jerking from the bullets received by his Double, who is far away.

We also find the Double in a series of films that Joëlle Kuhne has examined in her thesis, which she defended in Strasbourg in 1999. In carrying out an innovative anthropo-filmic analysis of the supernatural characters linked to the element of water and inspired by the Melusinian theme—the union of a mortal with a supernatural being—Kuhne succeeds in clarifying the background of the beliefs that feed these films, notably the belief in the Double.[10] Her work should be published in the near future, but unfortunately without all the illustrations that support her argument.

Belief in the Double seems assured of an unparalleled continuity, given that it is adaptable to technological developments. This is certainly due to the fact that we are dealing with a fundamental element of the imaginary. It would be interesting to see the results of extending our investigation of this subject to contemporary literature, art, and cinema.

Preface to the 1996 Edition

OVERVIEW OF STUDIES

Since the publication of this study on the Double (alter ego), the subject has not been taken up by other researchers. Fairies, most notably Melusine, continue to give rise to works in this field, but they are always approached from a literary perspective and from there enter into the scope of inquiries into the marvelous, the fantastic, and the archetypal.[1]

Historians have taken an interest in witches as sociocultural and religious phenomena, mostly endeavoring to discover the motives for and methods of the witch trials and the personalities of those involved. I must point out here Martine Ostorero's excellent book, *Folâtrer avec les démon*,[2] which looks at the sabbath and witch hunts in Vevey, Switzerland in 1448, and Wolfgang Behringer's book on Chonrad Stoeckhlin (1549–1587),[3] a man who meets a ghost and becomes one of a group who witness their external souls (alter egos) moving far away while their bodies are asleep. Even though Behringer is completely unfamiliar with the idea of the Double, the book confirms for us that at least three nocturnal legions exist. Stoeckhlin specifies that there are the *Nachtscher* (Night Troop), to which he belongs; the *Rechte Fahrt* (Just Voyage), which leads the dead to their place of rest; and the *Hexen-fahrt* (Witches' Voyage). People who double themselves belong to the first and third troops. When it came to the Sabbath, however, the inquisitors never took the trouble to make these distinctions.

Werewolves experienced another destiny. Charles Joisten, Robert Chanaud, and Alice Joisten devoted an exhaustive study to the werewolf, and though they limited their research to the Dauphiné and Savoie regions, it did open up new perspectives on these areas.[4]

The purpose of this inquiry is to confirm those ancient elements that readers discovered in my original book, and to bring to the fore new material to be analyzed. In this sense, Dauphinan and Savoyard werewolves are exemplary because they attest to an astonishing commonality of belief in Europe—most notably concerning the role of the caul (amniotic membrane)—that figures so importantly in ghost stories. The pieces of information gathered in the Alps, for instance, have their counterparts in Scandinavia. Catharina Raudvere showed this in her worthy thesis on the representations of the nightmare in folk beliefs, in which she confirms the similarity between the *mara* (nightmare) and the werewolf.[5] What is more, Raudvere supplies us with texts that prove the homogeneity and logic of the caul/placenta-wolfman-(night)mare complex.[6]

Thanks to Raudvere's book, which Ronald Grambo (Oslo) had the kindness to send me, I was able to read several important studies on the werewolf. If you share in the belief in (night)mares, you will find in the works of Raudvere, Grambo, and van Haver numerous charms designed to protect yourself.[7]

Michèle Simonsen has devoted several excellent pages to the relationships between the werewolf, pregnant women, and a curious but very common Scandinavian ritual in which the placenta of a foal plays a part,[8] and which we find again in Catharina Raudvere's body of work. Here is a typical Danish account:

Werewolves attacked pregnant women in order to free themselves from their curse; they opened the bellies of such women in search of a male fetus, which they meant to eat. There was a farmhand not far from here—Georges the weaver—who was suspected of being a werewolf.

Girls could escape the pains of childbirth by crawling naked across the fetal membrane of a colt.

I also refer to the monumental work of M. van den Berg on nine-teenth- and twentieth-century folk legends from the Anversois. Even though any diachronic perspective is absent, and even though he does not address the concept of the Double, his typology of the nightmare and the werewolf is of great interest because it is based on an enormous body of work. Not only does it complete what other Germanic accounts teach us, but it also illustrates the law of ecotypes.*[9]

Let me also point out Jeanne-Marie Boivin's study on the Bisclavret, the name of the werewolf in a lay by Marie de France. There, the wolf-man and another hero of the poetess, Muldumarec, the bird knight, both literary representations of the belief in the Double, are very rightly connected.[10] In addition, there is much of related interest on *Arthur and Gorlagon* in the memoir by Sandrine Conti.[11]

Specialists will find food for thought in the collection of analyses and the translations I have recently published, in which I supply the fundamental materials used in the development of my concept of the Double.[12] Those who are particularly interested in the survival of the belief in European literature may refer to the newly published collection of Déborah Lévy-Bertherat. The works she cites include those of Chamisso, Dostoevsky, Maupassant, and Nabokov.[13]

"Books have their own destiny." Here is one that allowed me to enter into contact with "soul doctors," those psychiatrists who even today are faced with the phenomena of doubling, traveling within dreams, and dreaming of such travel. Dr. Philippe Wallon's excellent study on the paranormal reveals that almost nothing has changed on the anthropological level, and the pages that he devotes to the Double very closely support what I have discovered about the Middle Ages.[14] What has changed is the interpretation of the events: Today, you are no longer burned at the stake for having traveled to far-off places in your sleep! In short, yet again

---

*[The law of ecotypes allows for the different outward look of a theme, legend, or belief according to the times and the country from which it comes. —Ed.]

we see the astonishing similarities among phenomena having to do with the human psyche, which gives us cause to reflect upon the "evolution" of man. As a matter of fact, we can see that these "voyages" in spirit or in body continue today in the accounts of those claiming to have been abducted by UFOs. The ethnologist Bertrand Meheust shows admirably well how hybrids of ancient folk beliefs and the "flying saucer" are created and observes that contemporary "fantasy mythology" represents the remnants—recombined and reworded—of ancient legendary themes.[15]

RESEARCH TRAILS

The body of writing on which our study is based can easily be broadened—first, by carefully reexamining all the accounts of visions and magic transports; then, by analyzing the relationships among these metamorphoses, most notably among those that tell of transformations into beasts, from the perspective of the Double.

Regarding visions, we can find, for example, some interesting material in Claude Carozzi, who, in his analysis of the soul's voyage into the next world, tackles the idea of the Double several times and offers us pertinent reflections on Saint Augustine's anthropology and on dualistic concepts of human beings (body and soul) and other concepts (body, soul, spirit).[16]

Nonscholarly literature must not be neglected in this process; it too can provide historical documentation for anyone working in psychological archaeology. Proof of this is, for example, the *Didot Perceval,* written around 1200–1210, in which fairies appear in the form of birds who, when wounded, assume human faces, as this summary shows:

Urban, who was charged by a fairy to guard a ford against any knight wanting to take it, is vanquished by Perceval, who asks him to put an end to this custom. When Urban complies, right away a great tumult arises, a thick vapor obscures everything, and a voice curses Perceval, who is then attacked by a flock of black birds. He fells one, which changes into a dead woman whom the other birds carry off to Avalon.[17]

Interestingly enough in relation to this tale, it is known that blood flow and wounds cause metamorphosis to end immediately.

Additional discoveries can be made in certain accounts of dreams corresponding to tales centered on the theme of the stolen goblet, which is sometimes combined with the motif of wounds received in dreams: In *Perlesvaus,* the young Cahus dreams that he enters a chapel and steals a golden candelabra; a black man, hideous and gigantic, *holding a big, sharp knife in his hand,* reproaches him and wounds him mortally with a slash of the weapon. Cahus awakes, screaming, to find the candelabra next to him and a knife plunged into his body: *Vez ci le cotel qui m'est cours desqu'au manche . . . ; por cest chandelabre sui ge navrez a mort.* [Here is the knife that cut me up to my shoulder . . . ; because of this candelabra, I am fatally wounded.]* A priest is summoned; Cahus confesses and dies soon after.[18]

His wound and the candlestick are solid proof that his Double, which is corporal, transported itself to the chapel. There is evidence on his body, therefore, of what had happened to his alter ego. Another detail, however, merits attention: In the "dream," Cahus is struck in his right side, but when he awakes, he discovers his wound when he raises his left arm *(son braz senestre).* This inversion remains unexplained, unless we entertain the possibility of a mirror somehow being involved.

Yet another example of a wound received in dream later appearing on the wakened dreamer's body can be seen in *Ála flekks saga.*[19] Cahus's story is also similar to one of the *exempla* in the *Dialogus miraculorum* by Césaire de Heisterbach: The soul of a sleeping young girl is transported to Jerusalem, where she attends Mass in the presence of a celestial army of Mary and Christ before reentering her body in the morning. When she awakens, she discovers that she has brought back a church candle.[20]

This account, referenced by F.-C. Tubach as an account of "soul carried to Mass," has deep roots in the belief in Double, though it expresses a Christian version of this belief (whereas *Perlesvaus* provides a romantic and fantastic version).

We should not assume from the example cited here that this belief is

---

*[The old French is retained here, followed by a simple modern English translation in brackets. — *Trans.*]

mainly one of Germanic countries and, to a lesser degree, of France. Spain offers us many examples as well, which have been collected by J. Sanchez Valdes de la Plata in the chapter "Of These Other Men and Lineages That Double Themselves and Appear in Several Places at the Same Time" in his *Chronicle and General History of Man*.[21]

What remains to be worked out are the complex but revealing relationships among man, the Double that is the zoomorphic domestic genie, and the Double that becomes a tutelary genie. What I outline in the chapter "The Double and Fairies" has proved to be much richer and more encompassing than the few traces that had been revealed at the time when it was written. It was upon these details that I have based my hypothesis of a sort of hierogamy, or sacred marriage. Certain legends, in fact, have preserved the idea that a supernatural being—like the Scandinavian *fylgja*—can be a living person's Double.[22] One such legend, collected by F.-X. Schönwerth in the nineteenth century in the Upper Palatinate, tells of two ladies of the woods *(Holzfräul)* living not far from Baker Trapp's house, in Tirschenreuth, who die when the mistress of the house passes on.

The Double can also be a domestic genie in animal form. In a Silesian legend, a man finds a large dead snake on the flagstone in front of the house on the day after his mother's death. When we understand that this reptile is one of the forms a domestic genie can take, the relationship between the snake and the living becomes clear. Likewise, we understand this relationship in the legend more clearly knowing that the reptile becomes a tutelary genie of a child from whose bowl he is allowed to eat, and that if the snake is killed, the child will die. Olaus Magnus attested to a belief in such relationships in 1555.

Traces of shamanism may seem much more numerous in medieval French literature than in the medieval literature of Scandinavia because very few scholarly studies on the subject are circulated from the countries of that region. Whoever reads Anatole Le Braz discovers the soul in the form of a mouse or a gnat.[23] However, in northern European countries, the bibliography on the subject is vast, and in it we find explanations of many of the marvelous motifs that run through French legends and ancient texts. But overall, it is important to remember that in order to have a more global view of the belief in the Double, which is widespread in all of Europe, it is imperative that we cross the borders between the Roman, Germanic, and Slavic worlds.

Without coming back to what I have shown in *Fantômes et Revenant au Moyen Age*,[24] I will focus on the area of northern Europe, which is very rich in vestiges of belief in the Double. Here again, however, we should not assume that this belief lives on only in Germanic countries. The following example, borrowed from a French manuscript in the Bibliothèque Nationale (Paris) and dated from the beginning of the fifteenth century bears proof of this:

Here is a vision that occurred in Brittany. A man, a baker by trade, passed from this world to the next and left his wife and children in this same line of work. So it happened that soon after his body had been put into the ground, his wife and children got up at night, as was their custom, in order to knead the dough and make the bread. While they were kneading, the man who had just died appeared among them and, after rolling up his sleeves to his elbows, he too began to knead the dough. He cheered them on, often in a loud voice, so that they could continue their work with all the skill and vigor they had when they started, but instead they fled, terrified, one here, the other there. As they ran, the neighbors gathered around to see the marvel that had frightened them so. However, they had yelled so loudly and made so much noise that they had chased away the dead man.

After that—though no longer at night—he appeared several times, lurking about the dwellings and throwing stones at people. He did not take the worn path but walked instead where the mud was thickest, so that he sank into it up to his knees and even to his thighs, which terrified people and surprised them so much that they did not know what to do. They did not know whether he was a dead man or an evil spirit.

So they went to the tomb where the baker had been buried, and when they exhumed him, they found his body covered in mud up to his thighs, exactly as they had seen him when he was roaming near their dwellings. They also noticed that his arms were covered with dough from the kneading he had done with his family. Having seen all this, they buried him again, but soon after, the dead man appeared as he had before. Finally, they decided to go once again to his grave and break his thigh bones. Thus it was done and *oncques puis ne fut veu* [he was never seen again].*

This is a good example of those accounts that Christianity had not yet influenced. What wanders in the mud and kneads dough is the dead man's Double, which continues to live as long as the man's body has not completely decomposed. At the end of the Middle Ages, under pressure from the Church, such occurrences were categorized as witchcraft and devilry. As such, they became distorted and the original concept of the Double, once so integral to them, became obscured. It was this process that has prevented any recognition or discovery of the belief.

Therefore, there are many discoveries still to be made regarding our ancestors and their beliefs, and there is a story to be written about these beliefs of old—a story that, once free from the imposition of the Church on historians, takes into account this so-called folk information.[25]

---

*[Again, the old French is retained here, followed by a simple modern English translation in brackets. — *Trans.*]

Introduction

We human beings, animals endowed with reason, have never been able to accept death, and the thought of our demise remains the fertile source of our self-reflection and our questions about the existence of a demiurge, a transcendence, and a hereafter. These questions, causing us anguish and forcing us to face the prospect of a return to nothingness, are met with different responses from each religion and each civilization. That we experience final dissolution has never been accepted, and our most cherished wish has always been that we not die completely, to borrow Horace's words, and that we live on in one way or another. But reality is inescapable; daily life proves that the body is ephemeral, perishable, and that it dies and returns to dust. So it cannot be the body that lives on. Hence, the idea has been developed and expressed—with more force or less force and clarity, depending on place, era, and ethnic group—that we are more than the body; that the body is only the physical encasing of the vital principle, the breath, a force, a spirit—in a word, a soul.

This intuition—a challenge to time and devouring Chronos, a revolt against the inevitable decrepitude of the body, and sublime because in some way it puts an end to existential anguish and gives meaning to life by making sparks of hope fly—does not suddenly and *ex nihilo* take form. It relies upon inexplicable phenomena such as dreams, premonitions, second sight, feelings of déjà vu—all phenomena that have reinforced humanity's belief in what we call today, for the sake of convenience, the *soul,* that immortal part of an individual, the link connecting one person to the entire cosmos.

1

After having repressed these issues in the remote areas of dreams and unreal imagination, especially during the Ages of Enlightenment and Reason, we are coming back to them at this time and engaging in the same philosophical and religious speculations that occupied our distant ancestors. Today, as in the past, we desire to penetrate the secret of secrets: the secret of death, or rather, of life after death. In other words, we want to reflect upon a dimension of ourselves that still largely escapes science, that will not allow itself to be imprisoned by laws, and that was responsible, approximately a hundred years ago, for the glory days of spiritualism.

This state of mind and curiosity has found expression in a blossoming of diverse works. Some of these, scholarly and well researched, are based on clinical observation and experimentation. It is appropriate to cite here the studies of the American Society for Psychical Research, as well as the collection of studies entitled *The Pursuit of Life after Death*, with, notably, the contribution of K. Osis and E. Haraldson, "Deathbed Observations Made by Doctors and Nurses."[1] In Innsbruck, Austria, the Institute of Paranormal Phenomena strives to find a scientific and rational explanation for all kinds of strange manifestations, as does the Institute of the Extreme Realms of Science in Fribourg-on-Brisgau, Germany. Other works have a more irrational, more subjective character and come from either people convinced by their own experience of the reality of events, or authors keeping a close watch on current fads. The Anglo-Saxons take the lion's share here, and cite, as matter of interest, only Raymond A. Moody's *Life after Life* and Robert Monroe *Journeys Out of the Body*.[2]

The release of films such as Joel Schumacher's *Flatliners* has caught the attention of the general public with this kind of questioning, and the press, discovering a subject it could run with, has given them extensive coverage, intensifying the discussion by bringing out of the shadows near death experiences, (NDEs) as well as the *Association pour l'Étude des États proches de la Mort** in Paris, France. In an interview given to the newspaper *Figaro* on January 11, 1991, sociologist Edgar Morin recalled the role a belief in the Double plays in an NDE:

*[Association for the Study of Near-Death States. — *Trans.*]

I see, therefore, three fundamental elements in this experience: first, the dissociation between the body . . . and an immaterial spirit or specter; second, a voyage toward another place via a tunnel; third, the great light. In the first place, the dissociation between the material body and an immaterial *Double*—which goes on to become a specter, a phantom, a spirit, and will continue to live after life—is found in a large number of archaic concepts of death. . . . This concept corresponds to life experience; ancient men became aware of their individuality starting from their immaterial Double, their reflection in the water, their shadow, their dreams (wherein the Double travels while the body remains motionless). It is this Double that frees itself from the body after the deterioration of the perishable body, and that goes on to live its own life—which is something I have shown recently through my studies of ghosts.

Experience of the other world is part of life and has to do with signals—perceptible from here—of a more profound and greater truth in which religions see the manifestation of the divine, or at the very least, proof of its existence. On July 8, 1918, wounded by an Austrian mortar shell, Ernest Hemingway recounted that he felt something escape from his body. What was it?

Anyone who studies the texts of classical antiquity and the Middle Ages, as well as more recent folk traditions, will discover, scattered throughout them, a thousand and one curious events that would be wrongly ranked among simplistic themes and legendary motifs, literary clichés and the marvelous. These occurrences seem to fall within the jurisdiction of these realms because we no longer understand them and have a doubly deformed view of them. Our lack of knowledge of ancient mentalities and our Judeo-Christian culture block our comprehension. In addition, we are prisoners of our century, of Cartesianism and received ideas, of prejudices toward the infamous old wives' tale! In fact, above all, we are missing the relationship of the elemental part to the whole. We have a few pieces of the mosaic, but are unaware of its design. That which used to be a product of a coherent culture, mentality, and belief no longer appears to us as anything but a fragmented form that has suffered centuries of abuse. Relatively speaking, our work thus resembles that of an archaeologist who tries to piece together a ceramic pot from its shards.

Even so, it is astounding to see that so many authors coming from so many different backgrounds so strongly assert that man is not limited to his body, and that so many writers create characters who have Doubles and whose alter egos are sometimes animals. It is astounding that so many poets speak to us about our shadow and our reflection as if each were our soul. Included in this hodgepodge are Edgar Allan Poe's *William Wilson*, Oscar Wilde's *The Picture of Dorian Gray*, Dostoyevsky's *The Double*, Guy de Maupassant's "Him," and Alfred de Musset's "The December Night." Ancient Egyptian religion speaks to us about the *Ka*, the Greeks speak to us of the *daimôn*, the Romans teach us that every man has a *genius* and every woman an *Iuno*, Christianity gives us a guardian angel, ancient Scandinavians knew the *fylgja*. It would be futile, without a doubt, to aim at discovering a genetic connection between all these examples from all these civilizations, but the similarity of these beliefs reveals to us that, along with the Double, we have the constituent elements of human thought connected to Jungian archetypes, or to what the folklorists call *psychic unity*. Is not this belief attested to by all eras, in all parts of the world?

Indeed, a gap remains to be filled where the medieval West is concerned. The clues are there, but we have not been able to see them—hidden, distorted, and masked as they have been, as has been everything that contradicts the dogma of Christianity, the West's dominant religion. Finding them again means working on a palimpsest, rereading the texts and refusing what they suggest and impose, so as to stick only to the facts. Decoding the message from the past that is hidden in its writings boils down to going beyond the *interpretatio christiana,* to discovering or rediscovering notions that sometimes escaped the writers themselves, who were most often clerics educated in monastic schools. It is by playing with differences in evolution, which in the Middle Ages contrasts Germanic civilization with Roman and Celtic civilizations, that the inquiry can be led to safe harbor.

Taking the Germanic traditions as its central axis aligns this work with my previous studies, but it is clear that we could refer to other cultural areas. It seems absolutely necessary to me not to limit ourselves to a single civilization, for in doing so, we risk running into the well-known adage *testis unus, testis nullus!* I will, therefore, depart from the geographic and temporal framework each time doing so will permit me to further our investigations.

As a matter of fact, it would be wrong to think that the belief we are tracking is limited to Scandinavian ice floes and Germanic forests. In such places, however, things are clear—or at least almost so—because Christianity has never succeeded in eradicating all that has to do with death and the hereafter. Having followed a slower historic evolution than that of the southern lands, the traditions of these countries have survived long enough to find the path to the written word and so, in turn, to become known to us. I will therefore take the following postulation as my starting point: The highly Christianized countries more quickly lost the exact meaning of the kinds of occurrences we are studying, but this in no way means that such occurrences did not exist in these countries.

Starting from this position, I have reread the Romance works whose Celtic origin is unquestionable, and I have been able to discern in them traces of the belief that we are here bringing to light. In taking a look at the peoples with whom the medieval West was in permanent contact— through commercial exchange, through wars, through invasion, or simply from being neighbors—I have been able to discover the root of the belief in the Double, and, taking this further, to see that this root is squarely planted in shamanistic concepts of the soul.* The people of our Middle Ages have always rubbed shoulders with peoples for whom

---

*A full study of shamanism does not fall within the scope of this work, but one essential feature of it, relating to our subject, should be recognized: its concept of the soul. Among all the shamanistic peoples (Turko-Tartars and Siberians), the soul is a triple entity. The lower soul dwells in the bones and leaves man only at his death, or, in animals, remains in the skeleton. The second is not as solidly fixed in the body; it can leave the body during sleep or on other occasions without the sleeper's awareness. The third soul separates itself from the body at the time of death and appears to humans in the form of a ghost. Several variations arise according to ethnic group, but the soul is never a single, indivisible entity. For more on all of this, see M. Eliade, *Le Chamanisme et les techniques archaïque de l'extase* (Paris, 1974).

shamanism is well in place: in the north, the Laplanders; in the east, the Avars, the Magyars, and the people of the steppes; in the southeast, the Turks.

My goal is simple: to write the history of the Double in the Middle Ages, to show the mind-set in which this belief is rooted, to see in it both diffusion and continuity, and to discover the implications of this. Others have already thrown themselves into this perilous adventure, but the scope of their studies focused most often on other times and other civilizations, and these studies have by now grown old.[3] Of our Western heritage there exist only rare articles, and gaining access to them is not very easy. Outside of the works of Régis Boyer—most notably his very rich *Monde du Double: la Magie chez les anciens Scandinaves* (1986)—the Middle Ages stand out by their absence. However, we cannot examine the folk beliefs and traditions of the eighteenth and nineteenth centuries very well without knowing what preceded them, for they include some very long-standing attitudes.

The belief in the Double—that is, in another self possessing a fairly large degree of independence enabling it to travel to faraway places— allows for the explanation of many phenomena, examples of which we all know, such as ubiquity or bilocation, the presence of the theme of twins *(Dioscuri)* in mythology, tales of metamorphoses, and more. Here is a text dating from about a hundred years ago that illustrates marvelously one of the manifestations of this belief:

> Near Philadelphia, not far from the windmills found on the Delaware River and about which I have spoken, there lived a solitary man. He was kind, but he resided in an isolated house and kept to himself and spoke little. People said strange things about him— for example, that he was able to discover what remained hidden to an individual.
>
> It happened that a captain had to set sail for Africa and Europe. He promised his wife, who was staying in Philadelphia, that he would be back after a certain amount of time and that he would write her often. She waited for these letters, which never came. The specified

amount of time passed, and her dear husband did not return. She was overcome with sorrow and did not know what to do. One of her friends advised her to visit the good hermit and tell him of her torment, and she followed this advice.

When she had told this man everything, he asked her to wait a moment until he came back with an answer to her questions. She sat down and waited. The man opened a door and slipped into his workroom. After he had been absent for a long time, the woman stood, went up to the spy hole of the door, raised the little curtain, and looked in: The man was lying on a sofa or settee, as though dead. She went back hastily to her seat. Finally, the man returned and told her that her husband was in London in a café and that he would be coming back soon; then he named for her the reasons that had kept him from writing her. Calmed, the woman went home.

What the hermit had told her would happen occurred at the exact time indicated. The woman's husband came back, and the causes of his delay and his silence were exactly those named by the good man. The woman was eager to find out what would happen if she visited the hermit with her husband. They arrived at the man's house, but when the captain saw him, he was frightened. Soon after, he told his wife that he had seen this man in London in a café on such-and-such a day—it was the day the lady had visited the hermit—and that the man had told him that his wife was very worried about him. He had given the stranger both the reasons his trip had been delayed and the explanations for why he had not written, adding that he would be returning home soon. This man, the hermit, had then disappeared into the crowd.[4]

I am going to examine and explain narratives similar to this, along with other tales that speak to us about exsomatic experiences, because they center on the Double as a true physical and psychic carbon copy of the individual from whom it issues—one of the last forms in which belief in a Double survives.

At the beginning of the century, Ed Morell, after having been pardoned, told of his out-of-body travels in *The Twenty-fifth Man* (1919), which inspired Jack London's *The Star Rover,* because those who write literature are always on the lookout for the strange and unusual.* Closer to home, the adventure of Erkson Gorique, as summarized here, deserves a moment of attention because it provides information about another manifestation of the other self:

> In 1955, Gorique went to Oslo to look into the possibility of importing Norwegian porcelain. He stopped in at the best hotel, and the receptionist told Gorique he was very happy to see him again. Gorique was astonished; he had never been to Norway. The next day, he visited a supplier by the name of Olsen, who likewise said he was pleased to see Gorique back again after the short visit he had paid him a few months ago. Filled with unease, Gorique opened his heart to his listener, who reassured him by telling him that this phenomenon was well known and that it was called vardögr, an apparition of a person that precedes the real person by a short period of time.[5]

It is possible to discover an important belief in the history of our ancestors only if we shed the weight of clerical interpretation obscuring the pagan substratum—that is, the interpretation representing the Church's true dictatorship and facilitated by the monopoly over fact that the Church exerts on the world of writing. We must also seek to put ourselves literally in the skin of the men of long ago in order to understand their mind's reactions; and we must acknowledge that the voices coming from the past contain the truths of that time—those that are found where language, the real, and the imaginary meet—in accounts that have been transcribed, for better or worse, and preserved. Finally, we must gather together these dispersed accounts. I am creating such a dossier, the fruits of a long investigation and closely related to my studies on phantoms and

*[Ed Morell was a friend of Jack London's whose experiences in prison and solitary confinement formed the basis of London's blast against the American penal system. —*Trans.*]

ghosts, dwarves, and elves.* I am presenting it and risking explanations, but refusing to reach a verdict on the degree of truth in each occurrence, which would be a measurement based only on the yardstick of the knowledge of our time.

One single thing is important here: Our ancestors believed in the existence of the Double, an independent alter ego freed from the body when the body is dulled by sleep, frozen in trance, weakened by illness, or immobilized in coma. So may each reader forge his or her own opinion in light of these collected documents. May each find in them the confirmation of his or her convictions, be they personal or the opposite. We cannot deny the existence of these texts—numerous, when all is said and done—and we must not remain unaware of their message for much longer; we must not silence it, even if it disturbs and calls into question the conclusions of much of the research on certain points that we will touch upon.

We will start, therefore, from events universally known—visions both Christian and pagan—then we will look at how these can be explained. Second, we will follow the Double in all its diverse fictional and historic disguises, which will lead to an examination of fairies, witches, and werewolves. Finally, we will take up related appearances of this belief. Because this material is rich and complex, I've included in the appendices any information that, in my opinion, is important; to include it in the body of this study would oblige us to juggle various centuries and places. Let us therefore allow the Double to carry us down paths strange and unusual—but oh, how enriching!—for, to repeat a phrase dear to the Anglo-Saxons: *It's a good tool to think with!*

---

*This book represents, for the time being, the last part of my exploration of pre-Christian European beliefs about death, their mythologization, diabolization, and recovery through fantasy literature. It is the follow-up to my studies on phantoms and ghosts, dwarves, elves, spirits, and the dead. Certain trails mentioned in these pages remain to be explored, notably the relationship between people and genies. The inquiry is underway.

Part I
The soul outside the body

1

The Ecstatic Journey

Writings of ancient times tell us of people who, for one reason or another, whether charisma or illness, go outside of themselves and see or learn that which remains hidden from ordinary mortals. Such people are called *ecstatics* from the Greek *ekstasis*, which literally means "straying of the spirit," and by extension denotes the act of leaving the body or, in other words, having an exsomatic experience, which is very often the experience of believers.

It is well known that faith moves mountains, but it can also elicit ecstasies and visions. The clerics say that when a vision does not take place in dream *(in somnis)*, it is defined as the voyage of the soul into the next world, a didactic peregrination if ever there was one, for in the Middle Ages its principle goal was to reveal to the fortunate chosen the correctness of Christian dogma and, possibly, the fate awaiting man in the next world.[1]

At the onset of the Middle Ages visions were not strictly reserved for ecclesiastics generally and those who belonged to the contemplative orders specifically. Therefore, testimonies of illiterate peasants do indeed exist, though the Church gradually co-opted them and claimed a monopoly over them. In the Church's defense, it must be said that it would have been quite difficult for it to allow such experiences—whether they are called *dreams* or anything else—to remain outside of its control, which is why, in the fourteenth and fifteenth centuries, visionaries were predominantly monks and cloistered nuns in search of mystical union.

However, when a cleric simply served as the scribe of these visions, these relatives of ecstatic experience, and they were not the direct products of ecclesiastic culture, we can discern in them another attitude, another culture, another concept of life and death. There are, nevertheless, enough common points between these attitudes and Christianity to cause a merging of one with the other, at the price of minimal adjustment and slight distortions. Let me now present a few important pieces of my argument.

CONDITIONS AND LENGTH OF THE VISION

Right from the start, the tone is set by the Venerable Bede (d. 735), whom Jacques le Goff holds as "the founder of medieval visions."[2] The visions that he reports in *Historia Ecclesiastica*—those of Fursy, an Irish monk who died around 650, and those of Drythelm, who finished his days at Melrose—take place in the context of illness.[3] Regarding Drythelm, Bede even says that he died one night and came back to life the next morning, when he proceeded to tell what had happened to him.

The theme of illness is fundamental in the history of visions. We could even go so far as to say that it is a constituent element of them. Gregory the Great (d. 604) refers to the case of Stephen, a Roman citizen whom illness led to the gates of death. His close relatives had already sent for an embalmer when, fortunately, his "soul" returned to his body.[4] And here is the gist of what Gregory of Tours (538–594) writes about Salvi, Bishop of Albi: "Having been taken with a high fever, he seemed dead; he was washed, clothed, and put on a stretcher, and he was watched over the whole night; in the morning, he began to move and, a few days later, he told of his vision."[5] Alberic of Settefratti, who entered the monastery of Mont-Cassin around 1211–1213 at the age of ten, had a vision while in an illness-induced coma for nine days and nine nights.[6]

Only rarely do people in good health receive visions. One such was the mother of Guibert of Nogent (1055–1125), who was lying along a riverbank, resting, when she dozed off: "It then seemed to her that her soul went out of her body in a noticeable way" *(sua ipsius anima de corpore sensibiliter sibi visa est egredi)*.[7] The case of Irishman Tondale must also be mentioned. His story was committed to parchment around 1148 by a certain Brother Marcus, monk of Ratisbonne. Preserved in more than 150 manuscripts, included in the works of about thirty authors, and translated into fifteen languages, the *Visio Tnugdali* is a noteworthy model.[8] We will not spend much time on Tondale's voyage into the hereafter, but rather focus on the departure of his Double.

While sitting at his table, Tondale exclaimed to himself that he felt himself dying *(ego morior)*, and after uttering these words, he collapsed, "lifeless, as if his spirit had left. His body showed all the appearances of a corpse: blank eyes, pinched nose, white lips, rigid extremities." He might very well have been buried, but those who were diligently palpating him felt a slight warmth *(calor modicus)* on the left side of his chest. He remained lifeless from the tenth hour on Wednesday to the tenth hour on Saturday, when, in the presence of the clerics and lay people who were preparing to bury him, "his spirit returned," and Tondale began to breathe weakly for about an hour. All were amazed, even the scholars, saying, "Is it not his spirit *(spiritus)* that left and then came back?" Then Tondale took communion, drank, gave thanks to God, and told of his voyage into the hereafter, a journey undergone by either his spirit or soul—the terms are used variously within such texts, which seemingly implies a certain confusion on the part of the copyists.

The texts suggest that there are two ways of allowing the soul to leave the body. One of these is involuntary: Sickness leads us to the gates of eternal night. The other way, more religious in nature, seeks to lower the body's resistance and so obtain, in fact, the same result as sickness. This mode seeks to break the soul's corporal encasing through the practices of asceticism, fasting, sleep deprivation, discipline (mortification), exposure to cold, and so forth, all of which are intended to eliminate the ties that unite the soul and the body through weakening the vital functions of the latter. This encourages visions, which depend—it goes without saying—on the faith of the person practicing these acts. The list of ascetic visionaries is very long. Among them are Ansgar de Brême (d. 865), who had his first vision after much prayer and a long period of abstinence, and Sibyllina Biscossi da Pavis (1287–1367), who whipped herself to the point of drawing blood, deprived herself of sleep, and endured festering sores. Many other examples can be found in the works of Louis Gougaud and Peter Dinzelbacher.[9]

The body must be in a critical state in order for the soul to become free, which is what happens during catalepsy, lethargy, or coma so deep that witnesses are convinced the Reaper has just struck. When Siagrius describes the ecstasy of Orm (1125), he specifies that the body suddenly became cold and stiff and looked exactly like a corpse *(subito corpus frigidum et inflecibile et simillimum mortuo efficiebatur).*[10] It is this corpselike rigidity that allowed the monks who were watching over Barontus in the winter of 678–679 to realize that his soul had left.

When the soul or spirit leaves the body, the duration of time that passes can last "from the period of time that passes between the first and the third *Agnus Dei* of Mass" to five weeks, as was the case with Njal, around the year 1000.[11] When visionaries return to themselves, they have no idea how much time has passed—which is normal, given that time in the other world does not in any way whatsoever correspond to ours.

But the question I ask is this one: What is it that leaves the body? Christians hesitantly alternate between at least two terms: *animus* and *spiritus,* or even *mens*—or else they get out of the whole affair without clarifying anything, as if the answer were self-evident. Let us try to see all this clearly.

A FEW LEXICAL REMARKS

My analysis is based on approximately a hundred visions.[12] Perusal of the texts highlights a curious fact that more in-depth research should be able to clarify. In the *exempla*—short, edifying narratives often serving as illustrations in sermons or as subjects for reflection in monastic "spiritual readings"—the actual escape of the entity that inhabits the body is expressed in only a very few ways. The less precise—in my view, of course—say any of the following: "He was brought before the tribunal, of God, of Christ" *(raptus fuit ad iudicium; ad iudicium Dei, ad tribunal Christi);* "in vision he saw . . ." *(in visione vidit; videbature siquidem in visione);* "he fell into ecstasy" or "he was sent into ecstasy" *(factus est in exthasi; raptus in exthasim);* or "he saw himself brought before the judge" *(vidit se duci ad iudicem).* The locutions are a little more precise—"He felt himself being carried away by spirit" *(sensit se raptum in spiritus),* with variations such as *rapta spiritu vidit se,* and *raptus spiritu,* and specify that this sometimes takes place at night *(quaedam nocte spiritus viri rapitur)* or include what the point of the carrying away was *(spiritu ad thronum raptus).*

The term *anima* is absent in the oldest of the texts I have perused, and in the political and secular vision, such as that of Charles the Fat, dated sometime around 889–890, a voice might say: "Charles, your *esprit* is going to leave you in a while, and a vision will reveal to you the just judgment of God and some omens concerning you, but your esprit will come back to you after a long time." And Charles would have recounted to the narrator: "Right then, my esprit was stolen away."[13]

It is said of Saint Fursy, whose vision most likely took place around 633, that his soul went out of his body from night until the cock's crow. Anima is present in those visions that take the form of a dialogue between the soul and an angel, as is the case in the *Chronical* by Hugo de Flavigny (1065–1140). We encounter the term in Tondale's statements—*anima mea corpus exueret.* Among the mystics it is much more frequent; for example, Catherine de Sienne (1347–1380) deplores that the soul cannot truly merge with God before death. It actually seems that, under pressure from the theologians, there was a specialization of terms for such visions: The soul, much more than the spirit, was perceived as being reserved for ecstatic peregrinations—voyages into the next world. This implies, however, a break with pre-Christian traditions, the followers of which would not have known how to speak of the soul because the concept was foreign to them. Where this matter is concerned, they more or less use spirit—animus, spiritus. Whatever name it might be called in the vulgar languages, it is basically a catchall word likely to satisfy anyone and everyone.

An English monk from the thirteenth century, the writer of the *Vision of Thurkill,* uses *soul* a single time in relation to rapture or ecstasy. Saint Julien appears to Thurkill and says to him: "Only your soul will accompany me" *(sola enim anima tua mecum abibit).*[14] Just as surprising is the intervention of the narrator, who makes a display of his knowledge of revelatory literature by mentioning the case of the Irish knight Audoneus (Owein) who, after having "gone out of his body" *(eductus a corpore)* saw "with his own eyes" *(oculis carnis),* in Saint Patrick's Purgatory, torture being inflicted upon sinners. I leave it to you to find the contradictions! The anonymous author also summarizes the *Vision of Edmund* (in 1196), a monk from Eynsham. For Thurkill, he uses only the verb "to go out of" *(a corpore eductus fuerat),* without saying what it is that leaves the body during the visionary's coma, which lasts two days and two nights. When Thurkill returns to his body, the writer says only that "the man was then brought back, restored to his body" *(reduc festinanter virum hunc ad corpus suum).*

In *Godeschalcus,*[15] which is the account of the vision had by the Holstein peasant Godeschalc from December 12 to December 15, 1190, the writer uses the term *animus* once to say that the cerebral functions of the visionary had stopped *(animo nil cogitante),* and he uses *anima* to designate that which leaves the body: "The soul went out of the corporal encasing" *(de vase corporis anima effusa est).* In the *Visio Godeschalci,* written soon after *Godeschalcus* but independently of it, it is also the soul that goes out of the body: "As soon as my soul had left my body . . ." *(dum anima mea corpore soluta fuisset),* the peasant says. This vision, of which we have two accounts taken directly from the mouth of the visionary—who is an *illiteratus,* a *rusticus*—offers us extremely unusual details, which we will now stop to look at for a moment.

THE VISION OF GODESCHALC

A peasant of the parish of Neumünster (Holstein), Godeschalc came down with a fever and, suffering much, he stopped eating and took to his bed. A priest brought him communion, the only food he had ingested in four days. "From Sunday to Wednesday, he lost consciousness; his face was pale, his tongue became quiet, his pulse slowed, his thoughts stopped and his whole body seemed to be without a soul. On Wednesday, his soul 'left the corporal vessel,' as the sick man himself said, 'to see the invisible and hear the untellable.'"

Whereas Saint Paul, in the same situation, wondered if he had been taken away in body or soul, Godeschalc does not doubt for a moment that his soul separated itself from his body for the entire duration of the vision—that is, five days—and he is sure that he was dead during this same period of time. The cleric notes, according to the witness statements, that God did allow a certain amount of movement in the body—the ecstatic's mouth was trembling *(os solum palpitavit)* even though his limbs remained immobile—to ensure that the ecstatic not be buried before the soul returned, "for the soul is of a single nature *(natura simplex)* and, not being formed of different parts, it does not allow itself to be divided and cannot therefore leave the body and stay in it, otherwise the man would not really be dead."

Godeschalc's catalepsy is thus interpreted in accordance with the current tradition. The adjective *exanimis* perfectly suited the state of his body. However, as in Tondale's case, a perceptible sign of life remained, which contradicts the narrator's and visionary's claim. There was no death. Of course, nothing is impossible to God—such is the explanation to which the anonymous cleric resorts.

The *Visio Godeschalci,* which is much more concise, states: "Godeschalc was sick for seven days; on the eighth, he was taken from the light of the world and five days later he came back into his body" *(ad corpus redit).* Because the witnesses observed a curious movement in Godeschalc's lips while his body was cold, stiff, and lying there like a corpse, they dared not bury him, thinking that his soul was still within him, simply sleeping. The writer of the *Visio Godeschalci* refuses to ask this essential question: "Only God knows if he had this vision corporally or if he was outside of his body," he writes, adding, however, that Godeschalc brought back from his voyage "proofs *(argumenta)* that could easily persuade even pagans to believe his words." What proofs is he speaking of?

Both accounts of Godeschalc's experience state that the ecstatic received several wounds during his peregrinations to the next world: His feet were torn by the thorns and burrs of the land through which he must have traveled; his left side was burned; and his headaches were attributed to the fetid vapors of hell. The interpretation that the clerics offer for these signs is eloquent: Both note that the skin on Godeschalc's feet was peeling, that his head was in pain and pus flowed from his nose and ears for six months or more, and that he could not sleep on his side. In addition, he was very weak and had no appetite. Twice the writers come back to the notion of proof.

In a fairly extensive commentary, the author of *Godeschalcus* shares his opinion with us: "The resurrection of a dead person is neither impossible nor new, and there is nothing remarkable about the spirit leaving and coming back" *(ire spiritum et redire).* But why does he not speak of the *soul* when he has always, until now, used this term? "Concerning the truth and dignity of the vision, it matters little, in my opinion," he goes on, "whether Godeschalc experienced it physically or when he was taken away *(in corpore an extra corpus raptus),* for he was taken away, and that is all that counts. The manner in which he was taken away . . . we must not be too concerned about that." A curious way to cut short an interrogation, it suggests that in Holstein during this time, the question of the soul leaving the body was considered acceptable, a point that the cleric who wrote the *Visio Godeschalci* allows me to clarify.

This writer does stick to the proof of Godeschalc's adventure. He notes that the man was completely exhausted for five weeks, that he was deprived of his senses and his reason, and that he was unable to eat. But a blunder in the text leads us to wonder if Godeschalc's soul really did come back. The cleric writes: "When this man's soul came back into his body, he remained exhausted for five weeks," but a few moments later, he states: "At the end of five weeks, the soul came back down little by little into his body" *(anima paulatim corpori suo condesendens).* Nevertheless, the impact of two of the narrator's remarks cannot be underestimated: "However, it is absolutely inexplicable that what happened in spirit *[in spiritu gestum]* be manifested in the body" *(in corpore appareat)*. This idea bothers the cleric, who comes back to it: "Here, as elsewhere, the reason is hidden: How could he experience physically what he suffered in his soul?" *(quomodo in corpore senserit, quod in anima pertulit)*. That is indeed the whole question, but in order to ask it, what was needed was a critical mind that faith could not prevent from reasoning soundly.

How do we explain that the body shows the marks of pain endured by the spirit or the soul without resorting to God, Satan, parapsychology, or psychosomatic theories in our explanation? How can some people have seen the other world with their own eyes, whether the eyes of the heart or spirit? In short, how do we escape the fetters of Christian tradition and interpretation so clearly presented in this summary of *The Vision of Thurkill?*: Thurkill was sleeping when Saint Julien appeared to him, wakened him *[a sompno excitavit]*, and said, "Here I am, as I promised you. It is time to leave." When Thurkill arose, he wanted to dress for the trip *(ad procinctum itineris)*, but Saint Julien said to him: "While you are away, your body will rest tranquilly on its bed, for only your soul will leave with me. So that no one thinks your body is dead, however, I will leave breath in it, which will indicate that it is alive."

Does not such a passage smack of fabrication, borrowing and transforming details into those particulars inherent in a Christian vision? The motif of being awakened does not hold together.

THE PROBLEM WITH PROOF

Wounds on the body that could serve as definitive proof of the truth of visionary phenomena gradually tended to become a constant in this kind of account.

We must, however, be sure to distinguish here between visions and apparitions of the dead. When a dead person visits a living person in order to let him know his fate beyond the grave, and when he is suffering in purgatory or in hell, he almost always leaves tangible proof of his visit. In *The Golden Legend*, Jacques de Voragine (1225–1298) reports the following: Master Silo of Paris, also known as Pierre the Bard, received a visit from one of his students who had died a few days before and who was now suffering the pains of hell. The ghost wore a cope lined with fire. A drop of sweat fell from him and stabbed a hole in Silo's hand *(manum perforavit)*.[16] In the accounts of apparitions of the dead, this motif is frequent; for example, it appears again in the eighteenth-century *Reun's Tale*.[17]

In accounts of visions that are inverse phenomena—a living person, in whole or in part, is transported to the other world instead of a dead person being transported here—wounds are rare. Likewise, in accounts of dream visions *(visio in sompnis)*, it is surprising to find wounds mentioned, for such visions do not involve travel. A narrative of this type is more closely related to visits from the hereafter or from hell, as the following example shows: At the Trinity Monastery in Caen, a woman lived a cloistered life, concentrating on certain shameful sins, until she died. One of her companions, sleeping in the room where she had given up the ghost, saw in a dream the dead woman burning in hell and being tortured by evil spirits. A spark from hell's fires hit her eye, waking her up. "It was confirmed that what she had seen in her dream," said Guibert of Nogent, "she had actually suffered physically; the real evidence of her wound came to confirm the authenticity of her vision" *(veritati visionis verax congrueret testimonium laesionis)*.[18]

The clerics who worked "for the greatest glory of God" built an edifying tradition, starting with elements that predated Christianty. But how are such events possible?

From his ecstatic journey, Fursy brought back burns on his jaw and shoulder. In 1104, a monk at the monastery of Fly, in the Beauvais quarter, had a vision during which a demon threw a rock at him, hitting him squarely in his chest. The monk felt such severe pain from the blow that "for forty days his suffering almost led him to the gates of death."[19] In another incident, one morning in 1197, Rannveig, the concubine of a priest, took a fall in her house and remained unconscious until that night. Once she returned to herself, she told of the vision she had just had, a story of having been wounded while crossing the lava fields of the other world, and her body showed traces of these burns.[20] According to yet another account, as she came out of her ecstasy that lasted one or two days, Elisabeth Achler (1386–1420) was sweating blood. We can connect all of these physical manifestations to the exhaustion and extreme weakness of the visionaries once they wake up, which recalls the weakness of shamans when they come out of trance, or the intense effects a person receives from a psychological shock such as that received by Adam of Kendal (d. 1223), Cistercian bishop of Holmeculter, who became stark raving mad and died soon after having seen in a vision a revelation of his fate in the other world.

If the clerics who took down such accounts rarely noted the wounds an individual brought back from an ecstatic voyage, there is an excellent reason why: The soul is incorporeal for Christians and thus cannot be marked in any way. The clerics wished to make people believe that ecstasy was a uniquely spiritual phenomenon—for witnesses to such an event saw the lethargic body before their eyes. This reasoning is exactly the same as that of the Inquisitors when they were faced with witches who had fallen into catalepsy. The motif of wounds to the soul fits very poorly with Christian dogma, unless we take into account the hypothesis formulated by Origen, an exegete and theologian who was born in Alexandria in 185 and who died in Tyre in 154. In his treatise called the *Resurrection* he states that by nature souls are spiritual, but when they leave their earthly body, they take on another subtle body, a form exactly like the body they have abandoned, which is, for them, like a sort of sheath or container.[21] Origen, however, does not speak at all of the corporality of this subtle body, nor of the three-dimensional physical encasing, yet his description applies marvelously well to the Double.

The existence, therefore, of the few dissonant testimonies I have mentioned prompts me to try to discover who in the medieval West possessed the gift of self-transportation into the next world, or the gift of going out of the body—for it is obvious that the essential point of the belief in which we are immersing ourselves is indeed the separation of the "soul" and the body, to use the Christian terminology, or of doubling, if we are to be content with pagan notions.

VISIONS AND DREAMS

All medieval literature is teeming with dreams, and superimposed on them are particulars and traditions that have come from Rome, Greece, and the Orient. Transmitted through a million channels, including the Bible and *The Commentary on Scipio's Dream* by Macrobius (who lived around 360–422), these particulars have tremendous reverberations. Their successful introduction in Christian literature stems from the fact that they have been taken for manifestations of divine or diabolical revelations. Between 210 and 213 Tertullian speaks of the demons who brought, in vain, false, troubling, and vile dreams. If Satan sends illusory dreams, God brings real, prophetic dreams.

It is nonetheless difficult to distinguish between good and evil dreams, and the Church's mistrust of them has been expressed since the year 314, at the council of Ankara, when divination through dreams was forbidden. Moreover, dreams considered to be true came to be called "revelations," and they tended to become the exclusive right of ecclesiastics and, *noblesse oblige,* kings. For all that, pagans still continued to dream and defend their vision of the world against all papal bulls, fiats, and so forth. But while both Christian and pagan bodies are asleep, other functions become manifest. I will not attempt to give a psychological explanation, for people of long ago reasoned in other terms. In any case, the explanation provided is almost always perfectly clear.

The distinction between visions and dreams was one made by the Christian culture of the Middle Ages. A person, whatever his religion, can have an ecstatic vision while his body is deep in coma or in lethargy, or, quite simply, when he is sleeping. If, in the first case, the soul leaves the body, it does not necessarily do so in the second, for the texts show us that the sleeper can receive visits—from God, saints, or relatives. Peter Dinzelbacher has attempted, with moderate success, to determine what it is that allows the distinction between ecstatic visions and dream visions.[22] The only pertinent criteria are the rigidity of the corpse and the ecstastic's total lack of consciousness, as well as his apathy when his soul returns to his body. Beyond these criteria, we have much trouble in distinguishing the two types of visions, and must therefore make use of diverse concepts for which both the key and common denominator are *revelation.* Having at our disposal texts that reflect pre-Christian attitudes and beliefs allows us to better clarify this concept.

In all cultures, dreams are the great means of communication with the other world, the invisible, the hidden side of things. The practice of incubation reveals this to us: People spent a night in a sanctuary, hoping that the supernatural occupant of the place would give them a prophetic dream. Through this means they sought to make contact with superior powers. Pagans and Christians alike engaged in this practice because knowledge of the future has always been—and, if you look at the specialized magazines and television programs, still seems to be—one of man's principle concerns. Most witchcraft rituals show this very clearly.

Let us return to Christianity, to the very Christian author Guibert of Nogent (1055–1125), a monk from Saint-Germer-de-Fly. He tells of his and his mother's dreams, saying of his own: "In my sleep, the demon very frequently introduced images of deceased people to my thoughts." Can this be classified as a vision? No, because it is the mind *(mens)* that is agitated by thoughts; there is no transport to some faraway place. On the other hand, he speaks of his mother's dreams in terms of visions: She "had the following vision. It seemed to her that she was in the church of our abbey." Guibert uses *visio* here, but a few lines later speaks of *somnium.* In the same chapter of his *Autobiography,* he tells us one of his childhood dreams—"One night, I dreamed that I was in a church dedicated in Your name [Mary]; next, it seemed to me that I was carried off by two demons"—and uses the term *visum.* He also writes of his mother: "Very frequent visions . . . allowed her to predict, a long time in advance, what was to happen," but these are really more like prophetic dreams.

Helped by Guibert of Nogent's hesitations, wherein I believe I recognize language corrected by the reflex of his Christian culture, I can clarify these terms in this way: True vision, ecstatic vision, entails the voyage of the soul into the next world. It is with Gregory the Great's *Dialogues* that this realm first became open to dreams; the distinction between sleep and catalepsy matters little here. Dreams, still according to

Christian interpretation, are dangerous: The soul does not leave the body, but receives images via what was called in those times *visio spiritualis* (applied to concrete things) or *visio intellectualis* (remaining in the realm of the abstract). The clerics had difficulty effecting any kind of distinction on this point. In the tenth century, Robert of Mozat testified that he "had this vision in a dream" *(in sompnis visionem hanc vidisse)*.[23] Dreams were suspect, in conformity with *Ecclesiastes,* which says: "For in the multitude of dreams and many words there are also divers vanities."[24] Understood as a means of gaining access to God, dreams could be useful, meaningful, even true, but they must then come from the Divine. They must go out through the "gates of horns" *(porta cornea)* and not by the gates of ivory *(porta eburnea),* to use a Virgilian image (*Aeniad* VI, 893). Dreams "short-circuit the ecclesiastic intermediary," says Jacques le Goff, and rightly so.[25]

What, then, did Christians ask when the Church did its best to impose its control over dreams, authority that was manifested in the watering down or mutilation of any accounts having to do with dreams? A hymn attributed to Saint Ambrose and sung at complines tells us the answer to this question: "May dreams and fantasies of the night recoil!" The prologue to the *Vision of Thurkill* contains a long passage that throws some light on the background of this debate: Many people had their doubts about visions, and they mocked and refuted visionaries. "There are almost as many mockers and skeptics as convinced and credulous people."

DREAMLIKE APPARITIONS

In Christian and pagan dreams, the most frequent detail is an apparition. Saint Martin appeared at Sulpice at the time of his death. After his assassination William, the prior of Cluny, appears to Peter the Venerable *in somnis,* "in a dream" (*De Miraculis* II, 25). Believers soon destined for martyrdom were visited by one of the saints. Leaving aside all religious connotation, what remains of these dreams, if not that one individual appears to another? Whether the apparition is living or dead has no importance whatsoever because each of us, depending on our religious convictions, decides this answer for ourselves. Here the soul is referred to; elsewhere, the spirit; later, the Double. I think I see here an inversion of the theme of ecstasy, of the voyage of the alter ego.

We are no longer looking from the perspective of a person who sends his Double far away, which the Norse language expresses by the term *hamför*, or from the point of view of the person whose alter ego regains independence and goes on to fulfill some cherished wish. No! We are now looking, in fact, at the arrival from the other end of the chain; we are with the unwilling host, close to the goal set by the Double. My reading, which relies upon non-Christian testimonies, allows us to see that it would be futile to insist upon separating ecstatic visions from dreamlike apparitions, for these are two aspects of the same phenomenon. At the same time, I better understand the work of the clerics, who, using theories from classical antiquity passed on by the Fathers of the Church, effected a reduction and a specialization: a reduction of the number and nature of characters likely to appear in dreams, and specialization of the monastic world in this mode of perceiving the Divine.

Let us keep well in mind that the creatures populating the dream world are men and genies, sometimes gods, and often saints, which confirms that sleep is favorable to communication with the other world. When we have learned, especially thanks to Régis Boyer's research, that to the pagan Germanic and Celtic mind-set—even though the field of research is still, in very large part, lying fallow—man remains permanently in contact with the supernatural side of reality through the intermediary of his Double or Doubles, then apparitions, visions, and dreams become not fabrications dictated by ethical, didactic, or religious considerations, but instead, evidence of reality. All of this sends us back to the fundamental idea of an alter ego. It is remarkably homogeneous and discernable beneath all attempts at acculturation.

The events that I have just presented through a Christain lens take on their full significance only when compared to similar occurrences in the pagan traditions, which I am now going to tackle. The phenomena are fundamentally the same and even have identical worth in the two cultures; only their interpretation differs. Visions, Christian ecstatic voyages of the Middle Ages, must not be rooted out from the pagan compost that has, in part, nourished them (an error committed until now with outstanding regularity, which shows how extremely difficult it is to completely disregard our own culture and religion). If the soul connects the Christian to God, the Double links the pagan to the entire cosmos, including the other world. But the other world, it seems, rather than being the world of the gods, is that of the dead, of those beyond the grave, from where all knowledge comes. It is the reservoir of the potentialities of each individual and each family.

2

Pagan Ecstatics

There is no reason that the ecstatic journey must be reserved for adepts of a single religion, much less a religion that has been imported and whose success is explainable only because it corresponded to indigenous beliefs on a great number of points. In the realm of dreams, apparitions, and visions, the parallels between pagan and Christian cultures are astounding. Because I have already provided many examples in part 1, chapter 3, as well as in my *Fantômes et Revenants* (Phantoms and Ghosts), I will be brief and refer only to those occurrences most accessible to everyone.

DREAMS

Dreams were part of daily reality in the pagan world. Everyone knows the story of King Herald the Black: He never dreamed, and so he sought advice to cure what everyone thought was a weakness. In *The Saga of the Jómsborg Vikings*, which was written around 1200, though its events unfold around the year 1000, King Herald's daughter tells Gorm that she will not marry him if he does not dream. Elsewhere, several texts emphasize that a person who is tossing and turning in sleep must never be awakened; rather, the individual must be left alone to "enjoy" *(njóta)* his or her dreams. Old Icelandic has an illuminating term for a man deprived of the ability to dream—*draumstolinn,* or "someone from whom dreams have been stolen," and uses two composite words to describe an individual who dreams greatly: *draumamaðr,* formed from "dream" *(draumr)* and "man" *(maðr).* It also uses the term *berdreymr,* "having clear dreams." Let me emphasize that this faculty can be hereditary, as emerges from a remark in *The Saga of the Sworn Brothers* in which Thorgeir says: "I see the future clearly in my dreams; it is a family trait."[1] Beliefs gathered in Northern Germany by ethnologists attest to the survival of this trait.

To the pre-Christian mind-set, sleep permits the free movement of genies, spirits, and Doubles, and distance presents no obstacle whatsoever. Immediate communication, sometimes taking the form of a semi-dialogue, can be established between people who are far away from each other. Again, in *The Saga of the Sworn Brothers,* Thormod receives a dream visit from Thorbjörg, one of his old friends, who tells him: "You are dreaming, but what will appear to you will seem as though it had appeared to you in the waking state." In the same saga, Thormod, *skald* of King Olaf the Holy (995–1030), finds himself in difficulty on an island. Not far away, Grim dreams that a man pays him a visit and says to him: "I am King Olaf Heraldsson, and I have come here because I want you to go and find Thormod . . . and save him." Olaf intervenes in *The Saga of Hallfred:* He appears to Hallfred in a dream, insisting that Hallfred come and join him, and another time dissuades Hallfred from fighting a duel. Even after his death, he returns to pour advice upon his skald. May no one be surprised! As long as the corpse has not completely decomposed, the Double does not disappear, which I have clearly shown in my studies on phantoms and ghosts.

Let us listen, then, to what the texts tell us about the events experienced by sleeping people. In many dreams, sleepers move, changing their whereabouts, even if only a few meters. Here is Glum, narrating what he has dreamed: "I was leaving the farm, without any weapons . . ."[2] And here is Atli, who awakes and says: "I seemed to have left dependence . . ."[3] Bödvar addresses these words to his mother: "You had a restless sleep, mother. Did something appear to you?" Thordis, Bödvar's mother, replies: "I took a witch's ride to many places this night, and I learned with certainty things I did not know before."[4] The locution *witch's ride* translates the Norse *gandreið,* a word composed of the verb *riðr,* "to ride," and *gandr,* whose meaning is not clear, though it possibly means "spirit" or "demon" and "stick." Here, the compound indicates that Thordis's Double went traveling while she was sleeping, and it is probably not too bold to assert that gandr may refer to the alter ego, given that the alter ego can ultimately take any form whatsoever, including that of a stick.[5] Nocturnal journeys are an inseparable part of dreams. Those who are not aware that they possess a Double—Glum, Atli, Bödvar—interpret what they have seen as a dream; but those who, like Thordis, have this knowledge, know with certainty that they have not dreamed, but instead have doubled themselves.

Along with involving travel, dreams are frequently prophetic. Also common is that the dreamer perceives the psychic Double of another person in animal form. Gunnar says to Kolskegg:

> "I had a dream both last night and tonight, and even though I do not want to announce who committed the murder, my dreams have let me know who it is. I dreamed two nights ago that a viper slithered away from a farm and bit Vesteinn to death. And the following night, I dreamed that a wolf who was running away from the same farm bit Vesteinn to death. I did not tell my dreams to anyone before now because I did not want them to come true."[6]

The snake and the wolf are in fact the zoomorphic Doubles of the assassin who, preoccupied with the murder he is preparing to commit, involuntarily emits his alter ego.

In contrast to Godeschalc, who doubles himself while he is in a deep coma, totally unconscious and nearly motionless, a healthy person stirs in his sleep when he makes discoveries through his dreams. Let us look closely at the following summary passage from *The Saga of Havard of the Ice Fjord:* Thorgrim, a sorcerer, is part of the expedition that is planning to kill Havard in Otradal. On their way, Thorgrim is suddenly overcome with sleepiness and cannot stay seated on his horse. "After having spread a coat over his head"—magic isolation—he falls into a restless sleep. When he returns to himself, he is very hot and says: "I was just at Havard's farm for a moment, but my mind became so distraught that I lost consciousness." During this time it is night at Otradal, and no one can sleep because Atli is so restless as he dozes. They wake him, a very rare occurrence in the texts, and when they ask him if he saw something, he answers:

> "It seemed like I had left dependence, and I saw some wolves coming from the South, running through the field, eighteen in all" — which is exactly the number of men led by Thorgrim — "with a female fox running in front of them. I have never seen such a tricky beast as she was. She was looking all around. . . . I know with absolute certainty that these were human spirits."

Let's do the math: The female fox guiding the troop is Thorgrim's zoomorphic alter ego, and the wolves are his companions' Doubles. Now, if Thorgrim really had allowed his alter ego to run, we are given proof of this by his sudden torpor, which does not strike the others, who were able to stay wide awake. This detail remains inexplicable. A variation in time allows me to clarify things a little: Atli dreams at night, whereas Thorgrim dreams in the wee hours of the morning. Atli's Double therefore goes to meet Thorgrim—whence the sleepiness—and the meeting of the alter egos precedes the real meeting by very little time.

It is not excessive to use another example to ensure that we get to the deeper meaning of these unusual accounts: Gunnar is on his way with his brothers. Sleep overcomes him, and he asks that they halt. He then slips into a deep torpor and begins to thrash about. They want to wake him, but one of his brothers opposes the idea. Coming out of his lethargy, Gunnar tells the others: "I dreamed that I was riding near Knafaholar. There I seemed to see a great many wolves, and they all attacked me." Soon after this, he fell into an ambush in which his brother Hjört meets his death, as the dream revealed would happen. The wolves, then, were his enemies' Doubles.[7]

With these testimonies in which animals play a significant role, we have entered a different area in the history of the Double: The term used in the sagas cited above is *fylgja,* the "psychic Double" (see part 1, chapter 3). In other words, what falls under the jurisdiction of dreams are merely occurrences of which the spiritual alter ego becomes aware while escaping from the body. But what causes this escape?

REASONS WHY THE DOUBLE LEAVES

Besides those cases where the alter ego leaves spontaneously in order to carry out a wish of his possessor, an account that is a lovely example of the mixture of pagan and Christian will allow us to broaden our knowledge.

The Bishop Sagas (Byskupasögur), which are little known in France, have the benefit of showing, relatively clearly, the clashes of paganism and Christianity, and the fusion and hodgepodge that result. These sagas bring us much information on specific attitudes because they are not cut from local and indigenous traditions. Let us say that the information found in them is comparable to that of the texts that discuss the catechization of the pagans in the early Middle Ages. In *The Saga of Father Gudmund Arason,* a surprising passage reveals the technique used by the clerics. This technique, however, does not succeed in masking the Double who intervenes:

> [A]nd that autumn, it happened that Gudmund said Mass for a man confined to his bed, and held holy relics over him. According to how it seemed to those who were there, he lay down on the bench next to the sick man, and he fell asleep while saying his prayers. His deacon was also lying on the bench close to him, and Father Gudmund slumped against him when he fell asleep. After a short time lying there, the deacon could not feel the priest lying on him, even though he saw clearly that he was lying there, and others saw him too. This lasted a very long time, and when Gudmund woke up, the deacon asked why he could not feel Gudmund though he was leaning on his chest the whole time he slept, but Gudmund did not want to tell him.
>
> That winter, rumors spread into the fjords from the west that a

man named Snorri, in the west at Skalavik, was under the spell of a giantess, and that this woman troll was oppressing him so much that he thought he would never escape her influence. That very same night about which we were just speaking—the night from Saturday to Sunday—Snorri went out alone to the holy service. The way was very long, and as he traveled, the woman troll attacked him, pressing and squeezing him and pushing him toward the mountain. So Snorri prayed to Father Gudmund to help him, if he was in God's counsel as much as he believed him to be, and to save him from this giantess. And at that very moment it seemed to him that a light came over him, and a man in a Church cloak followed it and, with the aspergillum in his hand, he sprinkled the giantess. Then the woman troll disappeared as if she were melting into the ground. And the light followed Snorri the whole way, until he reached the farm. He thought he recognized Father Gudmund Arason accompanying this light.

Now, it turned out that the moment when Gudmund appeared to Snorri and the moment when the deacon felt that he was weightless were the same.[8]

The interpretation is obvious: Gudmund's sleeping Double answers Snorri's call for help, and the exterior sign of the priest's doubling is his weightlessness. Gudmund refuses to explain to his deacon what happened, but that is perhaps only a typical clerical technique. Most important, from this we learn that Snorri's thought *(hugr)* instantly reaches and communicates with Gudmund, and that Gudmund's alter ego materializes right away, exactly where its presence is desired. This immediate communication indicates that all Doubles are linked to each other in the invisible.

PROFESSIONAL ECSTATICS

Not all men know that they have a second self, and not all master the technique of liberating it at will. While the Doubles of some individuals leave the body through sleep or illness and roam where they please (either on their own initiative or to answer a request), those of other individuals have as their function the task of fulfilling missions that a person or the community sets for their possessors due to the control they exercise over their own alter egos. These people are professional ecstatics who know how to break the ties that bind the body and the Double. They can "leap out of their skin" *(springa af harmi)* or "out of their spirit" *(springa af moeði)*—so say the Norse sagas.

An example can be found in The Saga of the Lakevale Chiefs, in which it is told how Ingimund, having lost his amulet, asks three Laplanders *(finnar)* to find it for him:

> Ingimund sent for the Laplanders, and there came from the North three of them. He said that he wanted to make a deal with them. "I will give you butter and pewter, and you will journey to Iceland to look for my amulet and to report to me the nature of that country." They replied: "That is a dangerous mission for young Samis, but since you are urging us to do so, we want to try. Now we must close ourselves up alone inside a house, and our name must not be uttered." And this is what was done. When three nights had passed, Ingimund came to them. They then arose, sighed deeply, and said: "We had some difficulties, and we had much work to accomplish; nevertheless, we have returned with information that will allow you to recognize the country if you go there. But we had much trouble in looking for the amulet."

They proceed to describe the journey their Doubles undertook while their bodies were sheltered in the house. Here they are able to emit their alter egos because they are Lappish or Finnish (Sami) magicians; these northern lands were renowned in the Middle Ages for their magi, whom the Christians called sorcerers. We should notice particularly the following details from the story:

- The Laplanders isolate themselves.
- They forbid others to talk to them.
- They sigh deeply when they return to themselves.

The first two points are practical details: When the Double is absent, the body is extremely vulnerable and, above all, must not be moved or touched, which would lead to its death. The third detail, the deep sigh, is the tangible sign of the alter ego's return to the body. Now we may complete the picture: When the Double wants to leave, the individual is overcome with sleepiness—it is even said, here and there, that he yawns. For those familiar with ancient traditions, yawning has always been proof of the alter ego's departure. One of Aesop's fables tells this story: A bandit desires to take for himself the fancy clothing of an innkeeper, so he sits down close to him on a bench and soon begins to yawn. The innkeeper is surprised, and the bandit explains to him that after three yawns he will turn into a wolf, and saying this, he yawns a second time . . .

Aesop, who lived between the seventh and sixth centuries B.C., is certainly using here, in a parodic way, a belief that was alive and well in his time. And what does this belief say? That metamorphosis into a wolf—understood as the departure of the zoomorphic alter ego—is preceded by yawning! The parallel is striking.

Yawning is a recurring and therefore significant motif. In *The Tale of Hauk Hábrók*, a female magician *(heixr)* yawns while feeling the bodies of those who consult her in order to detect future wounds: Her alter ego apparently projects itself into the hereafter and transmits to the body the information it gathers.[9] In *The Saga of the Féroïens*, when Thrand finishes his magic session—his Double has gone to the other world to look for the people who were assassinated by Thorgrim and his sons in order to make them appear—it is said that "he got up from his chair and let out a deep sigh." At the beginning of the session, "he asked that no one speak."[10]

In other times it was believed that yawning allowed the soul to fly away and evil spirits to take possession of your body, which is why people crossed themselves when they yawned. It was also said that "a spell has been cast upon" a person who yawned frequently. If a sick person yawned, it was thought that he was exhaling his soul and that he thus was condemned to die.

Historia Norwegiae (The History of Norway), a twelfth-century chronicle, devotes a whole chapter to professional ecstatics. Entitled "The

Finnish" *(de Finnis)*—that is, the Sami, a people of Lapland—it illustrates the pagan and magical character of these people. Pay close attention to these details of the text:

> The Laplanders worship a vile spirit called *gandus* [the Norse *gandr*], thanks to whom they make prophecies, see far-off things in space and time, and discover hidden treasures. A Christian doing business with them was sharing their meal when suddenly the hostess died. Not in the least disconcerted or affected, the "dead" woman's companions explained to him that she had been a victim of a hostile gandus and that they were going to bring her back to life. One of them was a magician *(magus)*. He spread a cloth on the ground and placed himself on it so he could pronounce the sacrilegious incantations, then he raised a bowl in his hands, found in it the figures of a whale, a deer [reindeer], a little boat with its own oars, and little skis with their own straps, "the vehicle that the diabolical gandus uses in deep snow, on mountainous hills, and in deep swamps." The magician then started his incantations, "singing and leaping, then throwing himself on the ground, black as an Ethiopian, foaming at the mouth like a madman, and with his stomach torn open and everything all red, he gave up his spirit."
>
> The other people then asked for the help of a second man expert in the magic arts, who proceeded as the first, but with success. The hostess then revived the dead magician, who explained that his gandus, having taken the form of a whale *(in cetinam effigiem)*, collided with an enemy gandus that had metamorphosed into sharp stakes driven into the bottom of the sea, and these stakes opened up his stomach.[11]

Everyone can recognize that there are shamans at work here, but most interesting is that the first magician, after leaving to seek the dead woman in the hereafter, changes himself into a whale, and that the wounds from the cetacean appear on his body. The text does indeed say *praeruptus ventrem*, which thwarts the intention of the narrator, who tries to get us to believe that the gandus is an evil spirit serving the magicians. The word *gandus* is problematic: It can mean "stick" as well as "magic" and even "wolf," and none of the etymologies suggested up to now is satisfactory. There is thus a tendency to acknowledge more and more that the term may not be of Indo-European origin but may stem from ancient ethnicities—the Europides?—whom the Indo-Europeans enveloped in two great waves. The "vile spirit" referred to in the *Historia Norwegiae* has all the traits of the physical Double *(hamr)*, whom people versed in the occult arts are able to dispatch to faraway places. Let us take the example of Thordis of Lönguness. One night, she has a particularly restless sleep; when she wakes, she says, "I had my gandr run to many places this night, and I have now acquired knowledge of things I did not know before."[12]

If the voyage to the hereafter still exists—the objects contained in the bowl in the example taken from the *Historia* correspond to the different means of locomotion that the magician's alter ego can be led to use—it disappears fairly quickly from the narratives. Around 1555, Olaus Magnus confides this to us:

When someone wants to know where his friends or enemies are, whether they be five or a thousand leagues away, he asks a Laplander or a Finnish person expert in this art [magic] to give him information on this point, and he offers him linen clothing or a bow. Accompanied by only his wife, the magician goes to his dwelling [thus isolating himself] and hits with a hammer in the manner prescribed a bronze frog or snake placed upon an anvil, and then swings the hammer in all directions, muttering magic formulas. He falls quickly into ecstasy and, in a very short time, is lying on the ground as if dead. During this time, the woman who accompanies him watches very carefully to ensure that no other living being, not even a fly or a gnat, touches him. Through the power of the incantation, the spirit of this man is taken away by the devil [*sic*] and, as proof that he has indeed fulfilled his task and transmitted his message, he brings back a ring or a knife from his voyage afar, which he gives to his "client," to whom he also gives the information requested.[13]

Starting from the sixteenth century, numerous corroborating testimonies confirm the principle traits of the accounts we have just read. In 1697, it is even specified, regarding the Laplander Jacob Smaosvend, who is charged with a "mission for information" by Johannes Dolling of Lubeck, that ecstasy comes to him after he has done a circular dance for a moment.[14] A work printed in Leipzig in 1704, whose title may be translated as *The Protean Imp,* contains a chapter entitled "The North Bothnians, Excellent Necromancers" in which we read:

> The people of North Bothnia, as well as those of Lapland and Finland, are the best necromancers [magicians, sorcerers]. They have the same appearance as the people who live in Bjarm [Karelia] and live beneath the pole and take at will any form and appearance whatsoever [allusion to doubling]. When they are given a linen shirt or another piece of clothing of the same material, or a bit of earth, they can learn what your enemies and friends are doing in countries very far away and unknown in these parts.[15]

That which falls under the jurisdiction of charisma or divine will among Christian visionaries is considered the fruit of a science as well as predestination among Laplander magicians. In all cases, the *conditio sine qua non* of the voyage afar is lethargy, the body in coma. On the one hand, it is the result of serious illness or asceticism; on the other, it is the result of a trance achieved through chant, dance, or a certain rhythmic music—but this applies exclusively to people whom the texts call Laplanders and Finns.

Pagan and Christian traditions come from the same unique source, and each clarifies, in its own way, the history of the Double. The phenomena witnessed or experienced are always the same—dreams, trances, lethargy, coma—and to study some of them without taking the others into account will only block further research. Before tackling the universe of the metamorphoses of the Double, we turn to the report of an occurrence presented as historical fact.

TEXTUAL RE-CREATION

Leopold of Gerlach (1790–1861), lieutenant general and aide-de-camp of Frederick William IV (1795–1861), told the following story to Franz Wallner, who recorded it in his *Memoirs (Aus Meinem Leben)*. It admirably illustrates the persistence of beliefs and their vitality when they are not separated from reality. Moreover, the truth of these events cannot be doubted, and their conformity with stories from many past centuries— stories that have no genetic link—allows us to enter directly into the daily life of the men of long ago.

The archbishop of Uppsala took a trip to Germany and stopped at our royal court, where he had the honor of being invited to his table by His Majesty. The conversation turned quickly to the excessive superstitions that still reigned in Lapland, where belief in magicians and in occult powers transmissible through heredity was well-rooted in many families at the current time. The archbishop himself had been sent into these parts several years before this as the head of an inquiry commission, in order to examine this unbridled irreligiousness and to extirpate it conscientiously. He was accompanied by a doctor and a high functionary on this mission. The archbishop stated:

"Due to the lack of some means of communication, our voyage was as long as it was difficult. Its goal was known only by us. Hiding it, we took quarters with a rich and hospitable man who had the sinister reputation of being a master of black magic. To our surprise, nothing in his appearance or his household justified this reputation. With usual Laplander hospitality, our host, a well-off man with an open countenance, gave us the best rooms and called for all that his kitchen and cellar contained in order to honor us. We were astounded, but no one—neither our host nor any inhabitant of the place—made a mystery of the fact that Peter Lärdal (such was his name) possessed supernatural powers and even that he was, quite simply, a magician. At the end of three days, while we were comfortably taking breakfast together, I turned the conversation to this subject, on the pretext of curiosity, and asked Lärdal if this reputation did not bother him. He smiled delicately.

"'My lord Archbishop,' he said, 'how does it serve you to try to hide the point of your question? You and these gentlemen are here only to find the reasons for this reputation and to hold me responsible for it.'

"'Well,' I answered with much energy, 'since you already know, yes, we are here to destroy this superstition and put to an end these senseless things.'

"'You can think what you want about it, My lord, but it certainly is not senseless!' said Lärdal, slightly shaking his head.

"'What do you mean?' I replied sternly.

"'I want to help you understand this belief. My soul, my spirit, whatever name you want to give it, will, right before your very eyes, leave my body and go to a place that you will determine. Upon its return, I will provide you with proof that my soul, at your service, went to the place that you indicated. Do you want to be certain about this?'

"The most contradictory feelings took hold of me," the archbishop went on. "I was afraid, being aware that I was encouraging a sacrilegious game, and within me I felt opposing desires: one, to unmask a possible deception and reveal it; the other—a violent one—to learn how this simple man would keep his word. Curiosity, the legacy of all of Eve's sons, carried away my fear. I conceded and charged Lärdal to send his soul to my house and tell me what my wife was doing at that moment and to provide me with proof of its presence there. It goes without saying that my companions were burning with a curiosity even stronger than my own and were completely in agreement with me.

"'Agreed, gentlemen!' said Lärdal. 'Give me a quarter of an hour for my preparations.'

"This time had barely passed when our host reappeared, holding a pot filled with dried herbs.

"'Gentleman,' he said, 'I am going to burn these herbs and

inhale their smoke. Be very careful not to try to revive me or touch me when I am in this state. Your success would be my inevitable death, for, in a few minutes, my spirit will leave my body, which will, by all appearances, be dead. In an hour, my body will be revived on its own, and will give you news of your country.'

"After an anxious silence during which none of us knew how to reply, the magician lighted the herbs and held his head over the narcotic and nauseating smoke. In a few minutes, his face was white as death, and after having twitched a few times, his body slumped into the chair and remained motionless, seeming in all ways like the body of a dead man.

"'My God!' cried the alarmed doctor, 'It seems as though he has poisoned himself. He really is going to die if he does not receive help immediately!'

"I had to hold him back forcefully to keep him from throwing himself on the unconscious man.

"'Have you forgotten that this poor man beseeched us not to touch his body unless we want to kill him for sure? Since we authorized him, reluctantly, to undertake this worrisome experience, we must wait until it has some success.'

"At the end of a breathtaking, interminable hour of tension, the color returned, slowly but visibly, to the lifeless man's cheeks; his chest began to rise and fall under violent movements, which, little by little, turned into regular breathing. Soon after, Lärdal turned toward me and said:

"'At this moment, your wife is in her kitchen.'

"'Of course,' replied the doctor, smiling. 'At this hour in our country, you know all wives are in their kitchens!'

"Without deigning to answer this ridiculous objection, Lärdal described to me, in detail and with painful honesty, my house and my kitchen, where, as far as I knew, he had never been.

"'To prove to you that I was truly there,' he concluded his account, 'I have hidden your wife's wedding ring in the bottom of the coal basket, for she had removed it to prepare a dish.'

"I immediately wrote home—this was the twenty-eighth of May—and asked my wife what she had been doing at eleven o'clock this same day. I urged her to probe her memory and give me a detailed account. Two weeks later—the letter took all this time due to bad routes of communication—my wife answered that on the twenty-eighth of May, at the specified hour, she was making a flour-based dish, that she would never forget that day because she had lost her wedding ring, which she had had on her finger not long before she began cooking, and which she had not been able to find again, despite much seeking on her part. It seemed to her that it had been stolen from her by a man who had briefly appeared in the kitchen dressed like a rich Laplander, but who, when she asked him what he wanted, had disappeared without saying a word."

Later, the ring was found in the bishop's kitchen, in the bread-basket.*[16]

The text speaks for itself. Note the manner in which the ecstasy is brought on, Peter Lärdal's recommendations, and the fact that the woman perceived him or, rather, briefly saw his Double, which is reminiscent of a phenomenon that the Anglo-Saxons call *fetch*.† In combing through travelers' accounts, we can find other examples that are just as telling. Johann Frischius relates in this vein the following anecdote, according to Brakius's *Historia Norwegiae:*

A fisherman from Lubeck came to speak about magic with a Laplander from Bergen, Norway, and the latter boasted of being able to send his spirit into far-off countries and to bring back news from there. So the Lubecker asked him, in order to put him to the test, to tell him what his wife was doing at the present moment in Lubeck.

---

*[The contradiction that exists in the wedding ring being hidden in the coal basket and found in the bread basket exists in the original text. —*Trans.*]

†[The *Concise Oxford* gives the following for *fetch:* "Person's wraith or double. (18th c.; orig. unkn.)"; for *wraith:* "Person's double or apparition supposedly seen shortly before or after his [*sic*] death; ghost; apparition. (16th c., orig. Sc., of unkn. orig.)." —*Trans.*]

The Laplander prepared himself right then for the trip and reported, a few hours later, that he had been to Lubeck, in the home of the fisherman's wife, and that he had brought back a knife as proof. He added that his wife had cut some bread with it and that she had poured wine into a carafe in preparation for the wedding meal of one of her close relatives. He also described the groom's clothes and his comportment and those of the bride and the guests, so that the fisherman was filled with surprise. Later, the fisherman discovered that everything had been exactly as the Laplander had said. During the time of his trip, the Laplander was laid out on the ground, as if dead.

In this chapter I have presented a few examples—I could easily give many more—of a civilization in which the Double is well known and well established. Such accounts leave at our disposal an important amount of information allowing us to understand phenomena that, according to the clerical interpretation of the Middle Ages, fall into the realm of witchcraft. I propose another reading—that is, a reexamination—of these phenomena in light of the traditions parallel to the Christian tradition that we've just seen. Before that, however, it is necessary to present briefly the pagan concept of the soul, which provides the key to understanding the Double.

3

An Unusual Concept
of the Soul

Once we have become aware of the unusual nature of ecstatic voyages, we cannot help but ask questions about the mental world that forms the humus in which these voyages are rooted, and here, the literature of the ancient Scandinavians can help us immensely.

Their literature teaches us that the Northern Germanic peoples did not create for themselves an idea of the soul that resembles our most common understanding of the term, the proof of which is that *sál* or *sála*, "soul," is a relatively late borrowing from Old Saxon. This culture thought differently about the spiritual principle that we call soul, and careful study of the lexicon of the other ancient Germanic dialects (Gothic, Old English, Old Saxon) reveals a certain unity of thinking among these peoples. Unfortunately, outside of the Norse language, only a few isolated terms have survived, and their meanings are very difficult to determine. We will begin, therefore, with the clearest particulars.

During the time of the ancient Scandinavians and Germanic peoples, at least three terms designated what Christians call the soul, without the semantics of the concepts overlapping exactly.[1] These are *fylgja, hamr,* and *hugr.* We will examine each, and then look into other medieval cultures where any analogies exist, which will lead us to show that epiphanies of the soul are not necessarily tied to human form.

THE FYLGJA

The *fylgja*, literally "the female follower," is the spiritual Double of an individual. She appears as a tutelary genie attached to a man or a family. A person can have several *fylgjur*, and in the Middle Ages it was believed that the more a person had, the stronger that person was. When the fylgja or fylgjur attack an enemy, they bring on irrepressible yawning and sleepiness. A passage from *The Saga of the Burnt Njal* illustrates this point: "So then Svann began to speak, yawning as he did so: 'Look here now, Osvif's tutelary spirits (fylgjur) are attacking us,' he said."

The spiritual Double can leave his possessor when the latter falls asleep. "The two Thorgeirs entered a wood," says the same saga. "There, they were taken by great sleepiness, and all they could do was sleep." The two men had left on an expedition against Gunnar, and "that night, Njal was at Thorolfsfell and could not sleep," says the saga. When he is asked what is bothering him, he answers, "Many things are happening before my eyes; I see a great number of the ferocious fylgjur of Gunnar's enemies." These are, of course, the fylgjur of the two Thorgeirs and their men.

The fylgja, psychic Double with tutelary functions, is closely linked to destiny in the Scandinavian tradition. A very lovely text, *The Saga of Gisli Sursson*, written around 1250–1260 but reporting events that happened between 960 and 977, tells of an outlaw, Gisli, pursued in his dreams by two women, one good, the other bad. The bad one, always seeking to rub him with blood, predicts only evil for him and begins appearing to him more and more often. These women are without a doubt alter egos: The good woman is Gisli's alter ego, and the malicious woman is that of one of his enemies. Just before his death, Gisli has two dreams. The good woman takes him on a gray horse—a psychopomp animal whose color indicates its supernatural and fateful nature—to a big house and says to him, "This is where you will come when you die." Gisli says of the bad woman of the dream, "She put a bonnet dripping with blood on my head, after having washed my head in the blood, and then she sprayed me all over with it." The mention of the bonnet, an object of the theme of the hereafter, reinforces the inevitable nature of the fatal destiny awaiting Gisli.

The fylgja's primary mission is to protect the person to whom she has attached herself, but she is not always immediately recognizable, as here:

> An had a restless sleep. He was awakened and asked what he had been dreaming. He answered: "A woman came to me, repugnant, and pulled me toward the edge of the bed. She had a large kitchen knife in one hand and a trough in the other. She plunged the knife into my chest, opened up my stomach, and took out the entrails."

Soon after, An is seriously wounded in the stomach. He is believed to be dead and is being watched over when suddenly his corpse sits up and says, "I dreamed of the same woman as before, and it seemed to me . . . that she was putting my entrails back in place and I felt good about this interaction."[2] The woman proceeds, therefore, with the inverse operation to the one that she had performed in the first dream, and it saved An's life.

The difficulty in precisely identifying the fylgja is also due to the very hesitations and inconsistencies of medieval writers. It seems that some of them saw the fylgja as corporal, as in the following passage from *The Saga of Thorstein with the Cow's Foot:*

> Thorstein, a child thought to be one of the lowest of peasants, one day entered the noble house where he was born as the result of an act of adultery, then abandoned. He ran into the room where his maternal grandfather was, fell, and heard his relative burst into laughter. He asked his grandfather the reason and heard the man say: "When you came into the room, a young white bear was following you. He was coming at you in the passageway, but when he saw me, he stopped. In your haste, you kept going and tripped over him. I am convinced that you are not the son of Krumm and Thorbrunn. You must have more powerful ancestors."[3]

That the alter ego precedes the visitor, be it friend or foe, is a belief that still exists today in Scandinavia. However, to show how tricky it is to distinguish between the two Doubles, hamr and fylgja, let us look at an example from the Swedish Laplanders: They believe that a spirit accompanies a man from the cradle to the grave and that it can take form, in certain circumstances, and appear as an alter ego or a close relative. This spirit is called *hambel,* obviously a deformation of the Norse *hamr,* and it is closely related to the guardian spirits that the Scandinavians call *vålnad* or *vård* (Norse *vörðr,* "guardian") and, in Norway, *vardøvl* and *valdøjer.** This "spirit" possesses the essential traits of the fylgja, the psychic Double: It has the same tutelary function and the same independence, but it is gifted with a certain corporeity in the most recent accounts: You can never see the *valdøgel* or valdøjer, but you can often hear it. You can recognize it by the sound of its steps behind the door or by its pushing on the doorknob just before a person enters. This is the sure sign of the return of someone who has been away from home for a long time.

When someone leaves, the door must be left open behind him so that the valdøgel can follow him. We do this when a foreigner leaves our house. Whoever goes traveling does not close the door behind him. This must be done only after he is already on his way. Opening the door behind the person leaving is called *se ud,* which means, "to follow with the eyes."[4]

It certainly seems that the animal nature of the Double predominates in the fylgja, whereas the hamr—Old English *hama*—is not necessarily theriomorphic. Hamr and fylgja are linked to sleep and trance, and they can travel to distant places. Hamr can act physically, whereas this is apparently impossible for the fylgja. And here is one more detail: The fylgja takes leave of a man just before his death, while the hamr remains attached to the body until its total disintegration and is thus, in this sense, related to the shamanistic soul of bones.

*These concepts must also absolutely be connected to the Finish *haltija,* deverbative of *hallita,* "to master, to dominate, to possess" (Germanic *halðiaz,* Gothic *halden*). Every man has a *haltija;* "It contains the name, the fortune, the destiny, the biological inheritance . . . of the man. . . . It is transmissible. . . . If it leaves the man after a certain period of time after death, this individual leaves the community of the living definitively," says A. Vilkuna, "Über den finnischen Haltija," in A. Hultkrantz, *The Supernatural Owners of Nature* (Stockholm/Göteborg/Uppsala, 1961), 158–65.

THE HAMR

In the case of the physical Double, the hamr, things are perhaps a little clearer because the examples in the texts are both numerous and telling.

Certain individuals, called *hamrammr,* "having a powerful Double," or *eigi einhamr,* "not possessing only one Double," are born with the ability to double themselves. The act of doubling is expressed in several ways, proof—if any is required—that it is well anchored in the mind-set of these times, for language is always a reflection of beliefs. We find *vixla hömum* and *skipta hömum,* "to change form," and the verb *hamask,* which indicates that the subject of the doubling is simultaneously active and passive. *Hamhleypa* means, more or less, "to flow into one's Double" or "to let one's Double run," and is a synonym of the phrase *springa af harmi,* literally "to go or spring out of oneself, one's skin."

When the alter ego travels, it runs risks, most notably that of not being able to reenter the body, which happens if someone disturbs the body while the alter ego is absent or if someone talks to the person whom the alter ego temporarily abandons. We find irrefutable proof of the corporeity of this Double in that the results of what happens to its body during its wanderings appear on its possessor's body once it has reentered this person. Here is an example:

> Dufthak of Dufthaksholt was powerfully skilled in doubling himself, as was Storolf, son of Hoeng, who lived in Hvall. These two had a disagreement about their pasturing arrangement. One night, around sunset, a man who was gifted with second sight saw a fat bear leaving Hvall and a bull leaving Dufthaksholt. They met at Storolfsvellir and started a furious fight. Eventually the bear got the upper hand. The next morning, the earth of the little valley where the bull and bear had met each other looked as if it had been torn up. Today this spot is called Öldugröf. As for Dufthak and Storolf, they were wounded, both of them.[5]

The zoomorphic Doubles of these two men get into a confrontation. Even though only a man gifted with clairvoyance can perceive alter egos, they are very much corporal, given that the little valley has been left with traces of the fight and that the bodies of the protagonists reveal the wounds for all to see. This passage is amazingly reminiscent of the more recent traditions of the Taltós, Hungarian shamans who engage in combat three times a year, or once every seven years, in the forms of horses, bulls, or flames.[6]

The Book of the Colonization of Iceland, one version of which— *Sturlubók,* "Sturla's Book"—is both credited to Sturla Thordarson (1214–1284) and named after him, introduces numerous characters who have the power of doubling: for example, Thorarinn Korin; Kveld-Ulf, grandfather of the famous Egill Skallagrimsson; and Thorkell Farserk. Elsewhere, the Icelandic family sagas, works that fall somewhere between chronicle and novel, mention many individuals who know how to liberate their Doubles. Examples can be found in the works of Régis Boyer and in my *Fantômes et Revenants.*

THE HUGR

It is necessary to say a word about the third component of the soul, the *hugr,* which roughly corresponds to the Latin *animus* and *spiritus.* "What this is about . . . is a kind of active universal principle," says Régis Boyer. "[I]t is more or less independent of individuals, but it can, on occasion, manifest itself directly or indirectly in man."[7] It can even manifest itself against people's will. It is this entity that takes on a form and animates the Double/hamr in order to go far away, either on a mission for a third party, or to fulfill a particularly strong desire. And what was said in Germany in the nineteenth century? "You must quench your thirst before you go to bed; otherwise, the spirit will go get something to drink while you are asleep."

In another Germanic language, Ulfilas (around 311–383), bishop of the Visigoths and creator of the Gothic alphabet, uses *hugs* (Norse *hugr*) for the Greek *nous,* "faculty of thought, mind, intelligence," in his translation of the New Testament. In the homilies of the early Middle Ages, *hugr* is used for *mens* and *animus,* from which it can be inferred that the term designates, above all, a spiritual principle, but the literature of the ancient Scandinavians reveals that it exists outside of man and besieges him.

To close these reflections on the concept of the soul in the ancient Germanic traditions, for the time being, I again take up Régis Boyer's illuminating synthesis: "Visited (hugr), inhabited (hamr), or accompanied (fylgja), it is perfectly clear that we cannot be reduced merely to our material dimensions, but that our dichotomous categories—real/unreal, material/spiritual, and in the extreme, life/death—are not suitable to us. If we are to grasp this concept in all its richness and uniqueness, we must, where physical and mental are indivisible, give up our unimaginative oppositions."

GREGORY THE GREAT AND THE SOUL

The idea of a single and indivisible soul, then, is foreign to Germanic paganism, the best representative of our far-reaching ancestors, and more generally, of the Indo-European peoples to whom this concept of the soul is fundamentally unknown. Christian scholars and theologians seek to define the soul, that is, to name the indescribable. Some slip on the deadly slope of heresy; others are led toward compromise. In short, the mixing of Christian dogma and the philosophy of classic and pagan antiquity does not happen without clashes, which, fortunately for us, have left behind some traces.

In his *Dialogues*,[8] Gregory the Great tackles the problem of the soul many times. He especially devotes the fourth book to this issue, wherein he addresses death and the hereafter, so it is much more likely than any of the other books to contain traces of paganism, local beliefs, relics, and recollections.

Indeed, he says, "All-powerful God created three vital spirits *(vitales spiritus)* [but *spiritus* can also mean "soul," as in the *Moralia in Iob*]: a spirit that is not covered in flesh; another that is covered in flesh, but which does not die with the flesh; and a third that is covered in flesh and dies with the flesh."

There exist, therefore, three spirits or three souls—such is Gregory's opinion in basic form. Nevertheless, the explanation given for this hard fact brings things quite quickly back to the straight and narrow. The first spirit is that of the angels; the second, that of men; the third, "that of domestic animals and all wild beasts." Man is therefore indeed the intermediary between the angels and the beasts, in conformity with Augustinian thought. However, the proposed schema can be read in another way: The angelic spirit corresponds to the psychic Double (daimôn, genius, fylgja); the second, the one that does not die with the flesh, to the physical Double (hamr) or the shamanistic soul of bones; and the third is simply the soul as the breath of life.

In principle, the soul cannot be seen — "The nature of the soul is invisible," says Gregory — but many who have "purified the eye of the spirit *(mentis oculum)* through pure faith and prolonged prayer, have frequently seen souls leaving the body" *(egredientes e carne animas viderunt).* He then cites some examples, among them that of a certain Gregory who had an ecstatic experience *(spiritus sublevatas)* "and saw the soul of Speciosus, who was so far away from him, leave his body. He announced this to the brothers [of the monastery] and left in haste [for Capua]. There he found his brother already buried and learned that his soul had left his body at the time that he saw it." We now know, thanks to pagan traditions, that Speciosus's psychic Double must have brought on Gregory's ecstasy so that he could deliver to Gregory the news of his death.

Mention is often made in Christian literature of the soul in the form of a bird. When Speciosus died, Gregory the Great writes, "He gave up his soul during his prayer. The brothers who were present saw a dove come out of this mouth." The motif is curious and, in any case, pre-Christian: The zoomorphic soul — and visible, at that — takes us back to archaic pagan concepts, those that we encounter specifically among shamanistic peoples.

When the Lombards hanged two of the venerable Valentio's monks from the branches of a tree, Gregory says, "That night, their spirits began to chant in a high and intelligible voice." This was attributed to a miracle of God, "who allowed these spiritual voices *(voces spirituum* [*sic*]*)* to reach corporal ears." Who will believe this? In fact, something survives, remains near the hanged men, and is heard—and we know it is the Double because, according to various ancient opinions, it stays near the body for thirty or forty days before going away.

Another Gregorian example is fascinating due to the perspectives that it opens. Armentarius was "taken away by those who surrounded him" *(sublevatus a praesentibus),* and had a vision from which he learned who was going to die from the plague that was devastating Rome. He brought back proof of his voyage to the sky: He spoke Greek, a language he had not known before. What does this anecdote mean, if not that the visionary received a gift during his ecstasy, his trip to the hereafter? According to the ecstatic's religion and his civilization, this gift is reputed to come from God or from the spirits. Ecstasy is a temporary death, an initiation. We can recall the pagans who slept on tombs in order to have revelations and came back from their sleep with gifts. We also find ecstasy in incubation and it is also seen in the practice of shamans, for whom the ecstatic state permits communication with the other world. In *The Saga of Thorleif, skald of the Jarls,* the pastor Hallbjörn is lying on a funeral mound, trying in vain to sing a poem in honor of the deceased. He falls asleep, and the dead man (Thorleif) visits him in a dream, unties his tongue, and makes him into a great poet.[9]

In short, the similarity between pagan beliefs and certain Christian traditions is astounding, and as to the Double, it is certain that there was a blending, which the texts we've collected so far do much more than suggest. Let us not forget the same message that can be concluded from all of these: The other world is open and accessible to Doubles, whether they are called soul, spirit, or something else.

Next, we will take up some examples of particular concepts of the soul in the Middle Ages that are also present in shamanism.

THE SOUL OF BONES

There exists at least one extraordinary example of the survival of a belief well known to shamanism: the belief in the soul of bones, that is, in a soul residing in the bones.

The Fascination of Gylfi, the second part of the *Edda,* which was written in prose by Snorri Sturluson (1179–1241), contains the following episode from the life of the god Thor:

> [Thor is traveling with Loki on his cart, which is being pulled by some goats.] At nightfall, they arrived at a farmer's house and obtained permission to spend the night there. That night, Thor took his goats and killed them both. Then they were skinned and placed in a cauldron. . . . [Everyone is having a meal.] Thor put the goatskins between the fire and the door and told the farmer and his people to place the bones on the skins. But Thjalfi, the farmer's son, kept one of the goat's thigh bones and cracked it with his knife to get to the marrow. . . . [In the morning, Thor takes his hammer, Mjöllnir, brandishes it and recites] incantations on the goatskins. They were brought back to life, but one of them was limping, favoring his back foot.[10]

Easily recognizable here is a shamanistic ritual designed to prevent game from becoming scarce by allowing the killed animal to be reborn from its bones. In the *Miracula sancti Germani,* which Heiric of Auxerre dedicated to Charles the Bald in 872, we find approximately the same story, but Saint Germain replaces the god Thor. Germain accepts the hospitality of a poor herdsman who kills his only calf to feed him. Once dinner is finished, the saint orders his host's wife to gather together the bones of the calf and place them on its skin. She obeys, and the saint brings the calf back to life.[11]

In the story of Saint Germain and King Benli, as told in the *Historia Britonum,*[12] a compilation of seven different opuscula completed at the beginning of the ninth century, Germain stipulates that the bones of the calf must not be broken *(et praecepit sanctus Germanus ut non confringeretur de ossibus eius),* a detail that Jacopo de Voragine does not provide in his version of the *Vita* of the saint, which he inserts in *The Golden Legend.*

In 1390 the Milanese Inquisitor Fra Beltamino of Cernuscullo questions Sibillia, wife of Lombardo of Fraguliati, and Pierina, wife of Pietro of Bripio. The women admit to having taken part in a nocturnal procession of Diana and Herodias, a scholarly transliteration of *Madonna Oriente,* which is the name provided by both women. Then Pierina specifies that during these nocturnal excursions there is a banquet for which cattle are killed. After they are eaten, their bones are gathered together and placed on the skins. Oriente hits the skins with the handle of her stick, and the animals come back to life. Of course, she adds, the cattle are no longer able to work.[13] Madonna Oriente's actions are amazingly similar to those of the god Thor, but a genetic link between the fourteenth-century Italian testimony and the Norse myth transcribed by Snorri in the thirteenth century is unimaginable. It must be imagined, then, that both come from the same reservoir of belief, the best examples of which are provided by shamanism with its soul of bones.[14]

Among shamanistic peoples (Turko-Tartars and Siberians), the inferior soul is said to reside in the bones. Even animals have such a soul, which is why their bones must not be damaged when they are butchered; their bones must be buried in a precise order to ensure that the flesh can cover them again and that the animal can be reborn and hunted anew. Today it is known that this belief is characteristic of hunting peoples and that is has a very long history.[15]

In classical antiquity, the same belief can be found in ghost stories, but it is hard to perceive. Take the story of the haunted house of Athens: If you dig in the place where the ghost disappeared, you will discover a skeleton in chains. Pliny the Younger, who tells this story, says the following of the meeting between death and the philosopher Anthenagoras:[16] "[T]hen a phantom appeared. It was an emaciated old man, covered in rags, with a great beard and shaggy hair. Chains fettered his feet and his hands, and he was rattling his chains."

So it can be clearly seen, then, that bones are the Double's carrier, and represent the refuge of the bony soul.

In *The Life of Saint Germain,*[17] which Constance of Lyon wrote around 475–480, the ghost who appears is not really described—he is "hideous" and "terrifying," but he is not a skeleton. When the ground is dug up, however, to satisfy his request for a decent burial, the only thing discovered is, of course, the bones of a skeleton. Christianity speaks, in this case, of souls in distress, but in my opinion, this story is about the physical Double who remains attached to the dead person, and it should be regarded as one of the manifestations of the soul of bones. In addition, more recent traditions almost always link hauntings to the presence of a skeleton hidden somewhere, a lovely storybook illustration of which can be found in Oscar Wilde's *The Canterville Ghost.*

LEUTARD'S MISADVENTURE

Near the year 1048, Raoul, known as Glaber, completed at Cluny his five books of *Stories* covering the years from 900 to 1004, which he dedicated to the priest Saint Odilon.[18] Among the marvels and other manifestations that the men of this time interpreted as signs of the Last Judgment was a blossoming of heresies. In the fourth book, Raoul gives a surprising account of an event that happened in Gaul around the end of the year 1000 and that remains, to my knowledge, the only such event:

> In the village of Vertus, county Chalons, lived a man of the people named Leutard who, as the end of the affair proves, can be taken for Satan's envoy. His audacious folly [heresy] came about in the following fashion.
>
> One day he was alone in a field, occupied with some farming work. Fatigue put him to sleep, and it seemed to him that a great swarm of bees penetrated his body through his secret natural exit. They then came back out through his mouth in an enormous buzzing and tormented him with a great number of stings. After they had afflicted him with their stingers for a long time, he thought he heard them talking and ordering him to do many things that are impossible for men to do.
>
> Finally, exhausted, he got up, returned home, chased his wife, and claimed divorce in compliance with the evangelical precepts.

In order truly to understand this text, you must overlook its Christian appearance, and thus eliminate both Satan and the verb *believe,* which throws doubt on the fact that the bees talk. It needs to be realized as well that the mention of the "natural exit"—in other words, the anus—is part of the arsenal of terms clerics use to demonize an event. Let us remember that demons are always linked to impurity, that they almost always leave a horrendous stench behind when they disappear, and—this is a significant detail—that they often appear in latrines. In fact, in his *Autobiography*, Guibert of Nogent (d. 1125) cites the case of a demon who faints in one.[19] And in Iceland, *The Tale of Thorstein Skelk* tells this: One night Thorstein went to the latrines, which have room for nine people. Suddenly, a *puki* (demon) sat next to him and declared that he had come from hell. He moved in closer and closer to Thorstein, but then the church bells rang, and, screaming, this demon went back underground.[20]

In an account like that of Raoul Glaber, every detail has meaning, especially given that it certainly seems to be a summary of occurrences. Raoul speaks of bees, noble and useful insects that, according to legend, came directly from heaven.[21] For Christians, the bee symbolizes chastity. In fact, Saint Ambrose (339–397) compared the Church to a beehive. This positive image was preserved for a long time, and an ancient Comtadine tradition maintains that the people of Saint-Roumanet (Vaucluse), who were besieged by the Huguenots, owed their salvation to some bees that were miraculously incited against the Calvinists.[22] So in having the bees intervene Raoul has certainly preserved an ancient aspect of local beliefs, without seeing the contradiction between their positive image and the negative acts (in his view) in which they are engaged.

To highlight the demonic aspect of certain events, flies are most often called upon, as in the story of Cunibert. This insect is Satan's, and Beelzebub is, in the *Malleus maleficarum* of J. Sprenger and H. Institoris, "prince of the flies." And when Otto, bishop of Bamberg (1103–1139) and advocate of Pomerania, proceeds to the lustration of the pagan temple of Stettin, the ancient Sedinum, evil spirits take flight in the form of flies.

Now let us return to Leutard and examine the chronology of events. Tired, Leutard falls asleep. He is lying on the ground, and this is when the bees enter his body. The underlying mythic structure is exactly the same as in the stories of men who lie down unknowingly where a shaman has been buried and are suddenly possessed by his spirit. The same structure also appears in medieval accounts of what is a Celtic, Germanic, and shamanistic ritual, in which individuals lie down on tombs in order to have a revelation.

The bees then begin talking to Leutard. If anything, this means that he suddenly understands their language, but this point is not of crucial importance. Whatever the hypothesis, we fall once again upon some familiar particulars: If Leutard hears their language, this is because he has just received a gift—the ability to communicate with the spirits. We thus have a selection or choosing process that is almost shamanistic: Leutard is chosen to accomplish a mission for the good of humanity, an essential characteristic of the shaman who is in the service of the clan, but as this mission is contrary to the dogma of the dominant religion, this notion of usefulness falls by the wayside. Yet Leutard's suffering favors the hypothesis of a choosing: The bees torment him with their stingers; no initiation can occur without pain. There is also his exhaustion when he returns to himself, exactly as if he were coming out of a trance. Understanding an animal language, undergoing suffering, experiencing exhaustion: We are very much in the realm of shamanism.

May you understand me well: I am proposing an interpretation that uses the events as support, but this interpretation in no way implies that Raoul Glaber or even Leutard was aware of what is hidden behind this unusual adventure, which above all else bears witness to the perpetuity of some very ancient mythic patterns.

THE CATHARS AND THE DOUBLE

With regard to the religion of the Cathars, a distinction must be made between that which comes under the heading of great theories, which we encounter in specialized treatises, and the popular beliefs that can be found scattered in the minutes of heretical trials.

In the *Register* of Bishop Jacques Fournier,[23] director of the Inquisition at Pamiers (Ariège) from 1318 to 1325, the heretic Pierre Maury reports, with the help of an exemplum similar to the legend of King Guntram, how the Cathars consider the relationship between the soul and the body:

One day, two believers were at the side of a river. One fell asleep, while the other stayed awake, only to see a creature that looked like a lizard come out of the sleeping man's mouth. Suddenly, this lizard, making use of a plank or a piece of straw extending from one bank to the other, crossed over the river. On the other bank was a donkey's skull that had been picked clean. The lizard went in and out of the skull through the many holes in it. Then, crossing back over the river, he came back to the sleeping man's mouth. He did this once or twice. Seeing this, the man who had stayed awake had an idea: He waited for the lizard to cross to the other side of the river toward the donkey's head, and then he removed the plank. The lizard left the donkey's skull and came back to the riverbank, but it was impossible to cross! Gone was the plank! Suddenly, the body of the sleeping man began to thrash about greatly, but he did not wake up, despite all the efforts of the man watching over him to pull him from his sleep. Finally, the man keeping watch replaced the plank over the river. The lizard could then retrace his steps and return to the body of the sleeper by passing through his mouth. Just then, the man woke up and told his friend about the dream he had just had.

"I dreamed that I crossed a river on a plank and that I entered a great palace with many towers and rooms. But when I wanted to come back to the place where I had started, there was no more plank! It was impossible to cross! I might have drowned in the river. Whence my agitation (in my sleep) until the plank was replaced and I could come back."

The two believers marveled much over this adventure and went to tell it to a perfecti who gave them the key to the mystery:

"The soul," he said, "resides permanently in the body of man; the spirit, on the other hand, goes in and out of the human body, exactly as the lizard who went from the sleeping man's mouth to the donkey's head, back and forth."[24]

Another passage from Jacques Fournier's *Register,* which Emmanuel Le Roy Ladurie does not mention in *Mantaillou,* sheds light on the above text, which is already remarkable in its idea of the spirit enjoying independence, leaving and returning to the body at will:

> Have you heard heretics saying, and have you believed that there are two rational substances in man, that is, two souls, or one spirit and one soul made such that one resides in the body during life and the other, the spirit, comes and goes and does not always stay in the man; that these impressions, waking dreams, reflections, and other phenomena having to with consciousness, are produced in man by the spirit; and that man possesses a soul due to the mere fact that he is alive?
>
> I heard the late heretic Philippe of Coustaussa and the believer Mersende Marty say that, while he is alive, a person always has a soul, but that when a person becomes a believer or a heretic, a good spirit comes, so that between the first soul and the spirit a sort of honeymoon is celebrated, the promoter of which is God. If after this the believer or the heretic gives up his faith or his heresy, this good spirit leaves the person and is replaced by an evil spirit. This, they said, is how the spirit enters and leaves a person. But the soul stays in a person as long as he is alive. I have not heard it specified whether they are talking about a human spirit, a created spirit *(spiritus creatus)* or the Holy Spirit, therefore God. However, they call the evil spirit that enters a person the devil.[25]

We can read between the lines of the following: The soul corresponds more or less to the vital principle, which explains the confusion of certain inhabitants of Montaillou, for whom "the soul means blood." The spirit is close to the Greek daimôn and the Roman genius, but it joins with an individual only after his conversion to the faith preached by the perfecti. This is either a concession to Cathar dogma or an attempt to conform a folk belief to the local religion. Whatever it is, for the people of fourteenth-century Montaillou man was inhabited by two entities, called *soul* and *spirit.*

It is interesting to observe the independence of the spirit and its ability to metamorphose, because both clearly indicate that we are dealing with the Double. In Upper Ariège and elsewhere around 1300, spirit and soul had one body. William Fort, a farmer from Montaillou, speaks of Arnaude Rives, living in Balcaïre, in the diocese of Alet: "Arnaude herself sees these souls! They have flesh, bones, and all body parts: head, feet, hands, and everything else. They also have a proper body at their disposal."[26] These souls take bodily form as ghosts or Doubles. We are very close here to Homeric concepts in which the *psuchè* takes the form of a corpse to produce a phantom *(eidolôn)*. Over and above any formalized religion, it is apparent that, for medieval man, the Double was well and truly a reality, though certainly on the margins of the great theological or mythical explanations and speculations. In Sabarthès, the soul is corporal. Pierre Maury states, "For as long as I have had access to reason, I have always believed that the human soul had form, shape, limbs, flesh, and bones, exactly like the human body."[27] Can a better description of the Double be found? Moreover, the people of Montaillou say that "souls are transported by birds," which takes us back to flight and metamorphosis, to the zoomorphic alter ego, even if, in accordance with Christian interpretation, demons are the ones who supposedly take this form.

In his study, E. Le Roy Ladurie concludes: "Thus, according to some, man has his personal lizard spirit, which presides over his waking life, even if it means standing back during sleep and dreams. Man possesses a soul in the form of the Double,"[28] which is not entirely exact. Placed in our context, the Ariègian particulars teach us that behind the terms *soul* and *spirit* is concealed the idea of a psychic and physical alter ego. The lizard spirit is the theriomorphic Double corresponding to the hamr of the ancient Scandinavians and the Finnish *haamu;* the image soul corresponds to the Greek eidolôn and the psychic Double, which is, however, lacking the explicit characteristic of the tutelary genie. But in Jacques Fournier's *Register*, it is said that the souls of the dead come back to watch over their sleeping loved ones.

At the heart of the microsociety depicted in the *Register*, one character is comparable, relatively speaking, to a shaman: the *armier*, the souls' messenger, who is charged with establishing and maintaining contact with the dead who surround us. Arnaud Gelis, armier for the Pamiers region, sees the dead and takes on their commissions concerning the living and vice versa, and if he does not fulfill his mission, the dead beat him severely with sticks.[29] Unfortunately, we do not know how he sees the dead, which limits his similarity to the shamans.

While no genetic link can be imagined between the beliefs of the Ariègian Cathars and those of the Germanic countries and the Siberian peoples, we find the same mental universe, irrefutable proof that this is about the survival of an extraordinarily ancient mind-set, of—I am tempted to say—an archetype. Either in its raw form or individualized and transposed into a psychological, philosophical, or religious framework, the Double is decidedly one of the constitutive elements of human thought. Because it is the link that connects us to the invisible, to the dead, the gods, the spirits, to the part of the individual that is a gift from the superior powers, and thus destined, the Double could have easily merged with the Christian soul. It proceeds from the same vision of the world, it places the human person in the divine order, confers upon him a teleological nature, a finality, and above all, abolishes the notion of a return to nothingness. *Nom omnis moriar,* "I will not die entirely," said Horace. His words certainly apply to our subject. One of our Doubles will immortalize us, suggest the texts, whether it be through the transmigration of souls or by another means.

Part 2
The Disguises of the Double

4

The Double and Fairies

One striking aspect of Roman and Celtic literature is the presence of fairies who function as destiny, female protectress, lover, and even wife. In the Scandinavian texts, apart from the translations and adaptations of French works, fairies are nonexistent. It is of some interest to our investigation into the Double to explain this curious phenomenon, especially given that careful examination of the accounts from medieval France will allow us to shed light on some narrative layers as well as on some beliefs analogous to those of the Germanic world.

Let us take another look at *The Lay of Lanval*,[1] written by Marie de France around 1170, and, putting aside all literary interpretations and linear commentaries, focus on the essential. Lanval leaves and goes into the forest, dismounts next to a flowing water, rolls his coat under his head, and lies down. He is deep in thought when two young maidens arrive. They invite him to follow them to their mistress, who says to the knight, "It is for you that I left my land, and my land is far, far away . . . for I love you more than anything in the world." She gives him a gift—wealth—but forbids him to tell anyone about their love. Before sending Lanval away, the fairy speaks these words: "Whenever you wish for my presence, there is no place, at least among places where one can receive his lover without villainy or offense"—very enigmatic—"where I would not come to you, ready to do your every wish; and no one will see me, save you, and no one will hear my words." When Lanval breaks his oath under the weight of circumstances, the fairy appears to everyone in the court of King Arthur, saves her lover from death, and then leaves. Unable to bear losing her, Lanval leaps onto the back of her horse behind her, and the palfrey gallops off. "It carried them away," say the Bretons, "to Avalon, an island both beautiful and magical."

The extent to which Marie de France—born in Normandy, a region of Scandinavian population, and a resident of England in the entourage of Henry II Plantagenet—was familiar with folk traditions and beliefs cannot be known. Her lays show evidence of them, but this poetess adapts and psychologizes what she gathers—the unsolidified material in the mold of courtly poetry—which makes the primary meaning very difficult to discover. But we may try to clarify *The Lay of Lanval.*

Lanval's encounter with the fairy takes place while the hero is cut off from civilization, in a forest that serves as the borderline between the supernatural world and the world of humans. He is lying down, and even though he is not sleeping, the theme of sleep is not far away. In order to find it, we need only replace the preposition *under* in the lay (v. 50) with its antonym.* When the fairy's handmaidens arrive on the scene, they show him their mistress's tent, which is set up close by—"look: her tents are near"†—yet Lanval has not seen it. The fairy knows the hero, loves him, and left the other world to find him, but what other world? She tells him that all he must do is turn his thoughts to her, and she will appear. So in fact, everything happens as if we have been catapulted into a dream world.

The anonymous fairy bears a strong resemblance to the Double/fylgja, the tutelary genie. In addition, a curious distortion deserves to be noted: Lanval's disappearance on the fairy's horse is the euphemistic expression of his death, which comes about because the fairy appears before King Arthur's court. Sometimes, as we will see later (part 3, chapter 7), the moment a man sees his alter ego, he knows he is doomed to die very soon. At a final level of analysis, beyond the literary adaptation

---

*[The Old French given here is *desuz,* referring to his coat which is "under" his head. — *Trans.*]

†[The Old French here is *veez: pres est sis paveillons.* — *Trans.*]

imposed by culture, the dominant religion (Christianity), and the poet-ess's circumstances, the idea of the psychic Double (fylgja) shines through, adapted here into a sort of hierogamy, or sacred marriage.

Marie de France seems to individualize the alter ego and to place it in the realm of the fairy world and the marvelous. But fairies, whose origins are complex, are referred to in Latin texts by terms that suit the Double as well—*fantasia, fantasma, dea phantastica, mulier fatata*—which also convey the ideas of dreams, phantom, and destiny.[2] What is more, these ideas are related to the visions we have during the first hours of sleep, pre-cisely as Hugucio of Pisa (d. 1210), bishop of Ferrara, said. We are, then, well within our rights to wonder if, in a "primitive" version of the tale that Marie de France has copied, Lanval has not fallen asleep, for the encounter seems at the start to be taking place in the other world, which is suggested in the lay by the forest and the presence of water, common borders between our world and the next. Leaving this lay for the moment, the next part of our inquiry will provide the justification for this hypothesis.

Another Melusinian legend—that is, one characterized by the union of a mortal and a supernatural being—is *Peter von Staufenberg*, written around 1310, and it provides us with other means of assessment.[3] The structure of the account is the same as that of the lay by Marie de France, but the tutelary role of the fairy is much more marked. During his first encounter with her, the hero hears these words:

My friend, I have been waiting for you, and I swear to you that I have faithfully accompanied you everywhere you have been since you mounted your horse. Since then I have been taking care of you on the roads and paths. In assaults and battles I have unceasingly protected you as one would a friend. In tournaments, I have watched over you well to ensure that nothing would happen to you. In all the courts where there was jousting, I protected you, generous knight, through your shield. I did the same in the Holy Land. . . . In Prussia, I guarded you from the Slavs and the Russians; in England and in France, I watched over you; and in Tuscany and Lombardy, I took good care of you. In all these places, I kept you from dishonor. Wherever your desire took you, I was close by, invisible. . . . Know that I have always wrapped you in my faithful vigilance.[4]

It is clear that she is his good genie, his tutelary genie, and she has not taken one step away from him since he left childhood—in fact, since his birth, if we refer back to Scandinavian traditions. This fairy is thus, in a way, Peter's destiny, his fortune.

"I can go wherever I want to be," says the fairy to the hero, who has only to call her—with his mind, I should specify, according to *Lanval*—and she will appear. This fairy is the Celtic counterpart to the Norse fylgja.

The fylgja is very often zoomorphic. Since the twelfth and thirteenth centuries, there has existed a direct relationship between fairies and certain animals: the wild boar, the doe, the stag.* These animals correspond, of course, to the hunting-related canons of courtly civilization and reflect its aristocratic culture, but they also have a pronounced supernatural character, which is indicated by their color—white, for example—or by an anatomical detail, or even by their strange behavior. They can metamorphose into human beings, like the knight in *The Lay of Tyolet* and King Lar in *The Wigalois* by Wirnt von Grafenberg. The essential function of these unusual animals is to lead a knight to a fairy, which experts in the study of folk tales referred to as the theme of the animal guide.

In *Partenopeu de Blois,* a novel from the end of the twelfth century, Mélior, a fairy who is given a very rationalized interpretation, swears to the hero at nightfall (the usual time for doubling in the Norse tradition)[5] that she created the wild boar that led to their meeting. In all the stories of this type, the animal suddenly and mysteriously disappears once its mission is accomplished, which is the moment the fairy appears before her chosen lover. To borrow the words of Jean Frappier, this animal, often

---

*The perusal of the Celtic texts by T. P. Cross (*Motif Index of Early Irish Literature,* Bloomington, Indiana, 1952, 256 f.) teaches us that fairies become bears, wolves, hares, eels, snake, etc. Common to the Germanic and Celtic worlds are metamorphoses into bear, wolf, horse, swan, or more generally, into bird, eagle, and falcon for the ancient Scandinavians. See in Cross motif F 234.1 and 220 ff., references classed under the rubric "external soul" ("the soul outside of the body, the soul enters and leaves the body").

white, is "a lure sent by the fairy to draw close to her, into the other world, the one whom she loves."* Laurence Harf comes close to the truth when, with regard to *The Lay of Graelent,* she conjectures that the white doe is a manifestation of the fairy.[6]

Celtic and Germanic traditions have many points in common, if only through the intermediary of England, where Saxons, Danes, and Norwegians were in contact with Celtic populations, or through the channel of mixed marriages that took place when a Scandinavian kingdom existed in Ireland and when the Shetland Islands, the Orkneys, the Hebrides, and the Isle of Man were Scandinavian, a point extremely well studied recently by Jean Renaud.[7] If we bring together these traditions, which many insist on attempting to keep separate, we can prove Harf right: Understood as the Celtic form of the fylgja (that there are no fairies in ancient Germanic literature should have made us think!), and certainly going back to the same common Indo-European reservoir of beliefs, the female tutelary genie and destiny both possess animal exteriors. Understood as the spiritual Double representing the part of man that lives in the other world, the part that connects him to the Whole— remember that Aristotle, Orpheus, Pythagorus, and Empedocles taught that the Self exists before the body and will continue after it—the fairy comes to reunite herself with the man she has chosen to accompany or follow (the verb *fylgja*). She makes a pact with him that binds both parties to honor it because it rests on reciprocal agreement. Of little importance here are the forms this pact takes or its bans on seeing or telling; all that matters is the deed. Look at this passage from *The Saga of Hallfred, the Difficult Skald:* Hallfred's fylgja appears before him soon before his death. He recognizes her, understands what must happen, and says, "I declare all ties between us now dissolved." She turns toward his eldest son and asks him if he wants her. In the face of his refusal, she goes to Hallfred's youngest son, who says, "I will take you," and then she disappears.

---

*J. Frappier, *Chrétien de Troyes* (Paris, 1968), 90 f. Frappier adds: "It is the same, taking into account a few variations, in the lays of *Guigemar, Graelent,* and *Guingamor,*" texts whose Celtic origin is beyond doubt.

In the lays that have been influenced by Celtic tradition, it certainly seems that belief in the pact between mortal and fylgja has been secularized in order to produce the accounts familiar to us. In these narratives, certain details resist analysis; at the time of their creation, there was a more concrete and fashionable way of expressing the ties that unite man to his psychic alter ego. This other self is brought back to its dimensions, to a human form and a human story, a story of love. The fairy/fylgja makes herself known, rather than confining herself to dreams. She comes looking for the man on whom she has set her heart, but she refuses to force herself on him and proposes a deal. Whether it be Lanval's lover or Hallfred's fylgja, the supernatural being, the Double, binds itself to a mortal only upon the agreement of the latter; it retains its daimôn nature.

Allow me to add two items in support of my hypothesis of a hierogamy between an individual and his Double. Studying the ways in which a shaman obtains his powers, Mircea Eliade reports on the traditions of the Goldi, a Mongolian tribe of eastern Siberia living on the banks of the Amur River, and on those of the Yakuts, a Siberian people living on the Lena River. A Goldi man explained to ethnologist L. Sternberg how he became a shaman:

One day, I was sleeping on my bed of suffering when a spirit approached me. She was a very beautiful woman, very slim. . . . Her face and her appearance seemed in every way like those of our Goldi women. . . . She told me: "I am the *áyami* [protector spirit] of your ancestors, the shamans. I taught them how to shamanize; now I will teach you too." Then she added: "I love you. You will be my husband, for I do not have one now, and I will be your wife. I will give you spirits who will help you in the art of healing. I will teach you this art and I will assist you myself. . . . If you do not want to obey me," she said to me, "too bad for you! I will kill you."

Since then, she has never stopped coming to my house. I lie with her as if she were my real wife, but we have no children. She lives completely alone, without relatives, in a little hut on a mountain. But she often changes where she lives. Sometimes she appears as an old woman or a wolf; that way, people cannot look at her without being terrified.[8]

Over the course of centuries, according to the unknown factors resulting from interactions between different cultures, the belief in the shamanistic protector/woman spirit crosses paths with the mythic theme of the supernatural nymph, or half-goddess who is both wife and teacher to the hero—without us being able to determine which is the original element in this blending. In the Middle Ages, this character reemerged in the Melusinian stories, but it exists throughout the whole Indo-European world, the most ancient examples of which can be read in the literature of Vedic India. Eliade suggests that the theme of the supernatural wife is a "derivation"—meaning "deviation," as well—or manifestation of the ecstatic experience.

According to the account of the Goldi shaman, the supernatural woman, or áyami, is comparable in many ways to the Norse fylgja and the Celtic fairies: They all choose a human for a lover, take over his life, and become his protector genie. Of course, different civilizations and imaginations produced very diverse accounts of this thematic character, but we will turn our attention to one particular detail.

In the theme termed by folklorists as that of the fairy mistress, the union of a mortal and a fairy remains sterile, except in those legends intended to glorify a lineage—the kind of legends that can be found in books such as *The Romance of Melusine* by Jean d'Arras—or to explain the diabolic nature of the members of certain families, such as the tales of the demonic countess of Anjou, an ancestor of the Plantagenet family, which Giraud de Barri reports in his treatise *The Instruction of Princes (De principiis instructione)*.[9] Lanval and Graelent have no children with their lovers; in *Désiré,* the children remain the property of the supernatural woman and disappear when she does. The presence of offspring lends a human dimension to the woman spirit; the disappearance of any children along with their mother is in some way the last vestige of the primitive belief from which these legends and myths emerge.

In the nineteenth century, J. Basanavičius recorded the following regarding a tale in Lithuania:

A son "without a part in life" *(bedalis)* left to travel the world and met Old Man God, who questioned him. "I do not know myself where I am going," he replied. "I have no part in life [no destiny], nothing is successful for me, I do not know where to go!" The old man took him on as a servant and sent him to get water at a spring. Three birds alighted there — three cygnets, according to one variation — who removed their feathers and went bathing in the form of women. The young man told the old man what he saw, and the old man said to him: "Do you know what that is? It is your *dalis* (part in life, destiny), who came to bathe." He advised the young man to steal the youngest bathers feathers and not to give them back until she promised to be his dalis. The boy without a part in life followed this advice. He married the woman swan and they lived happily ever after.[10]

The tale of the woman swan — well known to the Celts and to Germanic peoples, found in *The Lay of Graelent,* and especially famous thanks to the legend of Wieland the blacksmith — here assumes its true mythic dimension:[11] Man is united with his destiny, captures it, makes it his own, and thus receives good fortune and wealth. Through the many variations of this myth, an original model exists with the following guiding threads:

- In the other world live (feminine?) beings, each of which chooses to be the tutelary genie of an individual and to accompany him. See the story of Peter von Staufenberg, above.

- The tutelary genie becomes the psychic Double, the diamôn, of her protected one and appears to him in dreams. See the dreams of Gisli in part 1, chapter 3.

- The Double represents her mortal's destiny and possesses human and animal forms. See the fylgjur who appear to the alter ego's enemy in dreams (part 1, chapter 3) and the animal guides who are most certainly the Doubles of fairies (part 1, chapter 2).

Either through the loss of the primary meaning of these details, or by the psychologizing and adaptation of them in literary works, they undergo a distortion of form but not content:

- The supernatural being chooses to be the psychic alter ego of a mortal and is anthropomorphized.

- Given that this being is closely tied to destiny, it merges with the fairies, who are themselves the successors to the Fates and the Norns.

- It retains, nevertheless, its animal form but no longer uses it except to draw the chosen one to a suitable place, the selection of which is not left to chance, for water is always present. Once there, it declares its love and is united with the chosen one.

- But because this "fairy" is simultaneously destiny, fortune, and tutelary genie, if the mortal is separated from it—by transgression or breaking of a taboo, or whatever the motif may be—the mortal meets with death, however euphemized. Lanval disappears into Avalon, Graelent crosses the river that separates the earthly world from the fairy world and never appears again, Désiré leaves the king of Scotland's court for that of his fairy wife; and in *Peter von Staufenberg,* the separation is fatal to the hero, who dies three days after having married a mortal woman.

Even though these details are not easy to define precisely, their similar presence in a number of tales is perceivable, and their origins can be summarized thus: In mythical times, there was a *hiérosgamos,* or sacred marriage, between a mortal and his psychic Double, the being who accompanies him from birth to death, remains after his body has died, and transfers itself to another individual, often to another member of the first mortal's family. What we have, then, are ecotypical manifestations of the belief in the daimôn, who is given to man by the gods.

Let us return for a moment to the issue of children. In the medieval accounts in which the hero crosses into the other world and stays with the fairy—after having been brought there via the pursuit of an animal—the couple remains childless, which supports the idea of a literarily adapted ecstatic voyage. We find a strong trace of this ecstatic voyage among the Celts, in an account entitled *The Siege of Druim Damghaire:* One day Cormac left to go hare hunting. In the course of the day, he lost his dogs and his companions, entered a thick fog, and fell into a magic sleep on a hill until a voice wakened him. He rose, and his languor disappeared when he saw a young woman of enchanting beauty. She greeted him, swore her love to him, and asked him to follow her into the other world: "Come with me! . . . so that I can have you . . . as my husband and bed mate."[12]

We can strip the narrative of its literary varnish: In the form of a hare, the woman spirit draws Cormac to a place where he falls asleep—a hill, here the Celtic vision of a fairy mound, that is, the other world—and she asks him to be hers. That she wakes him up after putting him to sleep does not stand up to analysis, and there is every reason to assume that here there is some influence of vision literature in which, when a supernatural being enters the scene, it is stated: "He woke him up and said . . ." *(a sompno excitavit dicens),* as in the *Visio Thurkilli.* It is Cormac's alter ego that reaches the next world while his body remains on the hill, the spot where a magical sleep—the transliteration of trance or catalepsy—left him lying. This is a detail that has its own importance: Well attested to among the Celts and the Germanic peoples is the ritual of lying on funeral mounds in order to receive a gift or revelation—in other words, to follow the practice of incubation.

Within this whole family of legends there exists the theme of the sacred union—the hierogamy between man and his psychic Double, whatever name it is given (daimôn, genius, fylgja)—which translates among the Siberian peoples as the obtaining of supranormal powers (allowing communication with the other world and with the spirits) and among the peoples of the West's Middle Ages as the fulfilling of desires (wealth, honors, and so forth). These are, very simply, the reflection of the desires of the society to whom the storyteller belongs.

Behind all these accounts, we can make out a simple and profound thought: Alone we are nothing; in order to exist, we must reunite two principles within ourselves—spiritual and material—and so join our-selves to our Double. I am not disregarding the theme of the soul, and the differences I point out are a result of the fact that I am approaching this concept from several angles with the help of several civilizations. Yet the structure remains the same; only the words change. In studying the mythic background of the Melusinian legends some time ago, I arrived at the conclusion that they actually were myths of the soul's trials and tribu-lations on earth before its reunion with the Universe.[13] In exploring the realm that is the subject of this book, I have collided once more with evi-dence of this, which reinforces its apparent truth.

The other world appears like a reservoir of souls, in the sense of the daimôn and genius, that are looking to incarnate or that are obliged to do so, and that are expressions of our destiny and supernatural dimension and of the tie that binds each of us to the cosmos and so to the gods and the dead. These "souls" on a quest for a body can be the souls of ancestors as well as the hypostases or auxiliaries of divinities. They play the role of the psychic Double, but also, in the case of the fairies, the anthropomorphized Double, and they are very close, in sum total, to the Christian guardian angel, over whose prehistory there still reigns great obscurity.

Now it is time to tackle one of the other manifestations of the Double, the one that is interpreted negatively: witchcraft, the negative counterpart to the fairy world.

The Double
and Witchcraft

THE WITCH AND THE DOUBLE

If ever there was a theme that has enjoyed extraordinary popularity, it is certainly the theme of the nocturnal flight of witches. Regarding it, there are two differing opinions: Some hold it as reality and some see it as demonic illusion. All of clerical literature is filled with scholarly discussion on the subject, which resulted in the connection of these flights to the witches' Sabbath, and ultimately led to the death sentences of people suspected of nocturnal journeying. Originally, night flying was not related to such a Sabbath that occurred on the Brocken River or on some Bald Mountain. Instead, it was part of a complex set of agrarian rituals, or, more specifically, a ritual of the third caste that was intended to ensure prosperity and fertility to the familial or village community.[1] The Church has demonized these vestiges of paganism and imposed its point of view, but without succeeding in blocking the ancient pagan cultural substratum from which arose the nocturnal wanderings attributed to some people.

In the ninth century, in a capitulary by Charles the Bald, we find the first echo of this demonizing tradition, which becomes very quickly widespread in texts, penitentials, and canonical decrees. Yet there is also such information as the following from Réginon de Prüm, gathered in 906 in his *Libri duo de synodalibus causis:*

One cannot allow that certain wicked women, perverted and seduced by Satan's illusions and mirages, believe and say that they go out at night with the goddess Diana, or with Herodias, and a great crowd of women, riding astride certain animals, covering large amounts of ground in the night silence and obeying Diana like a mistress. . . . An innumerable crowd lets itself be taken over by this madness and holds it as true, wanders off the straight and narrow path, and ruins itself in pagan wrongdoing. . . . For this reason, priests must preach to the men of their parishes that all this is absolutely false and that such fantasies in the minds of the faithful come not from the spirit of God but from Evil. . . . Man wrongly thinks that everything happens not in spirit *[in animo]* but corporally *[in corpore]*.[2]

Burchard, bishop of Worms, takes up this same point around 1010, insisting on two or three occasions that all is illusion; those who believe in such things are "deceived by the devil" *(a diabolo deceptae)*.[3] The tone is set, and the collections of canons by Yves de Chartres (d. 1116) and by Bolognese master Gratien (d. before 1179); *The Polycraticus* by Jean de Salisbury, bishop of Chartres (1176–1180); and the penitentials all spread this view and feed the great manuals of the Inquisition, most notably *The Witches' Hammer (Malleus maleficarum)* by Jacques Sprenger and Henry Institoris, published in Magdebourg in 1486 or 1487. *The Inquisitor's Manual (Practica inquisitionis)* by Bernard Gui (1261–1339), which was made famous through Umberto Eco's *The Name of the Rose*, reveals but one allusion, which is nevertheless interesting because it does not concern witches: Sorcerers, seers, and invokers of the devil will be questioned, writes Bernard Gui, "on the subject of fairies who bring good fortune, or, it is said, who run around at night."[4] The Inquisitor here makes reference to a tradition attested to in all of the medieval West: that of fairies visiting houses at night and ensuring the prosperity of all therein if certain precautions were taken, a tradition demonized by the great Christian offensive against paganism.[5]

The Life of Saint Germain (d. 448) is included in *The Golden Legend (Legenda Aurea)*, written by Jacopo de Voragine around 1250, but the text contains some interpolations that can be compared to the primitive *Vita* composed by Constance of Lyon around 475–480:

> One day, after he had received supper in a place, Saint Germain was surprised to see that the people were getting the table ready again, and he asked for whom they were preparing a second meal. When they told him it was for the good ladies who come at night [that is, fairies and witches], he resolved to keep watch. During the night, he saw a crowd of demons in the form of men and women who came to sit at the table. He forbade them to leave and woke up the household to ask if any knew these people. They are all our neighbors, the people answered him. So he ordered the demons to stay there, and he sent someone to the houses of each one of them. They were all found in their beds.[6]

It is clear that these are not demons—the Christian interpretation of an event that the narrator does not understand—but, rather, the Doubles of the sleeping neighbors, and they are gathered there to participate in what the household members call the meal of the fairies. In demonizing the phenomenon, Jacopo de Voragine interprets a pagan belief from a clerical and canonical perspective, and as such, everything is forced into the realm of demonic illusion, for everyone knows that Satan is the great deceiver, the master of supernatural illusion who can take human form at will. It is easy to shed light on the pre-Christian substratum here. But it is much more difficult to do so in the following exemplum. Etienne de Bourbon was a Dominican most likely born in Belleville-sur-Saône around 1180. He was charged with duties of the Inquisition in the diocese of Valence around 1235, and died in 1261 in the convent of Prêcheurs in Lyon. In constant contact with people when he traveled what is the current Rhone-Alps region to preach to the heretics, the testimonies that he collected along with his personal experiences provided him with material for many exempla, which are very precious data for those historians who know how to study such material without looking through the distorting prism of Christianity. Etienne narrates this:

A woman lost two children in a row before they reached their first year of age. Rumor claimed that *stryges* [witches] sucked the blood out of them. The hapless mother said: "When my third child reaches the end of his first year, I will watch over him the whole night that brings that year to a close. I will put on him the iron cover that I use to cover my cooking pot when it is on the fire [this metal is reputed to make spirits flee], and I will stick a hot iron in the stryge's face when she comes, so that she will be recognizable the next morning.[7]

This detail reveals to us that this woman does not doubt for a moment that a stryge can enter her house at night, and it suggests that a marking from a hot iron, the mark of infamy, is a common means of recognizing women suspected of witchcraft. Here we return to the text:

The woman did what she said she would do, and around the middle of the night she saw a small, old neighbor woman riding a wolf and then saw her enter through the closed door *(vidit intrantem per jan- uam clausam vetulam quamdam sibi vicinam, lupum equitantem).* As the old woman approached the cradle, the mother put the burn- ing iron on her face, and the neighbor woman left, emitting a great cry *(cum ejulatu maximo recessit).*

The next morning, the mother went to the old woman's house, accompanied by some neighbors and a couple of bailiffs. They forced the gate [the fact that the old woman does not come to open the gate implies that she is in a deep sleep] and arrested the woman with the burned cheek. She denied everything, claiming that she was not at all aware of having committed the crime of which she was accused *(dicens non esse se impositi criminis consciam).*[8]

Up to this point, all in the account is clear: It is the physical alter ego of the old woman who acted while her body was sleeping. Two details indicate this: The inflicted wound that is discovered on the cheek of the old woman, and the fact that she entered the home through the closed door. The first detail is like one that appears in *The Saga of the Salmonvale*

People: A ghost named Hrapp is on the loose. Olaf waits for him and attacks him, stabbing him with his spear, but the recalcitrant dead man pulls out the tip and, sinking instantly into the ground, disappears. When Hrapp's tomb is opened, he is seen holding the iron of the spear in his hand.[9]

In Etienne de Bourbon's account there is a very archaic motif that is found throughout Germanic tradition: that of the wolf as the witch's mount. Here this seems to be an accentuation of the evil nature of the old woman: She allies herself with wolves. We can look now at the ending of the account and see how it is distorted in the interest of making it fit what is known and accepted by the Church: The bishop, who knows that the old woman is a good parishioner, suspects some devilry and orders the demon to show himself. The demon, appearing as the old woman, takes the thin layer of burnt skin from the old woman's face and places it on his own face (*tunc demon, similitudine vetule se transmutans . . . pelliculam combustam a facie vetule removit . . . et sibi imponit*).

This epilogue, the sole purpose of which is to reveal the demonic hoax, seems inspired by one of the Latin words for witch: *masca,* "mask." Faced with the belief in the Double, the Church escapes by cleverly side-stepping it altogether: It is all a diabolical illusion — *illusio, ludificatio diabolica.* Following, not long ago, Jean-Claude Schmitt, who speaks of the unmasked devil, I let myself be taken in by this argument. Only in the course of my own inquiry into the alter ego was I able to clearly assess the meaning of accounts such as this one.

A final word on this telling: The old woman defends herself against having committed this crime, which we can interpret as her true lack of knowledge about it or as her desire to hide her knowledge, but her good faith, according to the wording and syntax of the text, does not seem to be in question. We can recall this: The involuntary ecstatic does not necessarily have a memory of what his Double does. Professional ecstatics — magicians or witches, male and female — do remember, for they have voluntarily sent out their alter ego.

This exemplum of Etienne de Bourbon must be linked to an account by Gautier Map. Born between 1135 and 1140 in the Severn River Valley,

Gautier studied in Paris from 1155 to 1162 before coming back to England to settle in the court of Henry II. He died on April 1, 1209 or 1210. His *De nugis curialium* (1181–1193) is filled with echoes of folk beliefs and superstitions from across the Channel at that time, as this example shows: Every year a knight lost his newborn babies, each of which was found strangled the day after its birth. Watching over them day and night was in vain. In the fourth year of these deaths, the child just born was encircled by fire and light—said to make spirits and demons go away—and all the people fixed their eyes upon him. A pilgrim comes upon the scene then and asks for hospitality in the name of God. He is welcomed and joins the others in their watch:

> Soon after midnight, all having fallen asleep, the pilgrim alone stayed awake and suddenly saw a respectable old woman approach the cradle and start the task of strangling the little baby. He promptly sprung forward and forcefully held the old woman until everyone woke and surrounded them. Many recognized the woman, and all those who did declared that she was the most dignified of the village matrons. . . . Asked her name, she gave no answer. The father of the child and many other people attributed her silence to the shame of having been found out.

Soon the pilgrim was asked to let her go, but he refused, protesting that she was a demon.

> He seized the poker from a nearby fire, marked her face with the sign of evil, and ordered that the woman whom they thought she was be brought to the scene. The matron arrived, and, while he kept hold of the woman he'd surprised, all marveled that she was the same as the prisoner, even to the burn on her face.

The pilgrim then explained that the woman he held must be the demons' messenger and the executor of their vile works, and that she was made alike to the other dignified and pious woman in order to ruin the dignified matron. "So that you will believe what I am telling you, see what she does when I let her go!" And the prisoner flew out through the window with great shrieks and lamentations.[10]

Once again, we have before us the corporal Double at work, but here it is demonized. There is the branding with the hot iron, and Gautier Map punctuates his narrative with details that direct the reader toward the conviction that Satan himself is leading the dance, including that the accused woman is held in high esteem by everyone. Moreover, the prisoner's final flight out the window accompanied by a great shriek is a fairly common motif in the Melusinian legends: Once discovered, the woman spirit or female demon—Melusine, for example—disappears in this way, or over the roof, like the count of Aquitaine's fantasy wife in the work of the chronicler Philippe Mouskès.

Gautier Map, however, does introduce an unusual motif having no counterpart in the accounts of devilry that I know: the prisoner's silence—which is poorly explained by shame and contradicts the shrieks it emits when it goes away.

Another detail of note is that sleep came over them all except the pilgrim, who is no doubt protected by his superior faith. This torpor is inexplicable, for there is a large group of people in the room, the fire is lit, and the lights are shining brightly. This slumber precedes the entrance of the elderly woman, which affirms the importance of this recurring motif: the irrepressible sleep that overcomes every person attacked by the spiritual Double of his enemies, a detail that is extremely well illustrated by all the Scandinavian sagas. (See part 1, chapter 2.) The sudden materialization of the old woman in the room—she appears literally from nowhere—is another detail that we have seen before, in the story by Gudmund Arason (part 1, chapter 2). All these clues indicate that what we have here is a story of the Double as revised and corrected by a cleric.

Starting from the tenth or eleventh century, it was noted that certain women were capable of entering into homes at night, flouting closed doors. Gervais de Tilbury (1152–1218), named marshal of the kingdom of Arles by Othon IV of Brunswick, speaks about this in his *Loisirs impériaux* (1209–1213), in a chapter in which he discusses nocturnal apparitions. He states that he is not in agreement with the opinion of those who rely upon Saint Augustine's *The City of God* because he personally knows some women in the vicinity *(mulieres agnosco vicinas nostras)* who journey far away, leaving their sleeping husbands' beds and traveling the world. Gervais cites the case of one of these women who, having taken on the form of a cat, was wounded, and her human body had the mark of the wound. Yet again, it is obvious that the cat was the zoomorphic alter ego of the woman in question. In short, with regard to accounts such as these, two opinions come face to face—that of the clerics and that of the common person.

I will not enter into the polemic, which, from the thirteenth to the sixteenth centuries, set the partisans of real demonic transport against the upholders of illusion, but I will point out that no opinion is truly definitive.[11] In the fifteenth century we encounter a bit of everything: In 1461, Pierre Mameur, prior of Sainte-Opportune, near Poitiers, and in 1475, Jean Vincent, prior of the Moustiers (Vendée), and Ulrich Molitor, notary of the Episcopal curacy of Constance, all sided with illusion. Alonso de Madrigal, known as El Tostado (Tostatus), bishop of Avila (1449–1455), was of this opinion as well in 1436, but he changed his mind four years later and astutely explained that the demon carried you away, which the Milanese Minorite Samuel de Cassinis denied in 1505. The same uncertainties were in the mind of the famous Alsatian preacher Johann Geiler von Kaiserberg (1445–1510).[12] Neither does the Lyonnais doctor Symphorien Champier (d. 1539) decide either way; he claims the coexistence of real flight and illusory travel, which is also Pedro Ciruelo's opinion in 1529.

Listing all those who have given their opinion on the subject, an excellent sampling of which can be found in J. Hansen's work, brings nothing further to the discussion and simply confirms the conflict among concurrent interpretations. As such, it is more interesting to focus on information likely to further our inquiry.

All supporters of illusion agree on one point: Women claiming to take night flights are dreaming—they are hallucinating—and all the proof that is needed is what happens when the women are ordered to confess in front of witnesses. Numerous texts tell us that these women fall asleep, enter into catalepsy. They absolutely do not leave the scene, but tell, when they come out of their lethargy, what they have done and seen while far away. Even when we allow for literary borrowing, the consistencies in the testimonies are very worthy of attention. Some time around 1435–1437, Jean Nider, a Dominican Inquisitor, relates such an experience: The "witch" gets into a little vat, anoints herself with a balm, utters the magic words and . . . falls asleep! This anecdote is found again in a sermon by Geiler von Kaiserberg and, in a similar form, in a text from El Tostado (1436) as well as in a text by Arnaldus Albertini, first an Inquisitor and then Bishop of Patti, in Sicily. El Tostado stresses the fact that the woman was lying motionless and was not transported— *iacuissit exanimis, neque fuisse de loco motam.* Even earlier, around 1250, Vincent de Beauvais, a Dominican connected to the royal family as a reader, was already gathering the following account in his *Speculum morale:* One day an old woman told her parish priest that, accompanied by other women, she had visited him at night and that the locked doors were no obstacle to their entrance:

> In trying to make her enter into a room with barred windows, the priest closed the door and began to beat her with the crucifix, saying: "Go away, witch woman!" And as she could not enter, the priest sent her away with these words: "You can see at what point you are stripped of good sense, you who give credence to the inanity of illusory dreams."

There are elements of the fabliau in the demystification that also ridicules the belief. In the work of another member of the Dominican order, Etienne de Bourbon (d. 1261), we find a more troubling text: One day a man told the priest of a Cevenole parish that he left at night with some women "who are collectively called the Good Things," adding that if the priest did not believe him, he would take him along, which is what happened. The priest was brought into a storeroom where some women were eating at a well-laden table brightly lit by candles and torches. When the priest blessed the table, everything disappeared; he found himself alone, closed inside the storeroom. But Etienne does not seek to understand how he was transported there. There are questions it is probably better not to ask.

As a general rule, flight happens during a person's sleep, exactly as in the Norse accounts of the travels of the alter ego (hamför). For Jean Vincent, a demonic sleep is what allows the women to imagine themselves being transported or metamorphosed into animals. For Martin of Arles, professor of theology in Navarre at the end of the fifteenth century, everything happens "in dream, not in reality, but in a fantastic manner" *(in somnis, non realiter sed fantastice),* and this is the fruit of moods and imagination *(fantasia).* The lawyer Jean-François Ponzinibus of Plaisance is of a similar opinion and puts forth an explanation that is quite psychological. As for Arnaldus Albertini (d. 1544), Majorcan canon, he notes that the demon more easily deceives "stupid old women and sick people," such as "melancholics, the insane, maniacs, shy people, children, and peasants." In the fifteenth and sixteenth centuries, particularly, all educated people wondered about the reality of the transport: Does it occur to the spirit *(in spiritu)* or in reality and corporally *(vere et corporaliter)?* Jacques Sprenger and Henry Institoris admit that "this transport poses difficulties . . . due to a single text, the *Canon episcopi,"* and they give examples of corporal travel, with the understanding that it only happens with God's permission *(Deo permittente).* "As to the mode of transport," they add, "it is this: Witches, under the devil's instructions, make an ointment from the bodies of children, especially those whom they have killed before they are baptized."[13] Note this change in tradition: It is said now that the ointment is applied to an object—the broom—and no longer to the body, an opinion which was widespread at the time and which can be read in the writings of Jean Nidier, El Tostado, Jean de Bergame (in 1460), and in the little anonymous treatises on the sect of the Vaudois. Jean Hartlieb, personal doctor of Albert III, Duke of Bavaria, gives us, in 1456, the name of one of these ointments: *unguentum Pharelis,* for which we possess a thousand recipes. In fact, at least three traditions were combined by this time: that of animals serving as transport—already attested to around the year 1000; that of a satanic balm; and that of a fantastic ride on a stick, a tradition that grew to include a broomstick.

According to my studies, the ointment-stick association came on the scene in the fifteenth century. We encounter it in 1428 at the Lucerne trial; in 1430 in the *Formicarius* by Jean Nadier; in 1456 in *The Book of the Forbidden Arts* by Jean Hartlieb; in 1460 in the work of Jean de Bergame; in 1475 in *The Chronicle* by Mathias Widmann; in 1477 at the trials of Villars-Chabod, near Annecy; and in 1494 in a trial that took place in Frankfurt.[14] If we extract the essential from the texts referred to here, which the reader may find in J. Hansen and C. J. Baroja or in the manuals of the Inquisitor, we have the following original characteristics of those who are transported:

- The body stays where it is.
- It falls into a cataleptic sleep that nothing can interrupt; as Alphonse of Spina stated in 1459, "The bodies of these women remain completely unconscious" *(corpora vero earum remanent sine aliqua sensibilitate).*
- This catalepsy is a common occurrence in certain temperaments.

The balm or ointment given by Satan or made under his direction then came along to obscure these ancient characteristics. The reasoning of the Inquisitors and clerics emerges quite clearly from the review of writings on witchcraft. Christian and scholarly tradition was their guide wire as well as their guardrail. The Bible rescued them from the business most of the time—one example shows this clearly: In order to demonstrate the reality of nocturnal flight, the ecclesiastics cite, in their support, the air travel of Habakkuk (Daniel 14:36–39), Phillip (Acts 8:39–40), Christ (Matthew 4:1–11), and Elijah (II Kings 2:1–13),* and when these sources are not enough, they call up the legends of Simon Magus, Saint Ambrose, and Saint Anthidius of Besancon.

---

*[These references are from the Catholic Bible, which contains extra chapters in both Esther and, as here, Daniel, which ends at chapter 12 in the Protestant Bible. — *Trans.*]

But where, then, does the stick come from? What is its origin? We can perhaps put forward an answer by looking at the Germanic traditions, which are our best evidence of pre-Christian traditions.

To designate a female magician, Norse uses different terms, among them *túnriða* and *völva*. The first means "she who rides the hedge" or "she who rides in the closed meadow," the sacred spot where the ancient Scandinavians had their place of worship. The second is formed from *völr*, "stick." From the time of early antiquity the stick—*völr*, *stafr*, or *gandr*—is necessary for magic practices *(seiðr)*, and one can see in it, without risk of error, the ancestor of the fairies' magic wand. Male and female magicians—I do not use the term *(male) witch*, as it applies only to black and evil magic—send out this stick to execute desired tasks and use it to get around, or else they assume its form, which is why the magic transfer is expressed by the term *gandreið*, the "*gandr* ride" or "on the gandr," as well as by the locution *renna göndum*, literally "to make one's gandr run." But we must know that *gandr* can also indicate a spirit of the same type as the shamans' auxiliary spirits. I am tempted to see in this stick as an equivalent of Hermes's *kerukeion*, Circes' wand, and Bacchus's *thyrsus*.

Balm seems to be a relatively recent invention or a revival from classical antiquity (Petronius). Without attempting to anticipate the continuation of this inquiry, I believe it served, above all, as a drug, a soporific, which allowed the witch to enter into the catalepsy that enabled a part of her to escape her body—in short, it liberated the alter ego. In a way, the ointment replaced the ancient ecstatic techniques. We must keep in mind that this was an added, adventitious motif that came along to hide a gift, a temperament, or a science. Starting from the fifteenth century, El Tostado claimed that the Sabbath was an invention due to various drug preparations, and the recipes gathered from throughout the texts confirm this point: Into the composition of these balms enter Solanaceous plants such as belladonna, henbane, and stramoine,* as well as other ingredients that modern amateur practitioners of witchcraft have capitalized on: snake

---

*[Stramoine is also known as jimsonweed, angel's trumpet, and moonflower of the genus *Datura* and the family Solanacea. —*Trans.*]

venom, toad spit, spiders, and so forth. Around 1545, Dr. Laguna, the personal doctor of the Duke of Lorraine, proved the torpid virtues of such a balm. For the rest, in a Toulousian trial of 1335, Anne-Marie of Georgel and Catherine Delort swore to having been transported without the help of any ointment. Catherine stated simply that she fell into an extraordinary sleep every night . . . every Saturday night, of course, the Sabbath day.

WHEN WITCHES DOUBLE

Recent analyses have shown that nocturnal flying by women led by female demons (Diana, Herodias) or fairies (Lady Abonde, Satia) proceeded from worship of the dead and then swung toward witchcraft under pressure from the Church.[15] Experiments from the thirteenth to the sixteenth centuries, conducted in the presence of witnesses, show that the suspected individuals fell into catalepsy. Minutes from the trials reveal that there were, in fact, two types of people involved: evil beings, stealers of seeds, destroyers of harvests, emissaries of storms *(tempestarii)* on the one hand; and on the other, people who fought them, the *Benandanti* and the Livonian werewolves, whom we will meet very soon. Lethargy is used as an excuse to keep these unusual phenomena contained within the realm of fantasy and imagination, yet we have to admit that another "truth" exists and that it can be found within the borders of Europe. In his *Daemonomania*, Jean Bodin (1520–1596) brings forth two important items for our inquiry. He writes:

> When I was in Nantes in 1546, I heard astonishing things about seven magicians who, in the presence of many people, declared that in the space of an hour they were going to report news of what was happening in a radius of seven leagues. They lost consciousness then, and remained in this state for three hours. Then they sat up and said what they had seen in Nantes and the area. They precisely described circumstances, places, actions, and people. Investigation revealed the exactness of their words.

Is this not exactly what the Scandinavian sagas tell us? The similarities in the events are astounding. Here is a second testimony from Bodin:

> Another event came along during the brutal persecution of witches which took place in Bordeaux in 1571, and which I remember well. There was an old witch there who confessed to the judges that she and her sister witches were taken and led to certain places each week. When one of the high judges, the Honorable Belot, wanted proof, she answered that she could not provide it if she remained tied. He ordered her to be untied, upon which, naked, she anointed her whole body and fell on the ground as if dead, deprived of her senses, and only came back to herself five hours later. She told of events that happened in foreign places, and it was discovered that she was telling the truth.[16]

The reality of faraway transport is certain, given that, according to testimony, what these women or men say when they come out of trance turns out to be true. But what the people of those times were incapable of understanding is that is it *the Double* who travels. Having before their eyes an unconscious body, they could not imagine something so foreign to their culture and religion, because for them a person consisted of a body and a soul—period! We may note a difference in the two testimonies of Bodin: In the first case, we are dealing with professionals of the ecstatic voyage; they do not need balm. In the second case, we have what we could call "occasionals," those who do not master the ecstatic techniques and so must resort to a soporific ointment.

In the sixteenth century several similar accounts can be found, most notably in the works of Bartholemew of Spina (*Quaestio de strigibus*, 1525); Andreas Laguna (1499–1560), Pope Julius III's personal doctor; and, of course, Giambattista della Porta (1541–1615), author of the famous *Magiae naturalis libri XXX* (1589), in which we can read the following:

> I met a woman of the type who, people claim, do enter houses at night and suck the blood of babies in their crib. [Porta proceeds to

the usual experiment and notes the woman's catalepsy, brought on by the ointment.] When she woke up, she told of marvelous things and said how she was transported over mountains and seas . . .[17]

Now let us go back several centuries and cross into the North. Witchcraft stories from this region and time are clearer, first because there the alter ego was not at all acculturated, and second because the storytellers conveyed information unambiguously, even if it was sometimes somewhat cryptic. In an episode from *The Saga of Fridthjof the Strong,* Fridthjof breaks the spine of two witches (hamhleypur) who have changed themselves into seals. Their bodies die immediately in the room they have used for their evil deeds *(seiðhallr).*[18] In *The Saga of Thorstein Vikingson,* Ingjald's alter ego is fighting in the form of a wild boar and is killed: "They saw then that Ingjald was lying there dead."[19] In the saga named after him, Kormak and his brother have just raised anchor when a walrus surfaces near their boat. Kormak throws his harpoon at the animal and the beast goes under: "We thought we recognized Thorveig's eyes then," Kormak says *(þóttusk menn þar kenna augu Þorveigar).* The walrus does not reappear, "but it is said of Thorveig that she remained in bed, struck by a mortal sickness, and the people told that she died from it."[20] The lesson is clear: That which happens to the theriomorphic alter ego has repercussions on the body it leaves, and the death of the one inevitably leads to the death of the other—plainly and clearly proof of doubling.

THE CASE OF THE BENANDANTI AND THE ROLE OF THE CAUL

One inquiry largely passed over in silence should have made more of a stir than it did: Carlo Ginzburg's on nocturnal battles, published in 1968, which shook up ideas and rendered null and void many conclusions.[21] In a small study Ginzburg presents the *Benandanti,* "those who journey to the Blessed Realm," individuals similar to sorcerers who represent the last manifestation of a third-estate ritual related to the mythic vision of the combat between winter and spring. The components gathered within this

Friulian belief are of interest because they far surpass the geographic limitations of this culture in which some extremely ancient traditions survived up to the sixteenth century. Moreover, it is not insignificant that the Friulians saw Celts, Germans, and Slovenes pass through their lands, and even establish themselves there, which caused no shortage of traces of their influences in local customs and attitudes.

On March 21, 1575, a heresy trial opened in Cividale against Paolo Gasparutto and Battista Moduco. These individuals claimed that they went out at night to fight against witches. Stated Gasparutto on Thursday, April 7:

> Once they were gone, if someone approached the bed where their body lay, in order to call one of them, he would never receive an answer and could not make the body move, even if he were to stay there for a hundred years; but if the person avoided looking at him or talking to him, an answer would follow.

Some individuals left for longer than others, he added, providing an interesting piece of information:

> For those who take twenty-four hours to return, if someone does or says something, the spirit remains separated from the body. Once the body is buried, this spirit becomes a wanderer, and we call him a *Malandante* [he who journeys to the Evil Realm].

These details are worth noting. During catalepsy and sleep, that which detaches itself from the body can be prevented from rejoining the physical container. The body, then, is in danger, but so also is the "spirit." Gasparutto stated that any of the Benandanti who revealed their activity or committed an error received a beating that turned them completely black and blue.

Battista Moduco appeared in turn before the Inquisitor Felix of Montefalco and confirmed Gasparutto's statements: "I am a *Benandante* because I leave with the others to fight four times a year, that is, with the changing of the four seasons, at night, invisibly, in spirit. Only the body remains here."

October 1, 1580, Maria Gasparutto, wife of Paolo, was called to witness, and this is what she said:

> One morning, around four o'clock, I needed to get up, and as I was afraid, I called Paolo, my husband, so that he would get up with me. Even though I called him probably ten times and I shook him, I could not wake him, and he kept his face turned upward [that is, he was lying flat on his back, a detail that has it own importance, as we will see shortly]. So I left him lying there and got up without him, and upon my return I saw that he had awakened and was saying, "These Benandanti say that when they leave the body, their spirit resembles a little mouse, and it is the same when they come back; and while it is without its spirit, if the body were turned, it would remain dead, for the spirit could not reenter it."

During the trial that took place in Lucca in 1571, a certain Margherita of San Rocco testified: "If by chance we were turned flat on our stomach, we would lose our spirit and the body would remain dead." At another initial investigation occurring in the same place in 1589, the old peasant woman Crezia of Pieve San Paolo stated: "I know a witch who was called Gianna. One day she fell asleep and I saw a rat come out of her mouth. It was her spirit that was leaving for I know not where."

We have just discovered two paths that we are going to follow, starting with the simpler one, the mouse spirit. According to a belief widespread in Europe, attested to very early in Germany in the legend of King Guntram (Gontran) and discernable until the end of the nineteenth century, out of the sleeping body—whether in trance or lethargy and almost always via the mouth—might come a little animal that is none other than the zoomorphic Double of the sleeper.

At the end of the seventh century, Paul the Deacon, Lombardy writer and member of a noble family that had established itself in Friuli at the time of the occupation of Italy, completed his *History of the Lombards,* in which he compiled all information concerning the Germanic people to whom he belonged.[22] He used, most notably, the *Origo gentis Langobardorum*—written around 671 and covering the period from Scandinavian antiquity to King Perctarit—and a now-lost work by Secundus of Trent (d. 612). The work of Paul the Deacon is important because, among the many legends *(Sagen)* it tells, there is one that is of particular interest to us—that of King Guntram:

> One day during the hunt, King Guntram fell asleep at the foot of a tree, his head resting on the knees of a faithful vassal. Out from his mouth a little animal came, who then tried to cross a nearby stream. The vassal made him a bridge with his sword and saw the animal cross and disappear into a hole in the mountain, then come back out soon after and slip back into the king's mouth. When Guntram woke up, he told how he had thought, while he was asleep, that he had crossed a bridge, gone inside a mountain and seen a treasure there. The vassal told him what he had witnessed. Then Guntram had the dirt dug up near the hole where the animal had disappeared and there discovered a treasure.

This story was taken up again by Aimoin de Fleury in his *Histoire des Francs* (1002), Hélinand de Froimont, Vincent de Beauvais (around 1250), and Jean Wier (1563). It is the product of a tradition about which Hannjost Lixfeld compiled close to two hundred testimonies from all of Eurasia and from the Middle Ages to the twentieth century.[23] It is sometimes recounted, in a form that has been adapted to place or ethnic group, by the Buryats of the Alta, as well as the Vodyaks and the Laplanders.[24] The central theme is always the same: The psychic Double leaves the body of a sleeper in the form of a little animal and goes off to wander and roam; upon waking, the man narrates what he thinks has been a dream.

The legend of Guntram is presented as a marvelous vision and, when all is said and done, as a literary version of the ecstatic voyage. But this voyage happens down here in this world, even though certain details suggest that this was not originally the case: Present are water, which symbolizes the border between the two worlds; and the bridge, which, according to Eliade, is a very familiar symbol of the paradoxical passage, the difficult passage, the narrow gateway, and which is present in a great many myths.

The Lombardi historiographer relates another anecdote giving us an additional view of the Double:

> While Cunibert, the king of the Lombards, deliberated with a great equerry about the way in which he could put Aldo and Grauso to death, he saw a fly on the window. He took out his knife to slay it, but missed and only removed one of its legs.
>
> Aldo and Grauso came at the king's summons, but on their way they met a limping man who was missing a foot. He warned them that Cunibert wanted to have them killed, so they took refuge inside a church. Furious to see that the two had escaped him, Cunibert promised to save their lives if they revealed the name of the one who betrayed him. Aldo and Grauso told of their encounter with the lame man, and the king understood then that the fly whose leg he had cut off was an evil spirit.[25]

That Cunibert unhesitatingly interprets the facts in this way clearly shows that he lived in a world where the zoomorphic Double was a reality. The mention of an evil spirit is the product of clerical interpretation and throws the event into the realm of the devil, when what we actually have is an alter ego in the form of a fly and, in accordance with the rule that all that happens to the Double happens to its possessor, the amputated leg yields an amputated foot. This motif appears frequently in the tales of werewolves and other zoomorphic myths.

We find the mouse again in the Saxon traditions of the Wartheland, Mecklenburg, and Bohemia. It is sometimes red (Thuringe), according to a testimony that dates from 1661. In the Baltic countries and in Upper Harz, the alter ego is a scarab or a dung beetle. In Switzerland and Wartheland it is a bumblebee, and in Prussia, a cat. Along the lower stretches of the Sieg it is a toad; in Wurtemberg, a bird; a spider in

Swabia; in Transylvania, a fly. Nonanimal forms remain rarities: In Switzerland, mention of a light is sometimes made; in the ancient duchy of Oldenburg, there is reference to smoke, which recalls *kapnos* (smoke), which the Greeks sometimes used as a synonym of psuchè and which must be connected to the whirlwinds that devastated the fields and in Estonia were thought to be witches to such a degree that the peasants dared not stab at them with their pitchforks.

Forbidding touching the motionless body and, especially, moving it and talking to it, very clearly echo Norse traditions, but this ban was not common elsewhere except in Germany in the nineteenth century. To my knowledge, outside of Friulia and Scandinavia, the minutes of trials do not speak of it. However, once again, the period after the Middle Ages reports it. Vera Meyer-Matheis has made an excellent study of it, and though she limits herself to German traditions, her writings prove that moving a body in lethargy can cause premature death. The oldest testament to this belief is found in a chant from the Poetic Edda, in which Odin prides himself on this:

> *If I see witches riding through the air*
> *I do something to make them lose their way*
> *And they never find their own skin again*
> *And they never find their own spirit again.*

The relative obscurity of this passage dissipates as soon as we know that it is the Double of the witch who travels, courts danger, and can be impeded from returning to the body. The Norse language has an adjective for this state: *hamstolinn*, literally "deprived of one's Double." This is what happens to those whose body position is changed while the alter ego is traveling afar.

In *The Book of the Colonization of Iceland*, Ingimund asks two Finnish magicians to leave for Iceland in order to find the whereabouts of his lost amulet. The men insist that they first be enclosed alone in a house, then they send their Doubles to the island, which the text expresses by the phrase *í hamförum*, "in a voyage of the Double." *The Saga of the*

Lakevale Chiefs tells the same anecdote, but the Finns state, "At present, we have to enclose ourselves alone in a house, and our names must not be uttered." And this recommendation is also found in *The Book of Sturla:* Lodmund lies down and forbids anyone to call him by his name. While his body remains unconscious, his alter ego goes out to cause a landslide.

But this alter ego that the ancient Scandinavians call hamr is not necessarily confined to human form; it can just as easily take the form of an animal when the possessor is asleep. Norse mythology tells us that the gods have this power—and what does mythology do, if not transcribe and express in a coded form the thoughts of men, their mind-set, their *Weltanschauung,* their beliefs? Hence, it is scarcely surprising to find this theme in the family sagas, and not in the false sagas *(lygisögur).* What is more, the writers of these texts were Christians, clerics or lettered men educated in monastic schools, who—how lucky for us!—did not completely obscure the beliefs of their ancestors, but reported them because those beliefs were part of their cultural identity. These are invaluable testimonies if ever there were any, because they help us to understand just those unusual events that we come up against in the witch trials and within the sphere of the trials' influence.

But not everyone can be a Benandante and "leave through closed doors." To do so an individual must be born with a caul,* that is, a sign at birth, exactly like those designated to become shamans, who are recognized because they are born with a tooth or a sixth finger on one hand, and so forth. The caul—the portion of the fetal membrane *(amnion* or *amnios)* that certain babies have on their head when they come into the world—plays a very large role in transport, for it allows the spirit to leave the body. Ginzburg's inquiry explains how in Norse a single word, *hamr,* can mean, at the same time, "skin," "Double," and "caul."

In the Norse lexicon, *hamr* designates not only the Double, but also the amnion, the placental membrane that encases the fetus and takes its form. The baby born with a caul was considered to have a particularly

---

*[*Être né coiffé* means "to be born with a caul" and also "to be born under a lucky star." For more on this second meaning, see page 99. — *Trans.*]

powerful alter ego that was very attached to him, given that it accompanied the individual from birth. This other self would thus be more active in the life of such a "predestined" person, so to speak. If everyone possesses a Double/hamr, some are capable of mastering it and using it, while others cannot, for it has its own life, and its independence becomes manifest during sleep or trance, brought on spontaneously or through dances, incantations, and so forth.

The caul was baptized at the same time as its possessor. To the question "How does one become a member of the company of Benandanti?" Battisat Moduco answered: "Belonging to this group are all those born with a caul." In 1582 at Udine, a woman was asked about a certain Aquilina who was suspected of witchcraft. "She must have been born with a caul," the last Holy Tribunal heard her say. Moduco permanently carried his amnion with him but, having lost it, he could not get to the nocturnal meetings for much longer. In 1601 Gasperina of Grazano admitted to possessing such a caul.

People born with cauls were thus thought to have been provided with a gift leading to the ability to double as well as the ability of clairvoyance, which then predisposed them to practice, whether they liked it or not, the professions of magician, sorcerer or witch, seer, and so on. But at their death it was believed that these people would change into ghosts unless certain precautions were taken. In German-language countries, evil dead people called *Unhür (Ungeheuer, monstrum)*, or "ghost," and *Nohier*, "he who draws the living into death," were born with a caul.[26] To release them, it was said that the corpse was to be decapitated and the head put at the foot of it, or else they were to be buried facedown.

This detour through ancient traditions and Germanic beliefs allows us to understand the connection between the caul and nocturnal flight. It goes without saying that every time we turn to these traditions of the North and Germany, rather than arguing in borrowed terms, we are flushing out from under cover a belief that, in all its forms, is common to all of Europe. And we use the most telling writings to allow ourselves to grasp with precision the coherence of the many mind-sets and attitudes toward this belief.

There is one last detail of importance concerning the caul: To be "born with a caul" has taken on the meaning of being lucky. In Norse, good fortune is *hamingja,* an agglutinative word composed of *hamr,* the Double, and the verb *gengja,* "go." The caul is thus the tangible mark of the destiny that is in store for an individual.

The multiplicity of terms designating the various components of the soul makes it difficult to separate the physical and psychic alter ego, but a few clues shed light on the background of their origins. Let us now, therefore, complete the register of meanings of the term *fylgja.* It means, physiologically, the placenta, the membrane that follows the delivery of the newborn.[27] The most recent German beliefs teach us that the alter ego is sometimes understood as the uterus. Around 1715 Hans Christoph von Ettner und Literitz said that the uterus can take on the appearance of a mouse and travel far away from the body at will, while the "person remains as if totally dead until it has reentered the body." Behind this, which at first glance seems a fabrication without foundation, there is most likely hidden a vague reminiscence of what the ability to double brings to some: the caul with which they are born.

The amnion thus predestines people for the capacity of doubling. Now we may see one of the forms that it takes.

THE NIGHTMARE

In my recent essay "Dwarfs and Elves of the Middle Ages," I tackled the issue of the nightmare and its connections with the being whom folk beliefs call *ma(h)r* (masculine and feminine), the last manifestation of the ill-intentioned dead.[28] While pursuing my research from a different angle, I noticed that my conclusions remained incomplete—as is the case with all the little demons of popular mythology, the ma(h)r has several facets. I had successfully traced the prehistory of the concept behind the ma(h)r, but I now know that the night-*mare* is also a Double, which we can see by working backward from post–Middle Ages testimonies.

In her inventory of zoomorphic alter egos, Vera Meyer-Matheis collected sixty-three accounts, which can be divided into two groups:

1. Twenty-two narratives are typologically similar to the one called
   The Legend of King Guntram.

2. The other testimonies concern the nightmare and witches, and they
   have the following structure: a) A person suddenly falls asleep. b) An
   animal leaves the person and disappears. c) When it returns, the person comes back to life. Witnesses know that the animal left the person in order to press or squeeze someone.*

Individuals whose alter egos journey in this way—which a pastor of
the ancient duchy of Oldenburg considers an unfortunate destiny,[29] recall-
ing the words of Burchard de Worms concerning werewolves—have various names in the German dialects: *schrottel,*[30] in which the notion of
malice survives; *schreckli,* which transcribes as "provoked fear"; and a
collection of other terms that closely associate nightmare and witchcraft,
such as *Trude (Drude), Drudenmensch,* and *Alp,* all current names for
nightmare; *Walriderske,* "She who rides the stick"; *Hexe,* "witch"; and
Marriden, "the riding ma(h)r," a synonym of *witch.* By way of comparison, we can note that Hungarian uses *lidércnyomas,* a word composed
from *lidérc,* "nightmare"; and *nyomas,* a term of unknown etymology—
and that pressing or squeezing is almost always the principle function of
witches.[31] The lidérc partially corresponds to the Romanian *zburăor,*
"who is born out of fear or terror, out of vexation or wrath, of bad humors,
worry, boredom, and great joy,"[32] which says a great deal about the role
of the psyche in these phenomena and beliefs. In Lithuania we meet the
slogutis (plural *sloguĉiai*), "She who oppresses dreamers."[33]

The animal that leaves a sleeping individual is taken for the spirit or
the soul and, according to the narratives collected by Meyer-Matheis,
assumes the form of a mouse fourteen times, a cat five times, various
insects five times, a little bird, and a whirlwind. In Germany there are stories about this last manifestation that speak of a peasant who shoots at a
menacing hail cloud and sees a witch fall out of it. The wound brings the

---

*[The French for nightmare is *cauchmar,* from *caucher,* "press" or "squeeze," and *mar,* which
le Petit Robert defines as "phantom," and which the author more fully explains in this chapter;
see below. —*Trans.*]

witch back to her original form. In addition, in his *Poetic Art (skaldská-parmál)*, Snorri Sturluson suggests "Wind of witches" be used in describing hugr, or animus/spiritus.

In Meyer-Matheis's study, one thing is clear: The *Truden* and the *Alben*, men and women whose other selves go out on excursions, are similar to witches in that they attack others through the intermediary of their alter ego, but they are not witches in the sense we mean today. They are actually more like ecstatics. Here is an example of this in a tale told in Ratibor:

> A very beautiful young woman who had many suitors often went to the ball, but it was noticed that she always left before midnight. [Think of Cinderella!] One day, her wooers retained her and would not let her go, and at midnight she became completely stiff and fell into a lifeless state. All attempts to bring her back to life were in vain. A young mouse ran into the room, ran across the young woman's face, and just then, the young woman came back to herself.[34]

In such narratives, for example, those collected in Hessen-Nassau, it is often specified that the lifeless person lies on his back with his mouth open, which brings to mind the story of the Benandanti. In the canton of Uri (from Helvetia, or Switzerland) it is told how a man turned over his wife's body after she had fallen into catalepsy, which caused her death: "Her spirit could not re-enter her because she was lying on her stomach." According to a tradition established at Saint Gall, also in Helvetia, those who wanted to rid themselves of Truden were advised to lie on their stomachs. All witnesses agree that the Double enters and leaves by the mouth. Catalepsy can happen anywhere, but it almost always occurs at night. One narrative tells that people did not see a servant come back, so they searched for her and found her collapsed on the kneading trough. In Upper Austria, this testimony was given:

> After the Truden left at night to squeeze sleepers, they would lean their bodies against the wall or door of the sleeper's house. The soul

would leave the body, go into the house, and press so violently on the sleeper's chest that he would almost suffocate. If, while the Trude was with the sleeper, its inanimate body was touched, it would fall backward and die, for the soul could not return to the body then. If the one whom the Trude is afflicting is awakened, and if the name of the Trude is spoken, the body that she has leaned in front of the door collapses, lifeless, and the soul becomes the devil's. It happened once that a farmhand came home late one night and saw, in front of the door, a woman whom he knew well. He called to her: she fell down right away, dead on the ground.*[35]

We consistently find the same recommendations as those in the Scandinavian sagas: The bodies of those fallen into catalepsy must be neither spoken to nor touched. Yet there exists no genetic link between the sagas and accounts gathered in the nineteenth century. Thus we clearly have a belief common to all of the European countries. To be a Trude is a decree of destiny; to press or squeeze, an obligation.

In Austria it was believed that a person could rid himself of this miserable curse by strangling an animal: The Alb was the soul of an evil woman under a spell who must, at midnight, leave her body to go out and torment people. She could be saved only if she was permitted to squeeze to death the most handsome horse or the most beautiful cow in the stable.

The choice of the horse was most likely not fortuitous: Aside from its psychopomp nature, it was commonly confused with the (male and female) ma(h)r. In modern German, *Mähre* means "mare" and *Mahr* "nightmare."

The oldest and most complete testimonies on Truden and Alben go back to the sixteenth century. In a work by Johannes Prätorius, printed in 1666, an alter ego appears in the form of a red mouse who leaves the mouth of a servant in the Werbach (Thuringa) region.

Fortunately, it is possible to protect oneself from nightmares—that is,

---

*[The author here uses wall *(mur)* at the beginning of this passage; then in the latter two instances, he uses door *(porte)*. He seems, however, to be referring to the same idea in all cases. —*Trans.*]

son does not become one as well. And if he has daughters and no sons, they will most likely be nightmares.*[37]

In the nineteenth century J. Grimm noted the following belief: "Out of six girls born in a row to a couple, one is a werewolf." (*Deutsche Mythologie* III, 477, no. 1121).

Doubling is thus also an atavism, with the form of werewolf reserved for men and that of nightmare for women! Who can deny from now on the importance of the Double in this whole complex of ancient beliefs? This example from *Les Evangiles des Quenouilles* remains either incomprehensible or completely marvelous and surprising to those unaware of the link uniting werewolf and nightmare: the alter ego!

---

*[The old French is as follows: *Se un homme a tele destinee d'estre leu warou (loup-garou), c'est fort se son filz n'en tient. Et se filles a et nulz filz, volontiers sont quauquemaires (cauchemars* = nightmares). —*Trans.*]

6

Metamorphosis: The Double and Werewolves

In studying the beliefs behind the theme of metamorphosis, J. Frazer and other researchers following in his footsteps developed the concept of the external soul, the "free soul" *(Freiseele),* recorded in Stith Thompson's catalog of folktale motifs. We have seen that the word *soul* lends itself to confusion and that it would be better to use the term *animus,* or, to be perfectly exact, *Double* or *alter ego.* We also know that the body is host to at least three entities, according to those Germanic traditions that are representative of the most ancient stage of these concepts: Every man has his animal fylgja,[1] a psychic Double that is in some ways the equivalent of the Greek daimôn and the Latin genius (see appendix 1); and we all have at our disposal a physical Double (hamr) skilled at metamorphosis. From antiquity to the Middle Ages, accounts of form-changing abound, and even if we can but rarely envision a genetic link between the narratives, the typology is the same, from which it can be deduced that a common belief stands at the heart of all these testimonies.

Various traditions in which classical antiquity plays a large part have been superimposed onto the animal metamorphoses of witches, most often their change into cats. Let me just say in passing that some in the Middle Ages knew Ovid quite well, just as they knew Apuleius. If the texts coming from Rome nourished medieval literature, they only explain one part of what we encounter in it, but they also present astounding similarities with our body of work. This is what we turn to now.

ON A PASSAGE FROM *THE GOLDEN DONKEY*

In *The Metamorphoses, or The Golden Donkey,*[2] Apuleius—a North African born around A.D. 125 and originating from Madaura, Numidia, the present-day Algerian city of Mdaourouch, in the Constantine region—says much about witchcraft. His hero Lucius states: "I was in the very heart of Thessaly, a country famous around the world for incantations, of which it is the birthplace."

Here is a retelling of the narrative: While Lucius was watching over a corpse to keep some witches from taking away any part of it, which would impede the ritual burial, a weasel came into the room and stared at him, but he sent her fleeing. Then, said Lucius, a "deep sleep engulfed me in a bottomless abyss." The next morning, while all were congratulating him on his successful watch, an old man arrived on the scene and announced that the corpse was not intact. A magician was sent for, who, through necromancy, made the dead man talk: "While this man [that is, Lucius] . . . was keeping careful watch over my corpse, some old witches who were lying in wait for my remains and who, to this end, had several times changed their form in vain . . . finally threw a thick cloud of sleep over him."

We can compare this account to the words in the texts of the Scandinavian Middle Ages, taking into consideration, of course, the law of ecotypes, which allows for the different outward look of a theme, legend, or belief according to the times and the country from which it comes.

Witches change form at will, but the only form referred to here is that of the weasel, which we must keep well in mind. It is said that they throw a "thick cloud of sleep" over Lucius, which, translated into the terms of our medieval body of work, means that the hero is overcome by sudden torpor, the unerring sign that enemy Doubles are on the attack. (See part 1, chapter 3.) Further, it is known that metamorphoses concern only Doubles, which I will address later; so it is the witches' alter egos that bring on Lucius's lethargy.

For the rest, Thessalian witches, "these atrocious chameleons," says Apuleius, "transform themselves into any kind of animal whatsoever. . . . They disguise themselves as birds, dogs, mice, and even flies." Let me say in passing that we encounter most of these animals in the German folk traditions collected between the sixteenth and the nineteenth centuries. All of these animals are forms assumed by the Double, according to many testimonies, when it leaves to carry out a task, which here is an evil one, given that it is stealing a piece of the corpse. Apuleius does not dwell on this point and seems to suggest that for these women, the power to metamorphose is second nature. Nevertheless, the animals that he mentions— to which must be added the weasel—do not at all correspond to what we would expect, that is, large predators, such as wolves, foxes, and so forth. Perhaps the size of the animal was chosen here according to the evil deed that was to be accomplished. We can well imagine that these transformations have a particular and specific significance that can be understood only with the help of other traditions. But Apuleius explains nothing and simply refers to the power of these witches' incantations.

But what, then, is the term *incantation* hiding? Does it refer to a chant? A psalmody allowing entry into the state of lethargy or trance, and, consequently, the liberation of the Double? The question remains unanswered, even though I am inclined to think, on the faith of other testimonies, that an incantation is really an ecstatic technique. Future research will perhaps one day allow us to clarify this point.

SAINT AUGUSTINE AND THE *PHANTASTICUM*

Even if critics, such as Fulgence, fifth-century bishop of Ruspe, or the Fathers of the Church headed by Saint Augustine, attempted—without being particularly successful as far as the *rustici* and the *illiterati* are concerned—to show the inanity of metamorphoses and to prove that it was all only devilry and illusion, the belief in the transformation of men into beasts (the epitome of horror, given that the image of God is denatured) was much too well anchored in the pre-Christian mind to be erased without leaving some traces. Celtic and Germanic literature conveys many vestiges of it that are not simply products of mythology. The thought of Saint Augustine himself, whose interpretation of such facts marks so profoundly the Middle Ages, is not devoid of ambiguity.

In *The City of God*,[3] Saint Augustine (354–430) studies the phenomena of metamorphosis by using as supporting evidence the mythological texts—Circes' spells, Diomedes' birds, Arcadians's lycanthropy, and so forth—as well as the testimonies that he collected from trustworthy men. In mythology, says the bishop of Hippo, metamorphosis is unreal, illusory; the demon deceives our senses.

Testimonies on the real should receive more extensive reflection, given that the issue of the power of demons is brought forward. Fortunately, this power is limited, and all that the devil does happens only with the permission of God *(Deo permittente)*. Yet it is at the heart of the Augustinian critique and explanation that we find the *phantasticum* that has perplexed more than one exegete and more than one translator, as the term exists substantively nowhere else but under Augustine's pen, which hinders all cross-checking. Let us look at the text (XVIII, 18):

1. Demons modify in appearance only those creatures of the true God so that they seem to be what they are not.

2. I thus do not admit in any way that demons be capable, by their power or their tricks, to transform in reality not the soul, but simply the body of a man into parts and shapes of beasts.

3. I believe that the phantasticum of man—which modifies itself in the waking state or in sleep according to the innumerable diversity of objectives, and, without being a body, nevertheless takes, with surprising rapidity, forms resembling bodies—can present itself, under corporal appearance, to the senses of other men when the bodily senses of the man are dulled or exhausted, in an unknown and

ineffable manner and in such a way that the body itself of the man is lying somewhere, alive certainly, but in a numbness of senses heavier and more profound than sleep.

In sum, thanks to a daimôn, individuals can change their appearance: Such is the profound meaning of the first point. The phantasticum leaves the sleeping or exhausted person and takes on a corporal form in which it appears to other people: Such is the lesson of the third point, in which Augustine clearly alludes to what can only be catalepsy, profound trance, *conditio sina qua non* of the Double's liberation.

Behind Augustine's complicated assertion, then, we can recognize the alter ego, which here is called the *phantasticum hominis,* the part of man that is most vulnerable to Satan's attacks. Under the pen of our theologian, this part is reduced to a vision imagined by the sleeper, to a noncorporal phantom that is emitted when the senses relax—an image, hence, that demons shape to make a specific a form. In order to mask the illusory nature of the metamorphosis—when there is one—the devils take on material tasks that the cataleptic or the dreamer cannot fulfill, "in such a way that this phantasticum, having manifested itself corporally in the figure of some animal, appears to the senses of other men, again in such a way that the man himself also takes himself for such."[4]

Moving on to a critical examination of the testimonies, Augustine relates the following story:

A certain Praestantius told that his father, having by accident eaten some of this poisoned cheese at home [made by some Italic innkeepers initiated in the deadly secrets of magic], had remained in his bed, as if asleep, and no one could succeed in waking him. A few days later, having awakened himself, so to speak, the father related what had happened to him as if it were a dream: He had been a horse and, with other beasts of burden, he carried to the soldiers provisions called *rhetica* because they were transported in a net. His tale conformed to what had happened and yet, for him, he had seen only his own dreams *(quae tamen ei sua somnia videbantur).*[5]

What is for us the proof of Praestantius's doubling—that is, the narrator verifies that things had happened as they had been told—becomes a useless dream, a demonic substitution, under the pen of the Bishop of Hippo: Demons took on the shape of the horses and it is they who sent a dream to the sleeping man. But Augustine cannot quite convince us, nor even quite convince himself. He crashes headlong into reality and emphasizes that "the facts are reported to us by people not unworthy of our trust, but by people whom we believe incapable of deceiving us." Hence, what he proposes is, quite simply, his interpretation of the facts.

Here is one final testimony that Augustine examines:

> Another recounted that during the night, before going to bed, he had seen in his house a philosopher whom he knew very well. The philosopher explained certain Platonic doctrines to him that he had refused to explain to him some time earlier in his own home, despite the man's request. And when this same philosopher was asked afterward why he had done in this man's house what he had refused to do in his own house, he answered: "I did not do it in this man's house, I only dreamed that I was doing it."

Augustine thus concludes that by a fantastic image *(per imaginem phantasticam)* what was shown to the man who was fully awake, the other man saw in dream.[6]

This account is extraordinarily close to the Norse traditions of the Middle Ages, and by using the concepts of the ancient Scandinavian world to decode the Augustinian example, we can say that the hugr (thought) of the philosopher took form (hamr) in order to answer the call of the man asking for explanations. A detail easily shows that this is not about a psychic Double (fylgja), but well and truly about a physical Double (hamr), whether Augustine likes it or not: The person who emits the alter ego is asleep and dreams what he did, but the recipient of the visit is awake and sees the philosopher's Double—moreover, without knowing that it is an alter ego.

These issues did not cease to haunt Saint Augustine, and he returned to them in other writings, most notably in his opuscule dedicated to Paulin of Nole, between 421 and 423, and titled *Care to Be Had for the Dead.*[7] In this opuscule, he addresses the subject of the living who appear in dream to other living people, and of the dead who appear to us in dream, and gets himself out of the whole business by speaking of images and human weakness. After discussing the visions people can have during delirium or lethargy, he concludes by suggesting that we not scrutinize these mysteries, which is a way of recognizing the failure of his explanations and interpretation.

The Augustinian interpretation of events having to do with the Double is exactly that which the clerics of the Middle Ages take up again in order to make this stance into true canon. Thus, every time the medieval Church comes up against similar phenomena, it speaks of illusion, images, dreams, phantasmagoria, and demonic manipulation.

ATAVISM AND DESTINY

In the pagan mind, then, humans possessed a Double capable of changing appearance by detaching itself from the body either during sleep or trance—or at will, as was the case with magicians and sorcerers, both male and female. According to this belief, it is thus perfectly possible that another person could—by appropriate means that fall under the jurisdiction of the occult—metamorphose you or me, just as it is possible for either of us to metamorphose someone else. Where things become complicated is that Christianization, of which Saint Augustine is a good example, resulted in the erasing and acculturation of this belief in most of the Western medieval countries, with the exception of Germanic areas. The ecclesiastics who recounted these stories no longer knew that the touch of a magic wand or an incantation spoken over the alter ego liberated it, that is, freed it from its ties to the body, and could condemn it to wandering about in the form of an animal.

In a Latin text dated from the thirteenth century and titled *Arthur and Gorlagon,* this highly contaminated belief can be recognized, but the witness is invaluable because he reveals to us a world of correspondences, for here we enter into the area of the plant Double: In an orchard, a little branch starts to grow the instant the king is born. Things are arranged in such a way that if someone breaks off the branch and strikes the king's head with it while saying, "Be a wolf and have the spirit of a wolf," the king is right then metamorphosed into this animal.[8]

In this telling we can detect the hint of a connection between alter ego and transformation, but it is so diffuse that it remains invisible to anyone who is not familiar with other traditions that can allow for cross-checking. In fact, the ability of metamorphosis is a gift, but for a Christian like Burchard of Worms (965–1025), it is more like a curse. He states:

> You believe what certain people have the habit of believing, in other words, that women whom the vulgar call the Fates exist or possess the powers that are attributed to them; that is, at the birth of a man, they do with him as they please, so much so that this man can, at will, transform himself into a wolf—which common stupidity calls the were-wolf—or take on any other form *(aut in aliam aliquam figuram)*.[9]

Burchard tells us clearly: Metamorphosis into wolf is only one form among others! This confirms, with a precision worthy of winning over the greatest skeptic's adherence, what is said in all of Norse literature. In introducing the notion of destiny (the Fates), which he takes up again— we must be aware of this—in the Styrian penitentials, and which he inserts in his *Decretum*, Burchard only clarifies things. We must note, in any case, that sorcery or magic are not involved here.

In Ireland a thirteenth-century Latin text also clarifies our issue quite well, and it had a certain amount of circulation, given that we find the content of it in a manuscript of Nennius's *Historia Britonum*:

> There exist certain men of the Celtic race who have a marvelous power that they get from their ancestors. By a demonic force, they can, at will, take the form of a wolf with large sharp teeth and often, thus metamorphosed, they attack poor defenseless sheep. But when people armed with sticks and weapons come toward them, they flee

nimbly and cover great distances. When they are of a mind to transform themselves, they leave their human body, ordering their friends
not to change their position or touch them in any minor way whatsoever, for if that were to happen, they would never be able to return
to their human appearance. If, while they are wolves, someone
wounds them or hits them, the wound or mark on their [animal]
body is found in exactly the same place on their [human] body.[10]

The importance of this text will escape no one, for it is found at the
crossroads of traditions. It confirms the interpretation that I have given of
the stryge woman who was marked with a red-hot iron, and exactly matches
up with what the sagas say: Do not move the body of a cataleptic, and do
not speak a word to him. Even though it comes from a different geographic
area, it corroborates the testimony of the penitential that Burchard follows
and brings to us a valuable piece of information: These people acquired
their power of doubling from their ancestors. Does this not mean that it was
transmitted through heredity? In the stories of the alter ego atavism plays a
role that is by no means insignificant. In all the texts related to the Irish legend of the werewolf, this point is emphasized. See *The Book of Ballymote*,
with the tale "The Children of the Wolf," or the *Topographia Hibernica* by
Giraud de Barri (1146–1223), or *The Suitability of Names* (Cóir Anmann),
in which the following can be read:

Laignech Fáelad was a man who had the habit of changing his
appearance into a wolf *(fáelad)*. He and his descendants were in the
habit of taking on at will the form of a wolf and of killing herds the
way a wolf would. He was thus named Laignech Fáelad because he
was the first of his race to take the form of a wolf.[11]

Now we will change geographic area. *The Saga of Egill Skallagrimsson*
also confirms the role of atavism:

There was a man who was called Ulf (Wolf), son of Bjalfi and
Hallbera, who was daughter of Ulf the Non-coward and sister of

Hallbjörn the Half-Troll. [See chapter 1.] Every day, when night was coming, Ulf would become hostile, unsociable . . . and he would be taken with sleepiness. It was said that he had a very strong ability to double himself.[12]

The anthroponyms Wolf *(Ulf)*, Female Bear *(Bera)*, Male Bear *(Björn)*, and the meaning of *bjalfi*, "fur," suggest that this family has the gift of metamorphosis. Moreover, the family possesses a strangeness expressed by the surname Hallbjörn, "the Half-Troll." *Troll* extends back to the giant race and, more generally, to the race of indistinct spirits. In another text, *The Saga of Hörd*, the gift of metamorphosis is attributed to this family in an apparently parodic way: "He was the son of Ulfhedinn with the Wolf Double *(ulfhamr)*, son of Ulf, son of Ulfhamr . . ." [13]

A careful reading of the texts reveals that it is the alter ego that takes animal form while the body lies somewhere without any apparent signs of life. Between 1202 and 1216, Saxo Grammaticus wrote simply: "In other times, magicians were extremely adept at changing their traits and at appearing in various forms." Until recent times in Livonia, it was believed that when the soul of a werewolf had gone off to carry out its evil tasks, its body remained as if dead. If, during this time, the body was moved accidentally, the soul could never return to it again and it would remain in the wolf's body until the wolf's death. In a tale from Tourangeau folklore, mentioned by Philippe Ménard,[14] it is said that werewolves "peel off their soul," that their bodies remain where they normally would be while the soul incarnates itself. The term *soul* is, of course, completely incorrect, but such is the result of historical evolution.

The writers of the Middle Ages neglect to relate many details having to do with werewolves. They keep quiet about something leaving the body and speak of transformation, but they cannot completely ignore that the wounds inflicted on a given wolfman appear on the body once it has metamorphosed back into a man. This point has caused significant deviation from the tradition that was reviewed and corrected by clerics who were incapable of understanding this detail and, to support their arguments, used the authority of the authors of classical antiquity—*auctores antiquissimi!*—which was built on long duration and on the written word. These clerics told of the transformation of unusual individuals by drawing inspiration from known models, for example, the story of Lykaon.

The biggest distortion to which the original tradition has been subjected comes from introducing into it explanations that are products of other perspectives, that metamorphosis is due in part to magic objects—a wand, in the lay of *Mélion*,[15] written between 1190 and 1204; a branch, in *Arthur and Gorlagon*. Another explanation says that it results from a curse, as in the account of Giraud de Barri, or from an evil spell, as in *William of Palermo* (from around 1195). The issue of the moon's influence, which Gervais de Tilbury brings up in the *Imperial Leisures,* must be put aside, for to study it here would be to depart from our topic.

At times, the adaptation of the belief to literature nevertheless allows us to see more clearly into all of this.

THE WEREWOLF'S CLOTHES

We now turn to the *Bisclavret*,[16] a lay composed by Marie de France between 1160 and 1170. Here is a summary of the text: The unfaithful wife of a knight sought to rid herself of her husband, who changed regularly into a wolf, and she questioned him. He answered her thus: "My lady, I become a bisclavret."*

She listened, and then asked him if he undressed or if he went clothed.

"My lady," he said, "I go completely unclothed."

"Where, then, my lord, do you leave your clothes?"

"That, my lady, I will not say, for if I were to lose them, I would remain a bisclavret forever. My misfortune would be irremediable until they were given back to me."

The woman, with the help of her lover, then stole his clothes from him, and he remained a wolf.

*[*Bisclavret* is the Breton name for werewolf. —*Trans.*]

One day, the king met the bisclavret during the hunt and, intrigued by his human behavior, adopted him and took him back to the court. There, the king very quickly guessed the truth when he saw how the animal behaved toward the adulterous woman and her accomplice. The woman was then forced to give him back his clothes.

The scene in which the bisclavret returns to his human shell is extraordinarily revealing. The return to the human state cannot be carried out in the presence of witnesses, which is explained in terms of shame:

> [An advisor to the king speaks.] "Sire, you are approaching this wrongly. Not for anything in the world would the bisclavret want to put on his clothes or transform his animal appearance in front of you. You don't know how important this is! He feels terrible shame. Have him brought into your chambers, and have his clothes brought with him; leave him alone for a goodly amount of time. Then we will see if he becomes a man again, all right."
>
> The king himself brought him there and barred all the exits. After a while, he returned, accompanied by two barons. All three entered the room, and on the king's own bed they found the knight, who was sleeping.

Behind the literary adaptation, events that are well known to us and that we have discussed in the preceding chapters stand out clearly. Sleep, an unexplained and inexplicable motif in Marie de France's account because it seems tied to the clothes having just been put back on, is, in fact, the normal state of the person who doubles himself. *Clothes are thus quite obviously a substitute for the body.*

No one has been aware of this point until now because no one has taken into account the belief in the Double. While this belief is well known to specialists of Germanic, Baltic, and Finnish civilizations, the results of the research of Scandinavian scholars remain unknown in France, perhaps due to a language issue (see appendix 1). From now on, it will be necessary to reconsider medieval metamorphosis stories: When they are not simple reminiscences of tales from classical antiquity, they in all likelihood have as an underpinning the belief that we are unveiling here. This belief alone allows a satisfactory explanation for a recurring trait in these narratives: The werewolf is simultaneously man and beast. He retains his human reason in his lupine form.

Some will perhaps refuse to consider clothes as a substitute for the body in a state of lethargy and will refer to the *Satyricon* by Petrone, in which the theme of clothing appears but in a much different context than in Marie de France's account. Well, then, let's talk about this text! For Petronius (A.D. 27–66), the candidate for metamorphosis must undress, then urinate in a circle around his clothes, and all this at night.[17]

In Marie de France's account, the bisclavret takes off his clothes and hides them, and it is in putting them back on that he regains his human form. How, then, can a wolf put on the clothes of a man? It is a little too easy to say that the tale thumbs its nose at such pragmatic questions, that we are moving within the realm of the marvelous, in a world where laws of causality are abolished, where all is possible. This is to be unaware of the internal logic of popular traditions, which have a lot more wisdom than we give them credit for! It also cuts short all future interpretation and is evidence of a lack of knowledge about the recovery or survival of pagan beliefs—popular or folk beliefs, if you prefer. If, as the clerics did, we assimilate the illiterate people and the rustics with the pagans, we must call all of this book's subject matter phantasmagoria.

In what way would the loss of clothing be a hindrance to the metamorphosed returning to human form? Do clothes carry magic power? Certainly it is fair to assert that to take off our clothes means to rid ourselves of our human nature, but in this statement are we not remaining on the surface, at the first level of all levels of complexity? On the other hand, if we admit that the body remains lifeless while the Double travels in wolf form, we discover that clothes are, in fact, the substitute for the body. This is why they must not be touched; this is why in putting them back on, the person becomes human again. To put on clothes, a prosaic and rational act if ever there was one, is the medieval and clerical—in a word, Christian—vision of the return of the zoomorphic alter ego to the body. But this is also Petronius's vision.

Where is he on all of this in the *Satyricon*? In it Niceros narrates to Trimalchio what he has seen: "The soldier got undressed and placed his clothes alongside the road . . . he pissed all around them and, suddenly, he turned into a wolf. . . . I went up to gather up his clothes, but they had turned into stone." The circle is a talisman whose power is increased even more by the apotropaic qualities of urine. This means that the soldier puts everything to work in the interest of protecting his clothes, but why do they become petrified?

The motif remains inexplicable unless it is related to one of the meanings of stones: the Greek *colossos,* a rock appearing in empty tombs as a substitute for the absent corpse and whose function is to fix the Double, the psuchè who wanders endlessly between the world of the living and the world of the dead for as long as the body has not received a ritual burial. The colossos does not intend to copy the traits of the deceased; it is not an image of the deceased. "It is a reality outside of the subject," says Jean-Pierre Vernant.[18] In doubling, the body remains as if dead—all the texts repeat this again and again. It is impossible to wake it up and, if we refer to vision literature, this "death" seems so real that the pseudo-dead person would be buried if a divine sign did not cause the people present to doubt the seeming reality. Between this coma and a death understood as petrification there is only one step. The theme is perfectly coherent: The transformation of clothes into stone is a form of substitution where the abandoned body's resemblance to a corpse is predominant.

We must remember in this regard that the Greco-Roman world was very familiar with the idea of the Double. Jean-Pierre Vernant and Maurice Halbwachs have proved this, and a tradition that can be found in Aristotle's treatises *De anima* and *De spiritu* tells that magicians knew how to liberate their Double in order to allow it to travel to the next world. It exits and reenters the body at will, leaving it lying still without breath or life, in a sort of cataleptic sleep, sometimes for many years. The Double comes back rich with prophetic knowing from these travels into the other world. In the Middle Ages the idea of the Double was swept away by the Church, which replaced it with the soul or the spirit; the notion of the Double was no longer admitted among the theological, doctrinal, and demonological schemas of the dominant culture and religion. The belief was too irrational; it had to either join the current canons or disappear.

This "normalization" of similar events according to Augustinian criteria is particularly clear in the work of Guillaume de'Auvergne, who was born in Aurillac around 1180 and who died in 1249. Named Bishop of Paris in 1228, he wrote his comprehensive survey *The Universe (De universo)*, wherein he discusses at length the devil and his traps, and he presents the werewolf as someone possessed:

A man was possessed. Some days an evil spirit would take over him and cause him to lose his reason to the point where he thought he was a wolf. During these periods of possession, a demon would throw him into an out-of-the-way place and abandon him there, as if dead. During this time, the demon would put himself inside a wolf or clothe himself in the appearance of a wolf, appear to everyone, and carry out terrifying massacres of men and beasts. All fled at the sight of him, fearing they would be devoured. The rumor flowed that it was this man who was turning into a wolf certain days, and the man himself believed it. Furthermore, he was persuaded that he was the wolf responsible for the massacres. But a holy man, learning of the story, arrived on the scene and explained to the people that they were wrong to believe in this man's metamorphosis into a wolf. He led them to the place where the man lay, as if dead, showed him to the spectators, woke him up in front of them, freed him from his possession, showed him, as well as the others, the wolf with whom he thought he was but one, as well as publicly confessing him.

The distortion of the pagan belief is very crude, but it has succeeded more than once in deceiving researchers who did not have comparable texts at their disposal.[19] We may look more closely at the basic facts:

Belief	Christian Interpretation
A man has the ability to double himself.	An evil spirit takes over him.
He isolates himself from the community to avoid anyone touching his body while it is in a state of lethargy.	The demon throws him in an out-of-the-way place and abandons him there as if he were dead.
His Double takes the form of a wolf.	The demon puts himself inside a wolf or clothes himself in the form of this animal.
The man knows that he has a wolf Double at his disposal.	The man believes that he is a wolf.
The Double reenters the body.	The holy man wakes the man and frees him from his possession.

Adventitious details are included to better hide the original facts. Hence, the werewolf gives himself over to terrible massacres—in short, he appears to be a Beast of Gevaudan before it even existed!*

After reading Guillaume d'Auvergne's account, how could we deny that the Roman world was aware of the Double? The evidence is not isolated. We may refer to the texts attributed to Etienne de Bourbon and Gautier Map, cited in the preceding chapter, and the passage from the *Life of Saint Germain* that Jacopo de Voragine inserts in *The Golden Legend*. The alter ego is not exclusively Germano-Nordic, even if in this cultural area it enjoys a particular renown. The method used by Guillaume d'Auxerre and those of his ilk is perfectly representative of the clerical milieu of the Middle Ages. Now that we have seen this, it should be possible for others to find the Double in many additional texts.

A LIVONIAN WEREWOLF

That werewolves are in no way what everyone thinks, that they do not correspond to the image created by pseudoscientists in search of the sensational, emerges clearly from the story of Thiess, the Livonian wolfman.

*[The Beast of Gevaudan was a wolflike monster who terrorized the region of Auvergne during the mid-seventeenth century. It allegedly killed more then one hundred people before it was exterminated. —*Trans.*]

Set in a geographic crossroads between the Scandinavian, Slav, and Mediterranean worlds, the true story of this man, whom Otto Höfler studied from a different angle, proves the quasi-general diffusion of the belief that we are tracking down. In 1692 the trial of an elderly man, Thiess, who was more than eighty years old, took place in Jürensburg. Thiess declared that he had been a werewolf and had been to hell with his companions in order to bring back seeds that had been taken away by a sorcerer named Skeistan. The reader will find the translation of this text in appendix 3. Those who have studied the minutes of the trial, H. von Bruiningk, Höfler, and C. Ginzburg, retained from it only what is related to the secret brotherhoods and the mythic battle between winter and spring or summer, the exact counterpart of what is told in the story of the Benandanti—without paying any particular attention to the name assumed by Thiess and company: werewolf *(werwolf)*.

Livonia, a Baltic province of European Russia, bordered on the north by Estonia and on the east by Lake Peipus, has continually been an important intersection where exchanges, both commercial and cultural, take place. At the end of the nineteenth century there still existed a very high proportion of Swedes in this country. While what we are calling a werewolf was considered a common phenomenon in the Scandinavian countries, metamorphosis of the Double became little by little fixed on the wolf, from which comes, for example, the introduction of a new word in the Norse lexicon, *varúlfr* (wolfman), under the influence of the Norse translation of the *Lays* by Marie de France.[20] Even in Germany *werwolf* first meant "he who knows how to change form," that is, to double himself. If we stick strictly to the facts, Thiess has this name because it refers to this ability.

In hell Skeistan hit him with a broom handle on which were tied horses' tails, and a witness attests that, at that time, Thiess's nose had a mark on it from being hit.

But how did this individual become a wolf? The judge asks how this spell was put on him. "A scoundrel of Magdeburg turned me into a wolfman by making a toast with me," replies the old man, who specifies a little later that he himself could put the same spell on an individual: "All you have to do is drink to someone's health and blow three times into the wine jug while saying these words: 'May what happened to me happen to you.' And if the other takes the jug and drinks, he becomes a wolfman and I become free." We find this mode of passing on the power in the work of Swedish bishop Olaus Magnus in the *Historia de gentibus septentrional-ibus* (1555), which proves its diffusion and vitality, but an explanation is missing. Perhaps I can provide one.

If I we use *The Saga of Thorstein with the Cow's Foot* to support this explanation, we can envision the transformation taking place through the saliva. In the Icelandic saga it is the saliva of the witch *(skessa)* Skjaldvör that procures for Thorstein the ability to change form.[21] If we refer to the more recent Lithuanian traditions and if we remember what was said in part 1, chapter 1, we can decode the expression that Thiess uses: "Drink to someone's health." Indeed, it is said (in Lithuania) that the man who runs around changed into a wolf can, when he drinks to his neighbor's health and pronounces the word *sveikata,* transmit to him his werewolf characteristics. All that needs to happen for this to occur is that the other replies, "Thank you!"[22] *Sveikata* means "health" and is also one of the names for the alter ego. It is thus a very strong chance that this second explanation is the correct one.

Returning to the trial of Theiss, in order to get to hell a person or beast must walk: "The werewolves went there on foot. . . . They had a wolf skin that they would wear. . . . They would go into the bushes, strip off their clothes, and be transformed straight away into wolves." The weight of traditions and canonical interpretations is undeniable, and it muddles the facts. Another detail: These curious lycanthropes do not eat raw meat; they cook what they kill! Scholarly and literary tradition seems to have played a considerable — and most likely conservative — role in the state-ments by Thiess or, at the very least, in the writing of the trial document. Everything seems to indicate that no metamorphosis occurred, for Thiess undresses and then dons a wolf skin, a detail that strongly brings to mind a passage from *The Volsung Saga:*

[Sigmund and Sinfjötli] went again into the forest to get themselves some silver, and they found a house and two men sleeping in it with thick rings of gold. These men had been the objects of unfortunate fate, for their wolf forms were hanging above them in the house. . . . Sigmund and Sinfjötli entered into these forms and could not get out of them: what resulted from this was the power which was attached to them; they took on the mannerisms and voices of wolves.[23]

The writer of the saga transforms and literalizes the belief in doubling and, as in all the medieval West, he speaks of a "wolf form," meaning, in fact, a lupine alter ego. We probably should link this approach with an anecdote that Giraud de Barri (1146–1223) tells in his *Topographia Hibernica:*

One day, the Irish began to howl like wolves against Saint Patrick who was preaching to them about the Christian religion. So that their descendants would have a visible sign of the lack of the faith of their ancestors, the saint obtained from God that certain among them would be transformed into wolves for seven years and they would live in the woods like the animals whose appearance they had taken on.[24]

Giraud then tells how a priest meets such wolfmen, who ask him for the last rites. The ecclesiastic is obliged to administer the extreme unction to the female wolf who is in the worst shape, but because he does not want to perform the rites for an animal, the male wolf raises the skin of the female wolf from her head to her navel *(pellum totam a capite lupae retrahens usque ad umbilicum),* and the man of God sees the body of an old woman *(forma vetulae).* For Christians of the twelfth and thirteenth centuries, werewolves kept their human nature under their wolf skin. Let us specify, however, that opinions diverge on this point: Some favor metamorphosis; others, the superimposing of the wolf skin onto the human body. In the Livonian trial Thiess seems manifestly incapable of saying, or does not want to say, exactly how he would become a werewolf. But one point is very important: He went to hell in order to fight against Skeistan. Yet, to my knowledge, true wolfmen cannot do this.

Only Doubles are in the position to reach the other world. What is more, this type of combat in the next world, during which the fertility of the coming year is at stake, is well known among shamanistic peoples. Decidedly, there is no end to this extraordinarily coherent complex of which the Double represents the central axis.

The tyranny of canonical interpretation cannot, however, mask the reality of these beliefs, the traces of which we can follow at least up to 1704. Olaus Magnus and other authors repeat that many werewolves are found among the Prussians, the Livonians, the Laplanders, the Finnish, and the Biarmians, that is, the inhabitants of the shores of the White Sea, therefore the Samis and the Zyrians—the Komi of today: peoples among whom shamanism is well established.

METAMORPHOSIS

Outside of the werewolf stories, medieval literature presents few true metamorphoses. Most of the time, they are attributed to the acts of magicians. This is the case in *The Unknown Beauty* by Renaut de Beaujeu,[25] in which the enchanter Mabons transforms the beautiful Blonde Esmerée into a *vouivre* (a sirenlike creature who is half snake and half woman) by touching her with a book. In the novel of the same name, Merlin changes the appearance of King Uther to that of the baron Jordain, whose wife the king covets.[26] In the magic act of Sigurd (Siegfried), there is an exchange of appearances between him and Gunnar (Gunther), so that it is Sigurd who crosses through the wall of fire that protects the castle where Brynhild lies sleeping.[27] But during all these transformations, the individual's eyes do not change, which allows us to recognize the person who is hidden in someone else's appearance.

In the ancient Celtic mythological accounts, metamorphoses are legion, but they result most often from the intervention of a god. In *The Battle of Mag Tured*, Midir and his wife fly away in the forms of two swans; in *Math, Son of Mathonwy*, from the *Mabinogion*, there can be found metamorphoses into deer, male wolf, female wolf, and eagle; likewise, *Manawyddan, Son of Llyr* men are metamorphosed into mice.[28]

It certainly seems that the issue of metamorphosis has always been poorly examined until now, because it has always been looked at from the Christian perspective (the same view used to look at the witch trials), and this for good reason: Metamorphoses in the style of Ovid were taken for fables by the mythologists. But some thought that there was real transformation of man into beast when there was none, and again for good reason—this universe of thought has more logic than one would think!—because they had forgotten that every individual possesses Doubles that are able to assume a zoomorphic form. The animal alter ego is thus at the disposal of whoever knows how to use it. The Finnish magician and the Icelandic hamrammr can choose the form under which they will run afar. The psychic alter ego appears in the form of a bear if he is well intentioned or friendly; in that of a wolf and even a seal if he is evil and looking to do wrong. From the moment when animal forms are at the disposal of an individual, it is logical to admit that the individual can bring on a metamorphosis, that is, a transport into another form, if he possesses the appropriate techniques and science.

Magic and witchcraft work on the Double, not on the real body: Such is the explanation that I propose. Through charms and conjuring the magician extracts the animal alter ego from the man and forces it to leave the body and roam the earth. When they know how to control their own Double, magicians (male and female) are also likely to act on the Double of others. Is it not telling that the history of witchcraft is filled with women changing into cats at night? Misunderstanding, lack of knowledge, forgetting archaic belief in the existence of theriomorphic alter egos, and the intervention of the Church and men of letters—all these caused metamorphosis to swing toward either the marvelous or the satanic, and the example of the werewolf is an excellent illustration of this.

Part 3
seeing the double

7

Autoscopy

Autoscopy refers to the phenomenon of perceiving your own Double as a separate being; of seeing your Double as a spitting image of yourself, a theme that played a very important role in German romantic literature.[1] We must nevertheless be sure to distinguish the spiritual Double from the material alter ego because they do not manifest themselves in the same way. If we refer exclusively to the texts of the Middle Ages, only the spiritual Double would have to do with autoscopy, while the material alter ego is completely involved in faraway transports or transfers. But there are more recent revealing texts regarding this topic.

We must note right from the start that an undeniable link exists between second sight, clairvoyance, and the psychic alter ego, which is often visible only to its possessor. According to the inquiries of twentieth-century ethnologists, date of birth plays an important role here: A seer may be born on Christmas or Saint John's night, during the twelve days of Christmas or during Advent, or on All Saints' Day, Saint Andrew's Feast Day, Ember Days, New Year's Eve (the Saint Sylvester), New Year's Day, a Sunday during a full moon or a new moon, and, regarding time, most often at midnight, the moment that is no longer today and not yet tomorrow, a true "no man's time" belonging to the spirits.[2] People gifted with second sight are very frequently born with a caul. They can also be recognized by their joined eyebrows or by a peculiar look in their eyes. Their possible birthdays imply connection between the world down here and the next world; they are bridges erected between the two worlds, and the Double has something of the same dual nature.

THE MATERIAL DOUBLE

Outside of ancient Scandinavian literature, I have not found, as far as the alter ego is concerned, a trace of the phenomenon of second sight; thus we must return to the testimonies of the sagas. In reading them, I notice that the term designating these charismatic people of a particular type is *ófreskr,** literally "whose eyes have a higher power," that is, they do not stop at appearances but pierce through them, discovering the hidden reality and triumphing over the physical categories of our universe. *The Book of the Colonization of Iceland* provides us with an example: Björn receives in a dream a visit from a mountain spirit who becomes linked to him. His wealth increases (we are reminded of Lanval, part 2, chapter 4, and narratives of the same type) and "the people gifted with second sight saw that the earth genies were accompanying Björn."[3]

In another chapter of the same book, only the seers perceive the metamorphosis of the witch Geirhild into a cow skin full of water.[4] And further, it is told in the account of the fight between the alter egos of Dufthak and Storolf (part 1, chapter 3), that a man possessing this gift sees the two men's zoomorphic Doubles.

The material double is sometimes visible to all and sometimes invisible. There is a lack of certainty on this point because the texts rarely tackle this issue. But if we use the *Historia rerum Anglicarum* by William of Newbury (1136–1198) as support, we can see the beginning of an answer to this particular point. Today we are no longer unaware that ghosts are, in fact, the material Doubles of the dead. In one ghost story, it is said of the deceased:

He began to come back in full daylight. He was the terror of all but was only visible to some. Most of the time, as a matter of fact, he

*The term is used in the locution *ófreske maðr,* plural: *ófreskir menn.*

would go before several people, allowing himself to be seen by only one or two, without, however, hiding his presence from the others.[5]

This is particularity noteworthy because it is the only testimony I have been able to gather regarding the issue of visibility versus invisibility, and it no doubt allows us to confirm that the Double is, in general, invisible. Likewise, in the story of the archbishop of Uppsala (part 1, chapter 2), the woman believes she perceives Peter Lärdal in her kitchen, but the apparition remains fleeting, corresponding exactly to the phenomenon that the Anglo-Saxons call fetch.*

The difficulty also comes from the fact that a person does not have only a single, unique Double. There are at least two: one physical and sometimes zoomorphic; the other spiritual and also able to take animal form. All the confusion that can ensue from this duality is immediately obvious. Here is example from another saga: While his friends and allies are fighting the enemy, Bödvar Bjarki remains calmly seated as a white bear fights next to his people on the battlefield. When Bödvar goes to the battle scene, the bear disappears.[6]

How do we interpret this incident? The saga makes absolutely no mention of trance or torpor. However, small details illuminate the narrative sequence: No weapon can break the bear's skin—one of the distinctions of the spiritual Double; and when Hrolf Kraki's men are surprised by Bödvar's absence, they are heard to answer: "He must be somewhere where he can be of great use to us." The theme of the Double underlying this saga reaches mythic proportions with the battle of Hrolf Kraki and Bödvar against the army of the dead sent by the female magician Skuld. Admittedly, the sleep motif is missing, but the disappearance of the bear coinciding with the appearance of Bödvar is significant.

There is, then, no particular reason that the material Double should be invisible, and Germanic ghost stories support this. When they are invisible, it must be due to a contamination by the spiritual alter ego, which remains, it well seems, imperceptible to common mortals. But on this

---

* [See page 42, part 1, chapter 2. —*Trans.*]

point all peremptory confirmation is subject to caution. The discovery of other texts will perhaps one day allow us to settle the question of the material Double's visibility.

THE SPIRITUAL DOUBLE

Without returning to what I have said in any preceding chapter, let us remember that the principle characteristic of the spiritual Double is to manifest itself in dreams, in animal form, and to disregard both time and space, for its appearance precedes the events revealed to the sleeper, whether they be close or far-off. This alter ego concretizes, in an immaterial form—if I can risk using this oxymoron—its possessor's thought (hugr). This is absolutely obvious when it appears in dream just before a battle.

When it enters the scene far in advance of an event's occurrence, the spiritual Double is even closer to the concept of destiny, to which it is related in one way or another. The following example shows this well: Thorstein dreams that a swan comes to rest upon the roof of his home and that an eagle joins the swan. Then another eagle comes along, and the two eagles kill each other. Finally, a falcon arrives and leaves with the swan. Thorstein goes to see a Norse expert in the art of divination, who tells him: "These birds must be the fygljur of men *(fuglar þeir munu vera manna fylgjur)*."[7] The swan represents the girl whom Thorstein's wife is carrying, and the dream summarizes what her life will be.

Connecting us to the other world—or rather, in accordance with the mind of our time, to the hidden side of the universe—the psychic Double has knowledge of the destinies of others through their potential alter egos. It is the Double who will accompany the individual throughout his earthly existence.

SEE YOUR DOUBLE AND DIE

According to a very strongly enduring belief, the person who sees his spiritual Double is destined to an imminent and unavoidable death. This apparition is a sign or a warning from destiny.* In modern accounts of similar events the distinction between the physical and the psychic alter egos is disappearing. In the Middle Ages only Norse literature offers us evidence of this distinction, which clearly proves that it is one of the best reflections of those Western beliefs that Christianity eliminated or acculturated in most countries. How, then, would the presence of this "superstition" in the Roman world be explained if not by a resurgence of repressed beliefs? What would we say about the following?: It was said at Commercy (Lorraine) in the nineteenth century that when a person was seriously ill, those around him must take notice if some owl—a barn or screech owl—came fluttering about the place. If we interpret such an appearance with the help of the Northern mind, we can go beyond simply observing that these are birds of bad omen and see in their presence one of the last manifestations of the spiritual zoomorphic Double that comes to take his leave of the man.

In the North, things are much clearer. *The Saga of the Lakevale Chiefs* tells the dream of Thorkel Silfri, who has the impression he is coming down the valley on a red horse that seems barely to touch the ground. Signy, his wife, says: "This horse's name is Mar, and Mar is the tutelary spirit of a man. If he appears red, it is because you will be covered with blood, and it may happen that you will be killed at this meeting."[8]

Needless to say, Thorkel finds death at the gathering he attends soon after.

In *The Saga of Burnt Njal,* Njal and Thord are sitting outside, near a field where a goat is pasturing. "I have the impression that this goat is lying down here in the hollow and that he is all bloody," says Thord to his companion who, we must note, sees nothing.

His friend responds, "Maybe you are about to die, and that was your tutelary spirit [fylgja] that you have seen. Be very careful!" "That will not help me at all," retorts Thord, "if it is death that awaits me." Soon after, he succumbs to death during the attack of Sigmund and Thrain.[9]

In *The Saga of the Salmonvale People*, Thorgils goes to the gathering

---

*The man this happens to is designated by the adjective *feigligr* (Old High German *feig*), substantive *feigð*.

of free men *(thing)* with Thorstein. Both men see a very tall woman coming to meet them. Thorgils stands before her, but she slips by and declaims:

> *May they be careful, the warriors,*
> *If they esteem themselves valiant,*
> *And may they also be careful*
> *Of Snorri's ruses;*
> *No one will be safe.*
> *Wise is Snorri.*

Then she goes on her way. Thorgils then speaks: "It has rarely happened, when you wanted good for me, that you have left a thing when I was going to it."

The next day, Audgisl assassinates him.[10]

There are other examples: When Hallfred the Difficult skald falls sick, his fylgja appears to him and they separate themselves from each other. And in a chant from the Poetic Edda of Helgi, Son of Hjörvard, Helgi, who knows he is destined for death, tells that he has seen a woman riding a wolf, and those were his tutelary divinities.[11]

The Saga of the Svörfud Valley Dwellers has given us a very beautiful scene. Karl and Gunnar are outside when suddenly the first becomes pale after having looked up at the sky: "What is the matter?" asks Gunnar. "I saw my cousin Klaufi [who is dead]; he was crossing the air, pulling a sleigh on which I thought I recognized myself," replies Karl. Then the two hear Klaufi's voice: "Cousin Karl! You will join me tonight!"

That same day, Karl falls under the blows of Skidi and his men.[12]

The fylgja, tutelary spirit and spiritual Double of the individual, comes thus to take her leave of the person whom she has always accompanied and who has arrived at the end of his existence. She appears in general as a woman, but greater in size than normal, which allows her to be distinguished from a common mortal. She may also appear as an animal whose fur is gray or red, the colors of the supernatural and bloodshed, which leaves no doubt as to the immediate fate of the individual. That she turns to another member of the same family after service to the first is dissolved, as in *The Saga of Hallfred* (part 2, chapter 4), indicates that she has existed before her protected one and endures after his demise—thus she is clearly an independent entity who binds herself to a person only for the time of that person's earthly existence, a detail that must always be kept in mind.

THE DOUBLE TAKES ITS LEAVE

Pagan and Christian literature often relate the visit, in a dream, of a person at the exact moment that person has died. This phenomenon is still well known today and it has always been considered proof of the existence of the soul. This appearance just as the body has died has even drawn the interest of philosophers. In his *Lectures on Metaphysics,* Emmanuel Kant states that "the soul is not dissolved at the same time as the body, for the body is only its form."[13] And Goethe said to Eckerman: "I do not doubt our persistence. All entelechy is a morsel of eternity, and the few years during which it is tied to the body do not age it."

In the Icelandic sagas the examples of such appearances coincidental with death are numerous. *The Saga of Thorir of the Hens* depicts Blundketill appearing to his son and announcing to him that he has just died. And *The Saga of Gunnlaug Snake-Tongue* narrates Œnund's dream, in which his friend Hrafn finds him, and Œnund is all bloody. Sometimes the raw details leave no doubt that the dream visitor is dead: Also in *The Saga of Gunnlaug Snake-Tongue,* the brother of An the Bow-Stretcher appears to him with a sword stuck in his chest.[14] *The Saga of the Salmonvale People* offers still more illustration of this theme: Thorkel has been shipwrecked and drowned with his companions. His wife goes to the church that same day. When she passes the cemetery gate, she sees a phantom standing in front of her. He bows before her and says, "Big news, Gudrun!" She replies, "Do not talk about it, you miserable thing!" Gudrun continues to the church, as she had intended, and when she arrives, she seems to see that Thorkel and his men have arrived. They are standing in front of the church, and she can see that seawater is running in streams down their clothes.

Thus in these sagas physical Doubles (hamir) of the deceased often appear at the moment of their death, or immediately after, as they have died: The drowned are soaking wet, the assassinated are bloody. But in more recent reports, this detail is scarcely specified, as in this example from before 1752:

> The same morning that His Royal Majesty August the Strong died at Warsaw, it was said that he appeared in Berlin before Mister Grumbkow, whom he loved very much and whom he told of his death as Mr. Grumbkow was in his bed. Mister Grumbkow went immediately to the king to tell him the news, and after the king asked him where he had learned it, Mr. Grumbkow spoke to him of the apparition, but His Majesty did not want to believe him. Then a courier arrived confirming the news of the death.[15]

We can note that distance, in this case between Warsaw and Berlin, in no way hinders the movement of the Double, which in general is indistinguishable from its possessor.

When the apparition of a Double does not take place during sleep, a few accounts show the host addressing words to his visitor, or the fiancé advancing toward the woman he loves, only to see her recoil and disappear into thin air.

The phenomena of its appearance to tell of a death are among the best surviving accounts of the Double. In German, the usual term for such visitations is the verb *künden,* "to announce" — meaning the announcement of death, of course. In Switzerland in the 1950s, an inquiry undertaken by Aniéla Jaffé, a student of Carl Gustav Jung, with the help of a major journal *(Der schweizerische Boebachter),* illustrates the power and diffusion of belief in this aspect of the Double.[16]

The amount of information gathered by Jaffé, Will-Erich Peuckert, and other researchers is enough to shake the most solid skepticism. But it is said that these things happen not only to those who believe in them — and has not depth psychology brought to the fore the role of the unconscious in such occurrences? In my view, one detail is especially significant: These beliefs possess a venerable ancientness, and they endure through the hell or high water of history.

SURVIVALS

As mentioned in part 2, chapter 5, Vera Meyer-Matheis has pulled sixty-five accounts of cases of second sight from collections dating from the nineteenth century and the first half of the twentieth, as well as from the depths of the archives of Marbourg devoted to folktales—and they are all, it must be emphasized, connected to death. The testimonies can be divided into two groups around this theme:

1. Nineteen accounts involve a person's visions of either himself or someone close to him lying in a coffin.
2. Forty-six accounts involve the vision of a funeral procession.

Here is an example from the first group, a 1930 account from the province of Hanover: "A peasant from Lutter went to work in the fields one morning with his wife. Suddenly, he saw a funeral cart carrying an open coffin in which lay a village woman, who died soon after."[17] And here, from the second group, is a 1903 account from Saint-Gall, Switzerland:

> Barthli heard one night a strong murmuring in the street. He quickly got up and looked out the window to see a very long procession passing. At the tail end of this, he saw himself running, having put on only one leg of his pants. He then gazed down at his body as he stood at the window and saw that he had put on his pants only halfway. He died a few days later.[18]

In the first group, thirteen out of nineteen accounts concern autoscopy and, more precisely, the vision of oneself in a coffin, but in six narratives, the person receiving the vision does not recognize himself, as translated by a recurrent motif: cutting a lock of hair from the corpse to discover who in the household is going to die. The next day, the person examines the inhabitants of the house and, after finding their hair is intact, he looks at himself in the mirror (or passes his hand through his hair) and discovers that he has cut a lock of his own hair. He is thus sworn to death, which arrives within twenty-four hours to seven years. Here is such a testimony taken in Lower Saxe, in the Münster region:

> On a farm in Ochtrup, a farmhand got up in the night to go to the threshing floor. There he saw a dead man in a coffin and did not recognize him. It occurred to him that this must be a vision and he wanted to know who the man was. He went for some scissors and cut a lock of hair from the deceased man, then went back to bed without saying anything to the others. While he drank his coffee the next morning, he closely observed those around him, but saw nothing and kept his secret to himself. Then, after washing, he went to comb his hair in front of the mirror and noticed that he had cut his own hair. He still kept silent about his vision, but soon after he told the farmer, "I'm leaving!" The farmer asked why, for they had always been friendly. The worker did not want to say anything more, or to stay, even for a higher salary. He packed his belongings and left. The farmer accompanied him for a bit of the way and while doing so, attempted to get the farmhand to change his mind, but his words were in vain. "I'm leaving," replied the worker without giving a reason, and the farmer had to be satisfied with that.
>
> Seven years later, they met again in the village market and greeted each other amicably, and the farmer invited his former worker to visit him. Because they had never argued, the worker knew it was time for him to reveal himself! He then told the farmer how he had seen himself in a coffin, and that this was the reason for his leaving. "Ah, you foolish man, you believe these things! Such nonsense does not exist!" The worker agreed then and went to the farmer's house soon after. But what must be, must be. He fell sick at the farm and died shortly after. The coffin was placed on the threshing floor, as was the custom.[19]

We cannot help but be struck by the common spirit of these testimonies and those of the Middle Ages. Even when taking into account the inevitable distortions that historic evolution introduces, it is still surprising to notice such similarity, which occurs over centuries only with a deeply rooted belief. And rooted it is—we have only to look at the reactions of the characters who receive the visions in these accounts. The vast complex of beliefs having to do with death is one of the things that has resisted demise and survived the best, until the relatively recent advent of the industrial era and the decline of the rural world.

In modern stories, it is no longer tutelary genies or the Double that appear to individuals. In these accounts, a person can see himself, as did the farmhand of Ochtrup, without recognizing himself. Hence the inclusion of identifiying elements such as hair or clothes. It must be noted, however, that when a person gifted with second sight perceives a dead man in a coffin or a certain individual in a funeral procession, he or she immediately knows what it is about.

The other world thus appears like a reservoir of Doubles. Time there is nonexistent, and everything coexists at the same moment. The other part of ourselves, which comes from this other world without totally detaching itself from it, materializes our potentialities and our destiny. When the hourglass that measures our life's time is empty, or when the candle that represents it is ready to be blown out, our psychic Double appears to us—much as the angel of death appears in the Judaic tradition. It then takes leave of us and returns to the nameless world from whence it comes, to enter into a sort of retreat there while waiting to accompany a new individual. This belief exactly confirms certain traditions concerning shadow and reflection, to which we now turn our attention.

8

Shadow, Reflection, and Image

As I said earlier, literature has never stopped being in touch with the real. This means that stories feed themselves with *realia:* We can rethink them; poetize them; adjust elements of them with the intention of pleasing, surprising, instructing, or inducing reflection on serious subjects hidden behind pleasant banter. Very often writers and storytellers, such as A. Le Braz in France, update ancient knowledge, either from books or from the oral tradition of the regions in which they live. It is thus hardly surprising that a belief like that of the existence of an alter ego, the vigor of which we have come to appreciate, would have found the path of literature—but in what form? It appears in the simplest: that of the shadow, reflection, or image, which has the benefit of being plausible for readers of these last two centuries because it fits so wonderfully into so-called fantasy literature. Adapted to literature, this belief from the depths of the ages has known a second youth and undergone its own metamorphosis, which clearly proves that it is not a fossil unearthed by authors with antiquated tastes who have trouble with all things new. However, only one part of the belief remains: The idea of the pluralistic soul and the alter ego has been erased in favor of the single and indivisible soul, which is as expected, for we are very far from the times in which wild thought, unaware of the laws of causality, has reigned. We are no longer *in illo tempore.*

THE SHADOW

The shadow[1] is by far the most well-known expression of the belief in the Double because great writers and poets have popularized this theme and lent credibility to it. Everyone knows *Peter Schlemihl: The Man Who Sold His Shadow* by Albert von Chamisso (1781–1838), in which the soul takes on the form of a shadow that the hero abandons to a mysterious gray man in exchange for a bottomless purse. *Anna,* a series of poems inspired by Swedish legend Nicolas Lenau (1802–1850), presents a woman who leaves her shadow with a witch in exchange for the promise of eternal beauty. A tale by Andersen (1805–1875) titled, in fact, *The Shadow,* shows how the Double of an academic acquires total independence, supplants his alter ego, and even has him condemned to death. In the Middle Ages a certain Gonzalo of Berceo rewrote the legend of Theophilus, the archetype of Doctor Faustus, and took the trouble to specify that, once the pact is signed with the devil, Theophilus loses his healthy color and even his shadow, though thanks to the intercession of the Virgin Mary, his shadow is returned to him. This refers to the merging of the shadow and the soul, which is the origin of the notion that the dead, sorcerers, and witches do not have a shadow at all.

The shadow has always been the visible form of the hidden side of man. It is the carbon-copy outline of the body, but it is made of a more subtle material, and writers and philosophers have expended treasure chests of imagination trying to describe it. It is not simply the silhouette projected when the body intercepts rays of light, but another self who has all the physical and psychic qualities of the self, enjoys all the same prerogatives, and at the death of its possessor goes away into the other world so aptly named the Kingdom of Shadows. Homer tells us that it keeps its feelings, appears to the living in dreams, and even speaks to them, as long as the body has not been burned to ash. When the dead Patrocles appears to Achilles, Achilles cries, "Gods! So there is yet a shadow and an image in the houses of Hades."[2]

Pythagorus, Plutarch, and many other scholars of classical antiquity agree that the deceased no longer possess a shadow, and that this is the mark of their new status. It is remarkable that the Greek *eidolôn* means both "shadow" and "phantom," and that there are several terms for soul, including *skia,* "shadow," used as a synonym for *psuchè*.[3]

The shadow of a living person is taken for the visible manifestation of her Double, and this Double straddles the world down here and the world beyond, which can be deduced from the significant amount of reports it has generated, among which those concerning the shadow's oracular function are not the least important. For example, during the cycle of the Twelve Days,* the shadow is carefully observed because the fate of the living is determined according to it. In Germany it is said that whoever does not have a shadow on Christmas night, or whoever's shadow is headless, will die in the coming year.[4] The Bulgarians believe in similar observations for the night of the Feast of Saint John, as do Jews for the seventh night of the Pentecost festival.[5] In the mountainous mining regions it is said that misfortune will soon come to the one whose shadow has a big head. Among the Wendes, people of Slav origin established in Lusace, it is believed that the fate of the man whose shadow trembles on a wall will be bad. In *Mon frère Yves* by Pierre Loti, a woman from Brittany asks her listener to change places because his shadow is giving her the impression that misfortune is going to strike him. Jacob Grimm tells a legend in which a woman is warned of a menacing danger by the gesticulations of her shadow.[6]

It is also believed that the shadow goes away when its possessor is going to die—think of the fylgja—which is why particular importance is attached to the sharpness of the shadow projected by a sick person: If it is well defined, he can hope to get better; if it has disappeared, this means it has preceded the man into the other world. We can now understand all the implications of the ancient Turkish greeting "May your shadow not grow smaller!" and its counterpart, the curse "You will no longer cast a shadow!"[7] In Jewish tradition it is stated that death is announced to Heaven thirty days ahead of its occurrence; from that time on, the shadow of the person becomes smaller and smaller until it disappears all together.

*[The twelve days between Christmas and Epiphany. —*Ed.*]

We cannot help but be struck by the coherence of all these beliefs, despite their widely diverse geographic origins.

What belongs to a man also belongs to his shadow. What affects one concerns the other, and this is where we observe the identity established among body, shadow, and soul. In Acts 5:15, and in all texts inspired from it, it is said that Saint Peter's shadow heals the sick.* The shadow is thus fully able to uphold the same charisma as the body, and this is logical within the mentality that we are studying, given that it is the body's Double. See also what Pliny the Elder tells us: A hyena who walks on a man's shadow deprives that man of words.

In a more recent era, we find the same gathering of ideas. In Argovie, Helvetia, if an individual's shadow falls upon the first stone of a building under construction, he loses his health because in doing so it is thought that the health of this person has been walled up. The same occurrence in Bulgaria indicates the person concerned will die thirty or forty days after and become the genie of the place being built. It must be noted in passing that the Saxons of Transylvania substituted a symbolic act for the walling up of a living person in a brand-new building: Either they would place the first rock on a man's shadow, or they would measure the shadow and bury the measurements. In Germany it is believed that anyone who has the misfortune of walking on his own shadow will die. In Silesia, as in Italy, people are careful not to walk on someone else's shadow; doing so means that person will stop growing. Elsewhere it is claimed that if your shadow falls on a dead person, you will become a vampire.

Mixed in with the soul in the lexicons of many peoples is the Double, which is why walking on another person's shadow is a serious offense in certain civilizations. A medieval proverb says, "What I do to him, may he do to my shadow!" This cryptic phrase becomes more clear thanks to this ancient Swabian provincial right: A serf humiliated by a free man could demand reparation for this prejudice; the offender would be placed before a sunny wall and the offended man would punch his shadow in the throat.[8] This example and the following one clearly prove that the shadow is considered the person's Double: During the time of

*For example, in the legend of Servatius (Saint Servais).

Emperor Maximilian (1459–1519) in Austria there existed the punishment of banishing shadows.[9]

From these beliefs and practices it emerges that the shadow is the visible form of an invisible reality. Copying the external shape of an individual, it also possesses that person's internal properties. In short, it attests in broad daylight to what is manifested in other forms at night. It is important to note that to the mind-set that concerns us, it is impossible to dissociate the shadow from the soul, for the shadow is the alter ego of both soul and body.

REFLECTION AND IMAGE[10]

In a great number of myths and legends, the central theme is the story of a man gazing at himself in a mirror, either natural or artificial, and the consequences ensuing from this act. For the Neo-Platonists, this act resulted in the equivalent of losing the soul's happiness. According to the gnostics, Adam lost his heavenly nature from having looked at himself in a mirror and fallen in love with his image. And everyone knows the story of Narcissus, who fell in love with himself after having seen his reflection on the surface of the water.

Great writers have returned to the ancient idea that the reflected image is the soul. The best illustration of this is without doubt provided by E. T. A. Hoffmann in *A New Year's Eve Adventure*, a.k.a *The Lost Reflection*—that the story is set on New Year's Eve is definitely not an accident!—in which he tells the story of a reflection that has been lost. As his text is a veritable summary of the belief we are tracking, let us look more closely at an excerpt here:

[Erasme Spikher has fallen in love with Giuletta. He is obliged to leave her, and she asks him to leave his reflection with her.] "At least leave me your reflection, oh my love! I will watch over it tenderly and it will never leave me."

"How could you keep my reflection?" he continued. "It is inseparable from me. It accompanies me everywhere, is sent back to me by all calm and pure water, by all polished surfaces."

"So," says Giuletta, "even this aspect, even this dream of your being that stays in this mirror here, you refuse to give to me, you who just a moment ago were yet speaking of belonging to me body and soul!"

"If I have to leave, may my reflection remain in your possession for ever and eternity!"

Giuletta held out her arms to the mirror. Erasme saw his image, independent of the movements of his body; he saw it slip into Giuletta's arms and disappear with her into the middle of a strange vapor.[11]

The Student of Prague by H. H. Ewers is another tale of a lost reflection: Balduin, the hero, lives in a miserable room, and for fun signs a contract with a certain Scapinelli permitting the latter to take what he wants in the room, which is bare except for a mirror. Scapinelli then shows Balduin's reflection in the cheval glass, upon which the image leaves the mirror and follows Scapinelli away. Margit, the hero's beloved, breaks off their relationship when she sees that Balduin no longer has a reflection. The young man, despairing, wants to kill himself, when his Double appears before him, sniggering. Balduin shoots him with his pistol, and the Double immediately disappears. Relieved, Balduin goes to the mirror and looks at himself. He then feels a very sharp pain in his chest, notices that his shirt is covered with blood, and crumbles to the floor, dead.[12] I leave to the reader the task of discerning the most important elements of this summary.

In a work of Oscar Wilde, *The Picture of Dorian Gray* (1890), we encounter another aspect of the same belief: Face to face with a painting of himself, the young hero expresses the wish to remain forever handsome and youthful, with all marks of age and sin being transferred to his image. The portrait then becomes the mirror of his conscience—in fact, of his soul and body. Dorian kills the painter of this fateful portrait, pushes the woman he loves to her death, and ends up slashing the canvas with a knife. Having become old at the same instant, he falls dead, the knife plunged into his heart, while the intact portrait shows him in all his youthful freshness. The portrait is Dorian's Double; the denouement leaves no doubt about this.

Finally, in *The Horla* (1887) Guy de Maupassant presents a man who cannot rid himself of his Double and whose appearance is not reflected in any mirror.

All these literary expressions can be better understood if we first comprehend the belief underpinning them: The soul passes out of its possessor, totally or in part, into every representation, pictorial or otherwise, which explains the fear felt by many people when they are faced with their own image. Here it is stated without specifying the implicit danger, "Do not let anyone paint your portrait!" There you are advised, "Never look at yourself in a cracked mirror!" Even today followers of certain religions and people of a number of diverse cultures refuse to allow themselves be photographed.*

There is a second reason for this fear, closely linked to the first: If the soul passes into the image of the body, anyone who has sufficient knowledge and science can act on the living through the channel of this Double, a point that I am going to clarify immediately.

THE VOULT

As R. Boyer has clearly shown, magic widely employed the notion of the Double for the ancient Scandinavians.[13] With regard to classical antiquity, A. Abt collected the principle testimonies for the use of wax figures *(imagines cerae)* in Roman magic.[14] In the Middle Ages people continued to believe that it was possible to affect other people at a distance through the use of a *voult*.

The word *voult* comes from the latin *vultus*, "face," and led to the French *envoûtement*† through the Middle Latin *invultuor*, "sorcerer who makes a voult." Marbode, who was born in Anjou around 1035, appointed bishop of Rennes in 1096, and died in 1123 at the Saint Aubin

---

*I was able to observe this in Kotor, Montenegro, in 1962 when I wanted to photograph a person in folkloric costume who had come to sell his products at the market.

†[English *bewitchment.* — Trans.]

monastery, makes mention of these wax images that were baptized in order to increase their potential, their magic "charge." It is claimed that the Jews killed Eberhardt, bishop of Trier, through this means. Pope John XXII (1316–1334) very particularly feared this form of evil spell, and on December 3, 1339, his direct successor, Benoît XII, ordered an extensive inquiry into the subject. Alphonse X of Castille and Léon (1252–1284), Charles VI (1380–1442), and François I forbade this practice under penalty of death. However, Marie de Médici and Leonora Concini were, in the middle of the seventeenth century, suspected of planning to drown Louis XIV through the means of a clay statuette, baptized in his name and stabbed through with a needle. In England the Duchess of Gloucester was accused of this crime under Henry VI, and Shakespeare makes allusion to it in *Richard III* (Act III, Scene 4). In Carinthia and the Tyrol the judicial acts speak of murder attempts from a distance in 1465, 1485, and 1493. In 1578 a priest was accused of having made three wax dolls, with the idea of killing Queen Elizabeth and other nobles of England.

Regarding Germany, the Inquisitors Henry Institoris and Jacques Sprenger report this in the *Malleus maleficarum:*

> At Innsbruck, a woman attributed her sickness to a bewitchment [envoûtement], and asked for help from the lover of her neighbor witch, who discovered the rose pot: "My husband and he went then to remove the evil spell. The potter, lifting the seal, told my husband to put his hand in the crack that appeared and to bring out whatever he found, which he did. The first thing he brought out was a wax figure as long as the palm of a hand, with holes all over it, the sides stabbed through with two needles, exactly at the place where, from right to left and vice versa, I was feeling the shooting pains."[15]

Carefully prepared and stitched, the wax figure—a simulation of the person—functions like a lover. It attracts the Double, fixes it, and then catalyzes the evil spell. When wounded the figure transmits its wounds to the alter ego, which, because the alter ego is one with its possessor, results in a negative effect on the person. If, in our times, modern sorcerers still make use of voults, which they call *dagydes,** they resort more and more frequently to a simple photograph of the person to whom they direct their magic, sometimes requiring some of their target's hair or nail clippings.

IMAGES AND THE DEAD

All representations of a living being, human or animal, result in attracting the Double of the person or animal or, to use a more contemporary term, his energy, his astral body. The hunting-related magic of the primitives embodied this same idea. As old as the world, this belief clearly explains the role that corpse substitutes played in the Greek and Roman civilizations. A dead person's Double roams in space and cannot reach Hades as long as the body has not yet received ritual burial. The fate of the physical body affects the Double's destiny. Says Jean-Pierre Vernant of one of Medea's cenotaphs dating from the thirteenth century B.C.:

> This practice of substitution corresponds to beliefs with which we are very familiar. When a man, having left to go far away, seems to have disappeared forever, or when he dies and his body is not brought back or the last rites are not performed on him, the deceased—or rather, his Double, his psuchè—continues to roam endlessly between the world of the living and that of the dead. . . . Substituted for the corpse at the bottom of the tomb, the colossos is not intended to reproduce the traits of the deceased, to give the illusion of his physical appearance. It is not the image of the dead person that it incarnates and fixes; it is his life in the next world. . . . The colossos . . . is a Double, like the dead person himself is a Double of the living person.[16]

Images—whether statues or paintings—are tied to the same belief, and the story of Acteon proves this for us: The shadow, the ghost

---

*[*Dagdydes* is a term now used by English-speaking witches. They are wax or plaster dolls into which pins are stabbed—in other words, voodoo dolls. —*Trans.*]

(eidolôn), of Acteon is harassing the population. The Oracle of Delphi orders an effigy to be made and attached with iron chains to the same rock where the ghost has appeared. This is done, and the specter stops bothering the people, so Pausanias tells us.

Shadow, reflection, image ensure the link of man to his fellow creatures, to the dead, and to the invisible world. Were this not the case, the examples given would remain inexplicable, and the shadow's oracular function would be, when all is said and done, merely a vulgar superstition without any profound resonance.

The shadow Double is the intermediary between the worlds. For example, in the ancient duchy of Oldenburg the following belief was popular: If, between eleven o'clock and midnight—the hour of spirits *(Geisterstunde)*—an individual appeared in front of a mirror while holding a lighted candle in each hand, and if this person shouted his own name three times, he would be able to see into the future. And in France this used to be said: On the night devoted to the magi, if a person wrote the names of the three kings in blood on his forehead and then looked at himself in the mirror, he would see himself as he would appear at the hour of death. Not long ago people in Germany were persuaded that reading the Bible in front of a mirror would chase ghosts out of the house. And finally, the mirror has been seen as an open window to the other world, but also as a trap for the soul. In all of Europe, there was a very telling custom: that of covering the mirrors in a home where someone had just died. It was feared that the soul might remain stuck in them, or else that the spirit of the dead person would be reflected, resulting in dire consequences.

When we read Hoffmann, Chamisso, or Wilde, an essential question arises: From where do they get what they are telling us? From books? No doubt, but only in part. From the depths of themselves? Probably, and here we are sent back to the great constants of our thought. But the expression of these archetypes is no longer found, save among writers and poets, in legends and superstitions, and these testimonies are the last vestiges of these beliefs, which are now buried in the unconscious.

Conclusion

The importance of the Double in the mind of our distant ancestors should now be clear. The Double stands at the center of a fundamental anthropological construct: the relationship of man with the other world, both its higher and infernal aspects. The impression of heterogeneity, which emerges from the thousands of events recorded in the texts, disappears once the ancient concepts of the soul are acknowledged. Beliefs that rightly could be considered scattered and unrelated pieces find coherence again once we have discovered their common denominator, once we have grasped the central piece of the gigantic puzzle whose pieces the storms of history have scattered.

If we examine cultures and civilizations that were late in being Christianized and were isolated from great historical events because they existed at the edges of the so-called civilized world (for instance, on the steppes of central Asia, on the tundra, and on the taiga)—cultures that have therefore preserved elements of genuine archaism, one of which, first and foremost, is shamanism—we may reconsider strange and unusual phenomena that were once considered demonic by clerics and marvelous by pagans and that became ensconced in medieval literature.

So man possesses Doubles, most often two of them. One, material and physical, has the power either to take on animal appearances or keep its human form; the other, spiritual and psychic, is also capable of metamorphosis, but appears mostly in dreams. These Doubles have the ability to reach the other world—or any place whatsoever in this world—in one or another of their forms, as soon as the body has been put to sleep, sent into a trance, or made to fall into catalepsy. It is difficult to distinguish precisely between the physical alter ego and the psychic Double, given that even our distant ancestors confused them, as has emerged from the evidence gathered over the course of this inquiry. Every ethnic group and every civilization thought of the Double in its own way, but within the geographic area we are working with here, all evidence seems to indicate that the foundation common to all forms of this belief is shamanism.

One question remains unresolved for the moment: How did shamanism come to be known on Western medieval soil? Was it brought by the Indo-Europeans, or did it exist before them? Whatever the answer, one thing is certain: We can find traces of it among the Greeks and the Romans as well as among the Celts and the Germans. Carlo Ginzburg has endeavored to bring to light the connections of this kind that exist within the Celtic world; I have presented the connections existing within the Germanic world; E. Rohde and M. Halbwachs established, some time ago, the connections of ancient Greece to shamanism.

The constellation of beliefs whose center pivots on belief in the existence of the Double is represented by the diagram shown here, which forms, so to speak, the synthesis of this book:

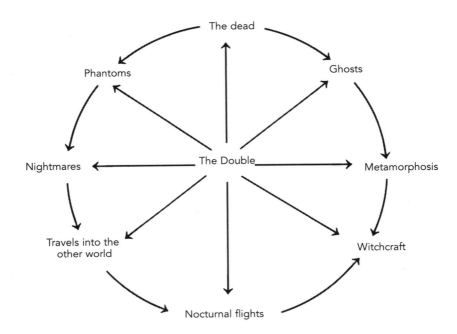

Death liberates Doubles; the physical alter ego yields a ghost, and the psychic alter ego is transformed into a phantom. Both conserve their capacity for animal metamorphosis, but one manifests itself in dreams and can function as nightmare, while the other appears in reality, as a material being. Nightmares and form-changing can also be the result of actions of the living; both have been attributed to witches. In such cases the travels of the Double to the next world—either to deceased ancestors or to spirits and gods—are secularized and demonized, becoming the nocturnal flights of evil-intentioned women who journey at night, flying across the sky in pursuit of Diana and Herodiad, or following lady Abonde to enter houses at night.

The Double does not die with the body. This is the explanation for phantoms and ghosts and the root of necromancy.

The Double is capable of changing into other forms, which is the origin of accounts of werewolves and animal metamorphoses.

The Double becomes independent once the body is at rest, and it may leave either to go about its business or to fulfill the desires of its possessor. This is the explanation for witches' and magicians' nocturnal and diurnal journeying and for saints' and mystics' ecstatic journeys.

According to the texts, these points are more or less developed, more or less obvious. Everyone is familiar with the theme of travels to the next world, whether it concerns descending to hell, traveling into the land of the fairies, entering a hollow mountain, or visiting places of atonement, as did Aeneus, Dante, Tondale, and Thirkill. The Double, in these cases, has very often disappeared when faced with the soul (which is the Christian perspective) or when faced with the body—as in the legend of Orpheus, one of the most ancient testimonies of shamanism's influence on the formation of such tales. And no one is unaware of the metamorphosis experienced or cited during the era of the great witch trials, or of the theme of the witches' Sabbath, the last incarnation of the ecstatic journey.

It must be admitted that belief in the Double has enormous power, given that it has survived over and across centuries and centuries. The victory of Christianity is essentially lexical: The term *soul* erased all other names for what was essentially the same concept, and everyone, even I, has been a victim of this lexical *diktat.* The Anglo-Saxons used the term that meant "external soul," the Germans *Freiseele,* and the French a term meaning "detachable soul" or "free soul." It was the lack of an adequate term that led to the improper, even erroneous, usage of the word *soul* when speaking of the alter ego, the second self, the Double.

The durability of belief in the existence of the Double is astounding. In Europe hundreds of accounts of zoomorphic Doubles—mice, flies, or baby birds—have been inventoried and recorded, with most taken down as real-life experiences. The belief is not ready to be extinguished, for spiritualism has fanned the flame. See the hypothesis of Léon Rivail (1804–1869), who was better known by the pseudonym Allan Kardec. It was formulated in 1857 in *The Book of Spirits:*

> Man is formed of three principles that are dissociated at death: the body, which dies; the soul, immortal principle that, at the time of death, attempts to disengage itself from matter—for it remains for a certain time a prisoner of the *périsprit,* the energetic encasing, being sometimes able to become visible and even to manifest itself in a tangible way; and the périsprit, which is the link between spirit and matter during the body's lifetime.

What Kardec calls *périsprit,* others call the *astral body.* Paracelsus spoke of it as the *Mumie,* alchemists termed it the *subtle body,* and the Kabbalist Jews spoke of it as the *zelem.*

If belief in the Double enjoys such vitality, it is because it responds to a human need. It carries a message of hope: We are not alone. The gods are concerned with our destiny, and we can communicate with them. We remain in contact with our deceased ancestors, and thanks to them, we know that death is not an end but instead a temporary retreat. The transmigration of souls is a product of the same mental world.

At this point in time, as we pitch like a drunken ship because we have been deprived of all transcendence, in this twilight of ideas, we have enclosed ourselves within a cavern of pragmatism and science. But, contrary to the Platonic fable, we no longer perceive reflections of the true world. We are no longer the One in the Whole, but the One without the Whole, and we live our earthly existence without being able to answer a question that our ancestors did not ask, protected as they were by a whole array of comforting beliefs: What is there after? In losing our Double, we have lost our soul, our relation to the cosmos, and, like new "Peter Schlemihls," we no longer know our place in the universe. Sadly, distraction replaces the beliefs and rituals that used to structure human existence, and all that remains is the eternal silence of infinite space.

Appendix 1
The Soul and the Double

Here I provide separately those facts that are the products of other civilizations that have, in one way or another, influenced the medieval West, and that corroborate the results of my inquiry.

The body/soul duality—which Ivar Paulson calls "dualistic pluralism," as opposed to a monistic concept of a single and indivisible soul—assumes a complex form among other Indo-European peoples (the Germanics do not have exclusive rights!). E. B. Tylor's works, and especially the work of Ernst Arbman, Björn Colinder, Åke Hultkrantz, Erwin Rohde, and I. Paulson to correct and further those of Tylor, revealed the existence of a pluralistic soul in the ancient mind-set.[1] Arbman and Paulson elsewhere undertook a well-researched study of the northern Eurasian peoples and have emphasized the close ties that exist among them between these concepts and shamanism. As I have stressed several times, shamanism was well known in the Middle Ages; the people of that time were in contact with shamanism's representatives (e.g., Laplanders). Starting in antiquity, there were exchanges and influences among peoples of these various geographic areas. We must also take into account the Indo-European invaders that passed through the territories of certain peoples before settling down in the West.

The presence of shamanism in European cultures and its major contribution—the belief in a pluralistic soul—could have another origin: It is possible that they were not imported. Today we know that communication with the next world is very developed among primitive peoples, whether hunters or herders. Shamanism might well have been in place before the invasions of Indo-Europeans and then included in the forms of religion that gradually developed. It has been dated back to the Neo-Paleolithic Age, and cave paintings—those of the cave of the Two Brothers, in Ariège, for example—support a native substratum. Of course, it is not this ancient shamanism that survived to the Middle Ages. Only remnants survived, bits and pieces that reemerged in the form of themes or legendary motifs often matching up with particulars from the Mediterranean basin. Hence, the motif of the bridge that must be crossed to get to the other world and, more generally, the theme of descending to hell.

First we will look at the Greek and Roman traditions, then we will concentrate on those of the countries bordering the Baltic Sea.

ANCIENT GREECE

Prior to the sixth century A.D., the Greeks used several terms for that which, in their view, animated the body. If we believe Homer, this is *thumos*, "passion, will, spirit" and *psuchè*, "life, breath," which escapes from the mouth of the dying person—the shadow image leaving the lifeless man (*Iliad* XXII, 466 and 475), breath image, or bodily substance. In Homer the concept of the soul is connected to more ancient beliefs and is in sharp contrast to them. This great poet also used the terms *phrén/phrènes*, "diaphragm, will, thought"; *êtor*, "lung"; and *kér*, "heart, feelings." Empedocles, who died around 490 B.C., used *prapidès*, "diaphragm," a word that designates, without clearly distinguishing between them, both an organ of the body and a psychic activity.

According to Homer, the psuchè is like a traced carbon copy of the body, and, at the time of death, it takes the form of the living person and becomes his Double (eidôlon). It is also the personality of the living individual. When the psuchè leaves a person it becomes an image, the immaterial materialization of the body, which explains the terms used as synonyms of psuchè such as "shadow" *(skia)*, "smoke" *(kapnos)*, and even "dream" *(oneiros)*. For Plato, the Pythagoreans, and Empedocles, the psuchè is represented by a daimôn, a supernatural being that leads an independent existence within us—see part 1, chapter 3, for the characteristics of the Norse fylgja—but, Empedocles adds, the psuchè is not to be confused with psychic life: "The individuation of this daimôn allotted to every particular human being, which discovers within a human its own destiny," notes Jean-Pierre Vernant, "does not modify its characteristic of mysterious power foreign to man, of the reality present at the heart of all nature . . . as well as in man."[2]

The soul is understood as the movement, motion, activity of the living person—the organs and the body are only its instruments—and as the activity of thought. For Plato the soul becomes the principle of life and thought, encompassing many attributes. In *The Republic* Plato divides the soul into three parts—reason, heart, and appetites—while emphasizing at the same time that it cannot be divided. In *Timaeus* he even distinguishes between a mortal soul and an immortal soul. Pindar (518–438 B.C.) conceives of the soul as a shadow, an image of life. "It sleeps while the body acts. When man sleeps, it shows him the future in dreams," he says, specifying: "Whereas all human bodies follow irresistible death, the image of life remains alive because it comes from the gods and from them alone."

All these often contradictory concepts, which partially appear again in Homer's *Iliad,* reflect the adaptation of a past stratum over which scholars ponder. Why does the ghost Patrocles ask that his body be burned? So that he can enter Hades! The Double/soul remains tied to the body as long as the body is not totally destroyed. Cremation was understood then as a purification rite, and it is true that it had become one, but it was originally a way of detaching the alter ego from the corpse, of facilitating its death, its passage into hell or into the other world. But what, then, are these ancient strata that are reclaimed and transformed by the Greeks?

At the beginning of the seventh or sixth century B.C., Hellenic civilization entered into contact with shamanism, which teaches that in humans there is a soul or a self of divine origin that can leave the body thanks to certain appropriate techniques.[3] The representatives of Greek shamanism are Abaris and Aristeus of Prokonnessos.

It is said that Abaris came from the Hyperboreans, that is, from the extreme north of Scythia, and that he was sent by Apollo and gifted with the powers of healing and predicting disasters. He never ate, Herodotus tells us, and he walked Apollo's arrow from one end of the Earth to the other. This miracle worker, whom Pindar makes a contemporary of Cresus, thus carries the arrow, the sign of magic air travel. The importance of this in the mythology and religion of the Scythians has been shown and its parallels to Siberian shamanistic rituals have been pointed out by Mircea Eliade. Using the name of Abaris as evidence, we can confirm, without great risk of error, that he belonged to the Avar race, a people of the Turkish family originating from the Caspian steppes, who were therefore in contact with central Asian shamanism. That, according to Herodotus, Abaris is Hyperborean simply connects him to the northern Asian shamanism of the small Ural-Altaic and Siberian tribes.[4] Whatever interpretation is accepted, we come back to peoples whom history pushed westward. It must be remembered that at the time of the great migrations, the Avars became Huns and arrived in Hungary. Thanks to archaeology, traces of their slow advance toward the west are fairly easy to decipher.[5]

Aristeus of Prokonnessos (sixth century B.C.) is just as well known.[6] In the grip of Apollinian delirium—that is, in trance—he saw himself transported to the land of the Issedones. Eliade recognizes the figure of a shaman in him.[7] Aristeus appears and disappears, he is seen in several places simultaneously, and he has the marvelous gift of falling into prolonged ecstasies. Pliny the Elder speaks of him in his *Natural History* and states that his soul leaves his body through his mouth in the form of a crow *(Aristeas animan evolantem ex ore in Proconeso corvi effigie).* Let me point out that the god Odin has two crows named Huginn and Muninn, or Thought and Memory, which for some time now have been recognized as his zoomorphic Doubles (hamr). We must also remember the theme of the soul in dove form, which was taken up again by the

Church and well illustrated by the iconography in manuscript paintings. Aristeus would have gone to the land of the Hyperboreans, the country from which Apollo came and about which marvels were told at that time, and were repeated by Ovid several centuries later.

Among the ecstatics, Hermotimus of Colophon must be mentioned. His soul could leave his body for many years and brought back prophetic knowledge of the future from its journeys. One day, his enemies the Cantharides took advantage of one of his catalepsies and burned his lifeless body. His soul never returned, which is astoundingly similar to what we have seen in other testimonies in this book.

There is also Epimenides who, after a long stay in the mysterious cavern of Zeus on Mount Ida, had contact with the spirits of the darkness. A thousand marvels were told about his strict fasts and long ecstasies. It was said that he was versed in enthusiastic wisdom and that he traveled the world, healing and predicting the future, which he came to know through his raptures. E. Rhode has already pointed out his similarity to the Greenlander Angegok, a shaman.[8]

All these "legends" turn on a central axis: the belief that something can be separated from the body and can then enjoy a higher existence, including contact with the gods and the spirits. Everything becomes clear once the word *soul* is systematically replaced with the word *Double*.

In the *Life of Apollonios of Thyane,* completed around A.D. 217, the sophist Philostratus does not neglect to note a few curious traits of this individual whom more than one researcher has recognized as a pagan version of Christ. When the Ephesians send Apollonios seeking to Smyrna, he does not want to defer the trip: "As soon as he had said 'Let's go!' he was in Ephesius, reliving the feat of Pythagorus who was once simultaneously in Thurii and in Metaponto" (IV, 10). Sent for by the emperor Domitan, Apollonios goes to him, defends himself against the accusation, and suddenly disappears in a supernatural way, only to reappear to his friends in Dicearchia (Pouzzuoli) that same night.

In *The Republic,* Plato echoes some beliefs on the detachable soul when he tells the story of Er the Armenian:

Wounded in battle, Er was found ten days later among the dead. He was brought to the house, unconscious and motionless. Two days later, when the people wanted to place him on the pyre to cremate him, he came back to life and started to speak of how men were judged after they died. He said that his soul, having been separated from his body, went with many people to a wonderful place, where they saw two openings, which were for those who had come from above the earth, and two other openings for those going to the sky. He saw the judges who were interviewing those who had come from this world. When Er's turn came, the judges told him that he must return to earth to tell men what happened in the other life.[9]

Such an account could have been written by a cleric of the Middle Ages. We need only change a few words to have a Christian vision!

There is no doubt whatsoever that the idea of a detachable soul, a Double, is a fundamental aspect of shamanism, whose influence on the Hellenic world is manifest. We will take as the last witnesses the enthusiast cults, that of Bacchus, for example. If the Bacchants fast, dance, sing, and shout to achieve divine delirium, it is in order to free their spirit Double from their body, as Maurice Halbwachs has clearly shown.[10] What is this technique if not a variation of the shamanistic ecstatic technique?

The legend of Orpheus is also connected to shamanism: Behind it the structure of the shamanistic voyage into the next world can be found.

From this brief incursion into the land of the ancient Greeks, we can conclude that this civilization was perfectly familiar with the Scythic—meaning shamanistic—concepts of the soul, and it knew that these concepts no doubt came to them through Thessaly, which had the reputation of being a country of wizards, and later a country of sorcerers. Everything indicates that the *Weltanschauung* that concerns us here comes from Northern Eurasia. Ecstasy, the journeys of the Double, the acquisition of knowledge, the power to work miracles, the impossibility of the soul (spirit, Double) to reenter the body if it is touched while the soul is still wandering—all of these elements structure the psychic universe that we are exploring.

CENSORINUS AND THE GENIUS

During the summer of the year A.D. 238, Censorinus, Roman rhetorician and grammarian, finished his treatise on *The Day of Birth (De die natali),* which he gave to his patron, Caerellius, for his fortieth birthday.[11] In this rich text, the oldest manuscript of which is owned by the Cologne chapter house's library, the genius is discussed, and what is said deserves consideration. The following lines are in some way a prefiguration of what Burchard of Worms wrote at the beginning of the eleventh century:

> Genius is the god under whose protection everyone lives, starting from birth. He is called genius, surely from *geno* [I conceive], either because he is involved in some way with our conception, or because he is himself conceived at the same time as we are, or again, because he looks after us and protects us.

In the hypotheses that Censorinus proposes, we find exactly, once more, the concept of the spirit guardian, the tutelary genie, and thus of the Norse fylgja and the Finnish haltija. Censorinus goes on:

> Some scholars were of the opinion that one must worship two genies, but only in houses where married couples live. Elsewhere, Euclides, a student of Socrates, confirms that in every case a double genie would be given to us, an idea that can be illustrated with the help of the sixteenth book of satires, by Lucilius.

So various opinions coexist. The one that claims man has two genies sends us back to the idea of the psychic Double and the physical Doubles; in other words, to the idea of a pluralistic soul. We can note once again the similarity of this opinion to those we have encountered in the preceding chapters.

Censorinus offers a highly valuable clarification:

> As a general rule, we sacrifice every year to this genie, for our whole life [an allusion to the celebration that we call a birthday]. The genie

is for us the attentive protector, and it happens such that he never goes far from us. He accompanies us from the time he takes us into his charge when we come out of our mother's stomach, until the last day of our life.

So the genius is a power that lives in each of us, and it is thought to predate each of us, like an immortal element within the individual. In this sense, it is very close to the Greek daimôn and Norse fylgja. It determines our personality, but it is neither soul nor life. It symbolizes, in a way, our spiritual being. The proverbial term *indulgere genio,* "yield to your genie," still expresses the notion of letting yourself follow your taste or wish, but it also emphasizes the idea of a supernatural visitor within us that imposes its will upon us. We should specify here that women have an *Iuno* that Pierre Grimal does not hesitate to describe as the "divine Double."[12]

It is very interesting to note the confusion that arises between genius and Lar, that is, between the genie and the shades of its ancestors: "May genius and Lar be identical and transmitted by many authors,"[13] says Censorinus, which foreshadows that which stands out about the Middle Ages: the fusion of the dead, Doubles, and genies.

The parallels between the Roman genius, the Norse fylgja, and the Finnish haltija, tutelary genies and spiritual Doubles—to which we must add the Christian guardian angel, *fylgjuengill* in Norse—are telling with regard to the concepts themselves and the similarity of the mentalities that produced them. It is clear that a Double, whatever its name and nature, is given to us for our whole earthly existence. It is fitting to recall here that for Plato, the Pythagorians, and Empedocles the daimôn is a divine principle whose function is to link our individual destiny directly to the cosmic order. We must not forget either that the psuchè also appears in the form of a daimôn, a supernatural being who leads an independent existence within us, as Maurice Halbwachs has clearly shown. This daimôn or genius appointed to a particular human being is individualized, but that in no way modifies its characteristic of a mysterious power foreign to humans, a reality present at the heart of all nature, a human destiny.

Again, it is clear that the notion of the Double is indissolubly tied to that of destiny, which the Norse lexicon was able to express with such clarity, given that these are words composed of hamr (hamingja), expressing the idea of destiny.

Censorinus is not the only Roman author to have spoken of the genius. The tenor of his message is also found in Martianus Capella (fifth century A.D.) whose *The Wedding Night of Philologia and Mercury* was a major work throughout all of the Middle Ages.[14] This book was among the texts studied in monastic schools; commentary and glossary were added in the ninth century by Jean Scot, Rémy d'Auxerre, and Martin de Laon. It is counted among the classics of the school of Chartres, and it was even translated into old High German by Notker the Thick-Lipped, who was born around 950 and who died June 29, 1022.[15] All of this indicates how much effect it had.

According to Martianus, a genius is given to every mortal and is also called Protector or Guardian. The people worship it, and every man has his own. It is called genius because it plays a role in conception, and *tutelator* because it watches over everyone, soul and spirit. It is a brother to the most faithful. It can also be called angel—that is, "messenger"—because it announces the secret thoughts of the superior powers *(arcana cogitationum supere anuntiat)*. The Greeks call it daimôn and the Romans "intermediary" *(medioximus)*.

In his translation four centuries later, Nokter draws this development in the direction of Christianity, replaces the superior powers with God, and leads the genius toward the angel by making use if its intermediary position: "The Latins call it *méteme* because angels are between God and man *(Latini námont sie méteme uuanda angeli sint mitte únder gote unde ménniskon).*"[16]

What we can consider an important testimony on the Double is thus integrated into Christianity, and the belief pursues its career in the new "clothes" of the angel. . . . It would take a gigantic amount of research to discover all that the medieval Church integrated and digested on the subject of native beliefs. A certain number of things have been discerned, but there are still so many shadows!

FINNISH, ESTONIAN,
AND MORDVINIAN TRADITIONS

It is interesting to gain awareness of concepts of the soul that peoples close to us, and those with whom people of the Middle Ages related, made for themselves. Such concepts from the shores of the Baltic Sea lend themselves well to comparison.

In Finnish, *henki* designates at the same time "soul," "breath," and "life" and is understood as the vital force necessary for movement of the body.[17] This entity disappears at our death, and when a person is close to death, the door or window is opened so that it can leave. For the same reason, in France there was the custom in many places of raising a shingle from the roof in the house where someone died. When an evil person died, the henki would leave in the form of a tempestuous wind.*

The henki can leave a person's body at times other than death. In such instances it exits from the mouth in the form of a small animal—a mouse, a butterfly, or a fly, as the forest-dwelling Finnish of Varmland believed. The henki possesses many traits of the Norse hugr, but the hugr is also related to another soul called *vaimas* in Finland. In the north of this country the inhabitants use this term for a quiver, such as an involuntary tremble or an eyelid that flutters suddenly, phenomena that the Carelians name *elohiiri,* "vital mouse," or *ihohiiri,* "mouse of the skin," the mouse being the spirit that can move throughout the whole body. In Norway's Verdal region in the sixteenth century people would say: "If you have tightness in the feet or arms, it is said that you have the hugr." The similarities among all of these are immediately apparent.

The Finns also use the term *haamu,* related to the Norse hamr, to designate the Double. The term means approximately "phantom, appearance,

---

*In French folk traditions Mélusine becomes a sort of tempest, and Georges Brassens remembers this when he speaks of her cries. Let us remember also that at the time of the fairy's flight, Jean d'Arras writes: "Then the lady, in the form of a snake . . . went three times around the fortress, and each time that she passed in front of the window, she let out a cry so strange and full of pain that everyone was crying with compassion. . . . Then she went in the direction of Lusignan in such a rustling and such a racket that it seemed, everywhere she went, that thunder and a storm were about to break out."

or form." The haamu can leave the body and reenter it, which causes sickness in its possessor. In the case of the haamu's prolonged absence, its possessor dies. We can lose this Double, for example, by looking at ourselves in water, such loss being due, it is thought, to the intervention of an evil spirit or a dead person. The disappearance of the haamu is followed by an illness that folk traditions call *kohtans,* or *kohtanstandi,* which can be translated as vertigo. The haamu engages in another phenomenon that we have already come across: "His haamu came before him," it is said when someone sees a person who actually arrives later than such a sighting. This entity leaves the human body in the form of a mouse or a little bird. As usual, above all, the body must not be touched during its absence, nor must the person be awakened; to do so ensures that the person will die. Along with the terms *kaave, kaavis,* and *aave, haamu* means "ghost," which confirms the conclusions we have reached in studying those who have died in the particular circumstances we have discussed.[18]

Finally, there remains the psychic Double, haltija,[19] corresponding more or less to the Norse fylgja. In Finland it is believed that this protector spirit is given to a person at a certain age, which recalls a passage in *The Saga of Hallfred the Difficult skald* stating that Hallfred's son, an adolescent, receives his father's fylgja after his father is doomed to an imminent death. The haltija accompanies its chosen one everywhere, aids his undertakings, advises him, and reveals future events to him in his dreams. The following table of correspondences delineates clearly the similarities we have discussed between ancient Finnish and Norse concepts of the soul:

Finnish		Norse
haltija	⟶	fylgja
haamu	⟶	hamr
henki	⎫ ⟶	hugr
vaimas	⎭	

Among the Aestii, inhabitants of Estonia who belong to the Ural-Altaic linguistic group, there exists *hing,* which is the equivalent of the

Finnish *henki* and designates the soul and the breath, as well as the psychic and physical Doubles. The term also means "life" and can refer to a person or an animal. When an individual passes away and the wind blows, they speak of the "wind of the soul," *hinge tuul.*

Vaim (Finnish *vaimas*) refers to the soul as the vital principle that abandons the living only at the final hour; the term corresponds approximately to animus. With the Votes,* the form vaim takes is that of animal, frequently that of an owl. One folk tradition tells us: "If someone dies at night, you must wake up the whole household because the vaim of a sleeper travels the world and can easily be carried off by the hing of the dead person." The separation is not very distinct between these two entities, whose domains overlap.

The unambiguous Double is designated by "figure" *(nägu),* "form" *(kuju),* or "shadow" *(vari).* It seems to distance itself from its possessor shortly before the person's death. When the alter ego of a man is seen though the man himself is not present, it is known that he is going to leave our valley of tears. In Northern Estonia this phenomenon is called *mardus (margus, marras),* which, by a coincidence whose secret is held in popular beliefs, sends us back to the night-*mare,* in other words, to the Double-who-presses.[†20]

Many *mémorats*—short accounts of a memorable event, reported as experienced by the teller or someone close to him—tell of a little beast (such as a fly, bee, butterfly, bird, or beetle) that leaves the body through the mouth of a sleeper and returns to reenter it later if the body has not been touched. One of them speaks of a young woman's soul, meaning her Double, running around in the countryside as a werewolf while her body lies as if dead. The alter ego can also wander like *Puuk.* In northern Germany, *Puk* or *Puck* designates a dwarf or a domestic genie.[21] In Norse, *puki* is a spirit, a demon, or a dead person. In medieval England and Ireland, Puck is a sprite of sorts, and we find him at Oberon's side in Shakespeare's *A Midsummer Night's Dream.*

The Double, it is said, can move from place to place like a whirlwind.

---

*[A people of the Finnish-Baltic region. —*Ed.*]

†[See the explanation of *cauchmar,* part 2, chapter 5, page 99. —*Trans.*]

In Livonia it is said that witches fly around like *völ*. When the alter ego functions as a nightmare, it does so due to anger, jealousy, vengeance, or love. Here are the correspondences between Estonian and Norse concepts of the alter ego:

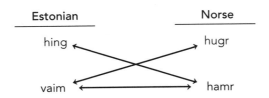

The Mordvinians, Mordins, or Mordouans—Finnish people from eastern Russia who divide themselves into two groups, the Erzya and the Moksha, and who belong to the Volga-Finnish linguistic group—have been Christians since the end of the eighteenth century. According to their beliefs, we have two souls (animus), designated by *ojm'e/vajm'ä*, "breath, inhalation, spirit, soul, living being," which are localized in various organs, the bones, and the blood, and a Double, designated by *tšopatša*. It is interesting to note that Vedic and even pre-Vedic Indians know several corporal souls: *prana*, "spirit of life"; *atman*, "breath"; *asu*, "life"; *manas* "senses"; an original self, and a Double. In ancient Iran there were *urvan*, the physical alter ego, and *manah*, the self, the psychic Double who leaves the body and leads an independent life while an individual is in trance or sleeping.

LITHUANIAN BELIEFS

In Lithuania, at least two Doubles can be found—*laimé-dalia* and *sveikata*—which can be noted because of the perspectives they open to us.

Laimé-dalia, literally "fortune-part," is a psychosomatic entity that is part of the personality.[22] It can reside in the human body or in a separate being and enter into the body of a swan or another animal. In folktales it becomes Dalia, a sort of personal goddess who is similar to the Norse fylgja and the Finnish haltija. The *dalia* is each person's chance, destiny, fate. Here we find the same destiny/Double connection that we find in the fylgja and hamingja (based on hamr) of ancient Iceland.[23] According to A. J. Greimas, Lithuanian traditions show how an abstract concept and even a theological idea can be anthropomorphized to become Dalia, the hypostasis of the syncretic Laima, the goddess of destiny and birth. She is a triple goddess, given that she has two sisters with whom she forms the Laimos group—and this new entity is a close relative of the fairies.

The Lithuanians' other Double seems to be *sveikata,* "health," to which we must certainly add *gyvastis,* "life." In the accounts that narrate a hero's battle against a reputedly invincible dragon, he must, in order to be victorious, find the place where the beast has hidden his life or his health. A hero may ask the maiden who was abducted by the dragon to question him slyly: "Go and ask where his sveikata is." The dragon gives himself away: "In the second kingdom lives my brother. If someone kills him, I will no longer have sveikata."[24]

In this instance, the brother is the Double. Here we find hints of the Dioscuri myth in which one, at least according to classical legend, is mortal while the other is not. In the text I have just cited, adventitious details arise to obscure that which is clear: The hero kills the brother, from whose entrails an egg falls, which allows the slaying of the other dragon. In a primitive version of this type of legend, it was likely a matter of simply putting to death the alter ego.

A testimony parallel to the preceding tale of the dragon no longer speaks of sveikata but of gyvastis. In this one, when questioned the dragon replies: "My life is in a far-away and deep place. In the ocean, on an island, is found an ox; in this ox there is a pigeon; and in this pigeon, an egg; and in this egg, my gyvastis."[25]

The notion of gyvastis also refers back to the Greek psuchè: If someone coughs and no one says "To your health!" his soul returns to Velnias, who is the devil in the Christian sense of the term, and in other terms most likely a god of the dead, for *vêlé* means "dead soul."

Appendix 2
Hambel and Vardøjer

In his novel *Anta, Memoirs of a Laplander* (published by Plon [Paris, 1989] in the collection *Terre humaine*) the Laplander Andreas Labba echoes many of the beliefs of his people. Among those beliefs that relate to the Double, there is the one that we know by the names of *hambel* and *vardøjer:*

[Jovva suddenly decides the go down to the village.] When Jovva had gone about halfway, he stopped near a little stream to make himself a cup of coffee and rest a little. Suddenly, Jensi, the old hermit, was standing before him. Jovva sat there as if petrified, his cup in his hand, then the apparition withdrew. . . . Even before he started walking again, Jovva knew that he would go to Jensi's house as soon as he arrived in the village.

At the same time, Jensi was sitting at the window of his big house mending his nets. Suddenly, raising his eyes, he saw Jovva pushing the gate. He immediately put his needle down to go meet his friend, but when he went outside, Jovva had disappeared. Jensi stayed on his dilapidated steps for a long moment, looking all around and crying out: "Come here, Jovva! Come on! Answer me, Jovva!"

He called in vain. Jovva was no longer there. So Jensi went back into his house. . . . The apparition troubled him. . . . Yet Jovva had definitely appeared before him, a Jovva in flesh and blood, but a Jovva who had vanished right after he appeared. . . .

As for Jovva, he was continuing on his way down toward the valley. He was now near the village. His old dog, who was going before him on the path, started barking when he came to a bend in the path. Jovva understood that he was going to meet someone. Maybe it was Jensi. He took a few more steps and saw Jensi coming toward him: "Let's hope he's really alive this time," Jovva said to himself. At that moment, Jensi saw Jovva and was surprised to find him with his dog, who hadn't been with him earlier.

The two men greeted each other, and taking each other by the shoulder, began to explain themselves. Jovva said: "Is it really you? I'd better touch you to make sure that you really are alive, that you are not the apparition that came to me when I was having my coffee!"

And Jensi said: "Me too, I saw you in front of my gate this morning, while I was mending my nets. But your old dog was not there. He must not have had the power to appear as quickly as your double."

Appendix 3
The Trial of the Werewolf

The original text for the following can be found in O. Höfler, *Kultische Geheimbünde der Germanen* (Frankfurt: n.p., 1934), 345–51.

JANUARY 1691, JÜRGENSBURG, LIVONIA

It seemed useful to me to provide the translation of this document, which is unknown in France, because it presents several interesting aspects: We see the judges getting bogged down in their routine questions, which tend to measure everything with the yardstick of Christianity; we can observe their inability to understand a mentality that is not their own; and we discover that certain werewolves are defenders of society. Above all, there is the almost complete acculturation of the ancient particulars having to do with the Double, just as in the Benandanti's case: There is no longer a question of a body in lethargy, and metamorphosis is here replaced by a wolf garment. There are also references to the time of year: the Feast of Saint Lucie, well known in the Germanic world for the passage of the Wild Hunt and the fresh upsurge of spirit activity; the Feast of Saint John, a celebration of the solstice, one of the two "doors" *(januae)* of the year — even though we do not know here if it is the summer Saint John's (June 24) or the winter feast (December 27); and Pentecost, the great celebration of spring renewal.

I have translated the most important parts of the proceedings of the trial, taking only the one liberty of offsetting the dialogue, whereas the clerk of the court placed everything in the third person. The spelling of proper names and their variations are respected. A few lexical difficulties have been resolved according to general meanings. *Seegen* means both "blessing, luck," and "fertility"; *zauberer*, "magus, magician" and "sorcerer"; *blüthe*, "blossoming, flower, seed."

In Puncto Lycanthropy and other forbidden and harmful Acts. Judges present: The Honorable Assessor Bengt Johan Ackerstaff, substitute for the provincial judge The Honorable Assessor Gabriel Berger.

Peter, innkeeper of Kaltenbrun, who smiled after taking the oath, is asked the reason.

Responsio: I see that my comrade, old Thiess, must also swear. *Quaestio:* Why would he not have to take the oath, like you, and testify presently on the theft in the church? *R:* Everyone knows that he visits the devil often and that he is a werewolf. How can he swear since he does not deny having been one for these many long years?

After hearing other witnesses, *ad dandum testimonium,* the old Thiess was criticized for this, and he simply acknowledged that he had been a werewolf in the past, but that he had not been one for the last ten years. He furthermore stated that he had already been questioned on this subject in Nitau, at the time when My Lord the baron Crohnstern and the Honorable Rosenthal and Caulich were still judges, when, at this time, Skeistan, peasant of Lemberg, now deceased, had broken his nose because the informant had brought wheat seeds back from hell, which the aforementioned Skeistan had thrown there in order to prevent the wheat from growing. The judges named above had done nothing to him, had made fun of him and let him go free because Skeistan had not appeared in court.

Before undertaking any further questioning, they gathered more information on this matter to find out if Thiess was in full possession of his senses and his reason, and if he had not been insane, whether he wasn't still, to which, in addition to those who knew Thiess well, the Honorable Bengt Johan Ackerstaff, representing the provincial judge, replied, saying that Thiess had lived on his land in the past and had been in his service for a few years, that he had never been lacking in good sense, that he had never denied what he was, and that, as the judges at that time had done nothing to him, Thiess had been a werewolf even more freely and that the country people had almost idolized him.

Ipse ad haec quaerebatur: Where and when did Skeistan hit him and with what? *R:* In hell with a broom handle that had horsetails tied onto it. The judge presiding over the session testified that at this time, Thiess had had a big wound on his nose. *Q:* How did the informant get to hell and where is it? *R:* Werewolves go there on foot, in the appearance of wolves; hell is at the end of the lake called Puer Esser in the bog under Limburg, about a half mile from Klingenberg, the domain of the gentleman who serves as substitute for the President. In hell, there are splendid places and guards who brutally beat those who want to bring back wheat seeds and the wheat brought here by the sorcerers. The seeds are kept in one purse [?] and the wheat in another.

Q: What do you look like when you change into werewolves? *R:* We have wolf skins that we simply put on. A peasant from Marienbourg who came from Riga brought me one that I gave to a peasant from Alla a few years ago now.

When questioned, Thiess did not want to give their names, and when asked *specialius,* he varied [in his statements], saying that they would go into the bushes, take off their usual clothes, and turn immediately into wolves, and they would roam around like wolves, pulling to pieces any horses and livestock they came across. But the informant never tore to pieces large animals, uniquely lambs, kids, piglets, etc. However, in the Seegewold region, there was a fellow, dead now, Tyrummen, very distinguished—the informant was nothing compared to him because the devil gives more power to one than to another—and this fellow attacked large livestock just because they were there: He attacked pigs in their fattening pens, carrying them off from farms and eating them with his company. There were often twenty or thirty of them together who would carry off loads [of beasts]. Then they would eat on their way and roast [their prey].

Q: How did you make fire and with what? *R:* We would take fire from the farms, and cauldrons, and we would make spits with wood and burn the fur; we did not eat raw meat. *Q:* Did the informant often attend such meals and banquets? *R:* Yes, of course. *Q:* What became of the small livestock? *R:* We ate it too. *Q:* Given that you were changed into wolves, why did you not eat raw meat, like wolves do? *R:* That is not our custom. We ate it roasted, like men. *Q:* How did you hold it, given that you had wolf heads and paws, according to what you are saying, with which you could not hold a knife, nor prepare a spit, nor carry out the other necessary tasks? *R:* We did not need a knife. We tore the meat with our bare teeth and put the pieces on bits of wood, when we could find some, and when we ate the meat, we were once again like men, but, in doing so, we did not use bread. We took salt from the farms, when we set off. *Q:* You would eat your fill, and the devil would eat with you? *(Prius affirmat, posterius negat?) R:* The sorcerers ate in hell with the devil, which the werewolves were not allowed to do. They would enter stealthily, take something, and flee with their loot because if they were met, the guards hired by the devil would hit us ferociously with great iron whips that they called "pricks,"* and they would chase us out of hell like dogs because the devil, *pro idiomate Lettico Ne eretz,* could not stand us.

Q: Since the devil could not stand you, why would you become wolfmen and go down to hell? *R:* Because we wanted to bring back from hell what the sorcerers had taken there, like livestock, wheat, and other seeds. Because the others and I had delayed doing it a certain year and had not gotten to hell while the doors were still open, we were not able to bring back the seeds and wheat taken by the sorcerers, and there was a bad harvest. But this year, the others and I acted in time and did what we had to.

The informant would have brought back barley, oats, and rye from hell himself, as much as he could carry, and so we would have had excellent harvests; however, more oats than rye.

Q: When did this happen? *R:* Before Christmas, the night of the Saint Lucie. *Q:* How many times per year do you meet in hell? *R:* Normally, three times: the nights of the Pentecost, Saint John's, and the Saint Lucie. Concerning the first two times, not always, but especially nights when the

---

*[The French here is *verge*, which means both stick and penis. —*Trans.*]

wheat is ripe because, at that time, the sorcerers take it right then and carry it off to hell, and the werewolves get to work in bringing it back. *Q:* So who were you with, then, the last night of the Saint Lucie? *R:* With people who had come from many villages, from the Rodenpei and Sunszel regions. We knew them and we asked them their names because different troupes were there. Skeistan Rein, the son of the man I mentioned earlier, had been part of one of them before me, but I have not seen him recently and do not know the reason.

When questioned about those from Jürgensburg, Thiess replied that they must have been part of another company because none of them were in his.

Q: How can the informant say that they brought back this year's good harvest from hell, which was carried away by the sorcerers during the last night of the Saint Lucie, since the wheat is not yet ripe and therefore could not have been taken? *R:* The sorcerers have their own time, and the devil plants a long time ahead. The sorcerers take a little, carry it off it to hell, and the werewolves bring it back. Our seed does not grow and it is the same story with the fruit trees—there are some in hell also—and fish. At Christmas, in hell, all the wheat is already completely green; so are the trees. As, during the last night of the Saint Lucie, we succeeded in bringing back a good part of the fish stolen by the sorcerers, we can count on good fishing this year. The sorcerers take the future seeds and carry them off to hell, but they cannot grow as much as those that are planted and grown in hell.

Q: Each time that you went to hell, did you find buildings that are there permanently? *(Affirmat.) Q:* Have you been able to see people living in the area? *R:* This place is not on earth, but below it, and the entrance to it is protected by a door that no one can find unless he is part of it. *Q:* Are there women and girls among the werewolves, and Germans? *R:* There are women, but girls are not admitted; otherwise, they would become *Puicken* [a variety of demons?] or dracs;* they would be bewitched and make the abundance of milk and butter disappear. There are no Germans in our company; they have their own particular hell.

---

*[*Dracs* are a kind of little people who live underground in Slavic countries. —*Trans.*]

Q: What becomes of werewolves when they die? *R:* They are buried, like other men, and their souls ascend to the sky. The devil takes sorcerers' souls. *Q:* Does the informant frequent the church, does he listen with reverence to the divine word, does he pray zealously, and does he take communion? *R: (Negat.)* He does not do any of that. *Q:* How can your soul go to God given that you do not serve Him but the devil, that you do not go to church, at least to confession, and that you do not take communion, as you yourself admit? *R:* Werewolves do not serve the devil because they rob him of what the sorcerers bring him; that is why the devil hates them, cannot stand them, and has them hunted like dogs, with great cracks of his iron whips. Sorcerers serve the devil and do his will, which is why they belong to him body and soul. Everything werewolves do is for the good of men and, if they did not exist and did not rob, did not steal the potential harvests from the devil, there would no longer be any harvest in the world at all—and Thiess affirmed this by oath, adding that the Russian werewolves had come earlier the year before and had taken the blessing (luck, fertility) of their country *(ihres landes seegen).* This is why they had a good crop, which was lacking in our country because we arrived too late. But this year, we preceded the Russians and we will have a fertile year, good in flax. Why would God not accept my soul because I do not go to church and I do not take communion? In my youth, no one told me anything about all this, no one taught me. I do not do any harm at all.

With great zeal, they showered him with advice and made him understand.

Q: Is it not doing harm to steal the livestock of one's neighbor, as you have acknowledged doing, and to transform in your imagination the image of God—man—into a wolf? To have missed taking the oath made to Christ, your savior, at the time of baptism, that is, to renounce Satan, his cohorts and his works? To forget God, to commit highly forbidden sins that disgust and offend other people? Not to go to church where, thanks to the sermons and the priests, you could come to know God and be in his service? You prefer to head toward hell while our pastor comes by the farms and urges you to pray and to go often and faithfully to church and allow yourself to be instructed! *R:* I did very little wrong to the live-stock. The others did a great deal more. It is true that the good pastor comes by the farms, instructs the people there, and prays with those who are there. I also have repeated with them what the good pastor would say, but then it turned out that he could not come any more. It seems that now that I am old, I have to learn this.

Q: How old are you and where were you born? *R:* When the Swedes took Riga [1691], I already knew how to harrow and labor. I was born in Courland. *Q:* Since the last night of the Saint Lucie, you went to hell again; why did you claim to have given your spell to a peasant from Alla a long time ago? *R:* I did not tell the truth because I do not have much strength left and I am old, but I will do it now. *Q:* What benefit did you reap from being a werewolf? Everyone knows that you beg and own nothing at all. *R:* Nothing! Not a single thing! A fellow from Marienburg put the spell on me by drinking to my health, and so since then I have had to behave like a werewolf. *Q:* Do werewolves receive a sign from the devil so that he can recognize them? *R:* (*Negat.*) He marks sorcerers, deals with them and feeds them the heads of dead horses, toads, snakes, and other vermin. *Q:* Since you are old and without means, you must think about death everyday: So, do you want to die a werewolf? *R:* No, before my death, I will put the spell on someone else, if I can. *Q:* How will you do it? *R:* I will do it as it was done to me: I will drink to some-one's health and blow three times into the jug, saying: "May what hap-pened to me happen to you." If the other person takes the jug, I won't be a werewolf any more and I will be free. *Q:* Don't you believe that this is also a sin and a demonic illusion and that you cannot give it to anyone except a person who, like you, knows nothing of God and is inclined toward it? *R:* It is true that I cannot put the spell on anyone against his will. But many have asked me, seeing that I was old and incapable, to leave them my spell. *Q:* Who asked you for it? *R:* They are far from here, some in the area of the Honorable Judge, others in Sunszel, and I wouldn't know their names. *Q:* When you and others were changed into wolves and looked like wolves, dogs must have attacked you and hunters surely shot at you, since you said that there were big ferocious dogs near hell?

R: We could easily escape the dogs, but the hunters could get us. The dogs of hell didn't do anything to us. *Q:* According to what you said, the fellow Tyrummen from Seegewold went into the peasants' farms and took pigs from their fattening pens; these farms are not lacking in dogs. Was he not attacked and bitten by them? *R:* If the dogs saw him! When that happened, the werewolves would run much faster than them and the dogs could not catch them. Tyrummen was a very bad fellow, and he did a lot of wrong to people, which is why God made him die young. *Q:* What became of his soul? *R:* I do not know if God or the devil took it. *Q:* What did you do with the wheat heads and the trees and everything you took from the devil? *R:* We would throw them in the air, and the blessing [luck, fertility] would come back to the country, on rich and poor alike.

Upon which, he was taught some things, and he was persuaded that all this was only illusion and trickery of the devil, which he could see, for example, in the fact that the people losing their livestock and their pigs from the fattening pens in this way would not hesitate to do some searching, and they would eventually find the traces, especially of the pigs, in the spots where they had been burned and eaten.

R: We did not steal close [to the farms] but far away, and who could have discovered us? *Q:* How is it possible that one of these big, fat pigs or one of these large, horned animals could be carried off by a wolf for twenty or thirty miles or more, through bushes and fallow fields, and even outside of Estonia, as you say? You must be able to see that all this is only false imagination, demonic duping and illusion. *R:* It is the truth. The fellow Tyrummen of Seegewold would be gone sometimes for a whole week. I would wait with my company in the bushes and when he had brought back a nice, fat pig, we would eat it together. In the meantime, we ate hares and other wild animals that we captured in the bushes. Now I now longer have the strength to run so far and capture and bring something back. I can have as much fish as I want, even if the others can't, because I have a special gift for that. *Q:* Don't you have the intention to turn to God before your death, to let yourself be instructed in His will and His being, to renounce these demonic practices, to repent your sins and so save your soul from eternal damnation and the punishments of hell?

R: (Thiess did not want to answer frankly.) Who knows where my soul will go? I am old. What can I understand about such things?

Finally, strongly pressed, he declared himself ready to abandon all that and to turn to God.

Notes

Preface to 2001 Edition

1. Helsinki, 1989 (FFC, 243). The reader may also refer to the clarification that I gave before the Centre du Patrimoine linguistique at ethnologique de Champagne-Ardennes: C. Lecouteux, "Le loup-garou," *Parlure* 12–13 (1998), 6–13.

2. Phillippe Wallon, *Expliquer le paranormal. Les niveaux du mental* (Paris, 1996). Note especially 154–87.

3. E. Bozzana, *Les Phénomènes de hantise*, new ed. (Chambéry), 91–98.

4. J.-M. Ertlé, *Sorciers, Magiciens, et Enchanteurs de nos terroirs* (Paris, 1996), 83–90.

5. Leszek Pawel Slupecki, *Wojownicy i wilkolaki* (Warszawa, Alfa, 1994), 279 pages, with illustrations on the werewolf.

6. C. Shinoda, *Jinrô henshintan: séiô minwa to bungaku kara* (Tokyo, 1994). Discusses werewolves and their manifestations throughout popular editions and literature in Europe.

7. C. Shinoda, *Le Métamorphose des fées* (Nagoya, 1994).

8. K. Watanabe, N. Pujol, "Histoires étranges des hommes-tigres en Chine, 1," *Journal of School of Foreign Languages* 13 (Nagoya, 1996), 83–97; 14 (1996), 78–86; 15 (1997), 139–63; 16 (1997), 88–94; K. Watanabe, O. Lorrillard, C. Nakane, "Traces de la légendes du loup-garou. Quatre exemples de métamorphose animale en Asie," *Nagoya Studies in Humanities* 27 (1998), 100–107.

9. Written and directed by the Wachowski brothers.

10. Joëlle Kuhne, *Personnages d'eau au cinéma*, Strasbourg Thesis, 1999–2000. Analyzes *L'Inhumaine* by Marcel L'Herbier (1923), *La Sirène du Mississippi* by François Truffaut (1969), the *Contes de la lune vague après la pluie* by Kenji Mizoguchi (1953).

Preface to 1996 Edition

1.   P. Gallais, *La Fée à la fontaine et à l'arbre: un archétype du conte merveilleux et du récit courtois,* Centre d'Études et de Recherches sur le Merveilleuz (Amersterdam, 1992); F. Dubost, *Aspects fantastiques de la littérature narrative médiévale, XIIe–XIIIe siècle* and *L'autre, l'ailleurs, l'autrefois;* 2 vols., Nouvelle Bibliotèque de Moyen Âge 15 (Paris, 1991).

2.   *Cahiers lausannois d'histoire médiévale* 15 (Lausanne, 1995).

3.   W. Behringer, *Chonrad Stoeckhlin und die Nachtschar, eine Geschichte aus der frühen Neuzeit,* SP 2095 (Munich, 1994).

4.   "Etres fantastiques des Alpes françaises," *Le Monde Alpin et Rhodanien* 1–4 (1992), 17–175. See also Alice Joisten and C. Abry, *Etres fantastiques des Alpes. Extraits de la collecte Charles Joisten, 1936–1981* (Paris, 1985), 171–82.

5.   C. Raudvere, *Föreställningar om maran i nordisk folktro,* Lund Studies in the History of Religions 1 (Lund, 1993), 111–13 and 258.

6.   p. 112: "*När en kvinna ville ha lätt för att föda barn, kröp hon genom en upständ fölhamn. Då blev första barnet en mara om det var en flicka, och en varulv om det var en pokje.*" Raudvere cites other texts explaining the origin of women who become *mara* and men who become *varulv* (wolfmen).

7.   R. Grambo, *Norske trollformler og magiske ritualer,* 2nd edition (Oslo, 1984), 109 and 142; J. van Haver, *Nederlandse Incantatieliteratuur* (Gand, 1964), 330–33; C. Raudvere, *Föreställningar om maran i nordisk folktro,* 136 and 158–70.

8.   M. Simonssen, "La Variabilité dans les légendes: les récits danois sur les loups-garous," in Marie-Louise Ténèze, *D'un conte . . . à l'autre: la variabilité dans la litterature orale* (Paris, 1990), 181–90.

9.   M. van den Berg, *De volkssage in de provincie Antwerpin in de 19ste em 20ste eeuw,* 3 vols. (Gand 1993). On the nightmare, see vol. 1, 279–94 and vol. 2, 1573–83 (typology); on the werewolf, see vol. 2, 956–70 and more specifically, vol. 2, 968 (becoming a werewolf); vol. 2, beginning on 962 (confusion with the spirit who lets itself be carried); and vol. 1, 261 (confusion with *mar*/wolfman).

10. J.-M. Boivin, "Bisclavret et Muldumarec, La part de l'ombre dans les lais" in J. Dufournet's *Amour et merveille: les lais de Marie France* (Paris: Unichamp, 1995), 147–68; see especially 166 f.

11. S. Conti, *Le conte d'Authur et Gorlagon: la figure mythique et rituelle du loup-garou,* Université Stendhal, Grenoble, 1993. I thank S. Conti, who very kindly sent me her unpublished work.

12. C. Lecouteux, *Au-delà du merveilleux. Des croyances au Moyen Âge* (Paris, 1996) (Cultures et Civilisations Médiévales XIII); as well as *Mondes parallèles. L'Univers des croyances au Moyen Âge* (Paris, 1994).

13. *Le Double, l'Ombre, le Reflet*, texts collected and presented by D. Lévy-Bertherat, *Cahiers de Littérature Générale, Recherches et Concours* 4 (Nantes, 1906). I thank Jacques Catteau (Sorbonne) for having made me aware of this book.

14. Ph. Wallon, *Expliquer le paranormal: les niveaux du mental*, Paris, 1996. See particularly chapters 4 (visions) and 5 (the Double).

15. B. Meheust, *En soucoupes volantes: vers une ethnologie des récits d'enlèvements* (Paris, 1992).

16. C. Carozzi, *Le Voyage de l'Âme dans l'au-delà d'après la littérature latine, Ve–XIIIe siècles*, Collection de l'École française de Rome, 189 (Rome, 1994), 173–80, 216 (animus in butterfly form), and 384–86.

17. Ed. W. Roach (Philadelphia, 1941), 966–1114.

18. W. Nitze and T. Atkinson Jenkins, eds., *Le Haut Livre du Graal: Perlesvaus*, 2 vols., 2nd ed. (New York, 1972), 29 f. See the analysis that F. Dubost gives of this passage in *Aspects fantastiques de la littérature narrative médiévale (XIIe–XIIIe siècle)* and *L'autre, l'ailleurs, l'autrefois*, 788–91.

19. Ed. Å. Lagerholm, Halle, Altnordische Sagabibliothek 17, 1927.

20. Tubach, *Index exemplorum* (Helsinki, 1969).

21. *De como hay algunos hombres o linajes de gentes que se multiplican y aparecen en muchos lugares en un mismo tiempo*, book 1, chapter 1 of *Crónica y historia general del hombre* (Madrid, 1598).

22. Ibid., 23. I took the following two testimonies from Dagmar Linhart, *Hausgeister in Franken. Zur Phänomenologie, Überlieferungsgeschichte und gelehrten Deutung bestimmter hilfreicher oder schädlicher Sagengestalten* (Dettelbach, 1995), 417, 296, 316, 461, and 288.

23. A. Le Braz, *La Légende de la mort* (Marseille, 1982), 129–43.

24. 2nd edition (Paris, 1996).

25. This error was made by J.-C. Schmitt in *Les Revenants, les Vivants at les Morts dans la société médiévale* (Paris, 1994). Schmitt abandons these folk traditions and concentrates on clerical literature, thus writing a history of ghosts according to the Church. See my review in *Cahiers de Civilisation Médiévale* 38 (1995), 73–75.

Introduction

1. K. Osis and E. Haraldsson, "Sterbebettbeobachtungen von Aerzten und Krankenschwestern," in A. Resch, *Fortleben nach dem Tode* (Innsbruck, 1981), 425–55.

2. R. A. Moody, *Life after Life* (New York: Bantam, 1999); and R. A. Monroe, *Journeys Out of the Body* (New York: Doubleday, 1971). See also F. Holck, "Life Revisited: Parallels in Death Experiences," in E. S. Schneidman's *Death: Current Perspectives* (Palo Alto, Calif.: Mayfield, 1980), 398–408; and E. Morin, *l'Homme et la Mort,* (Paris, 1976).

3. Readers may consult to their own advantage: W.-E Peuckert's "Der Zweite Leib," in *Niederdeutsche Zeitschrift f. Volkskunde* 17 (1939), 174–97; Vera Meyer-Matheis's *Die Vorstellung eines Alter Ego in Volkserzählunguen,* dissertation, Fribourg/Br., 1974; G. Maspero, "Histoires des Âmes dans l'Egypte ancienne," and "Une formule des stèles funéraires de la XXIIe dynastie," in *Bibliothèque Egyptologique* 1 (Paris, 1893); O. Rank's "Der Doppelgänger," in *Imago* 3, no. 2 (1914), 97-164; H. Gaidoz's "L'Âme hors du Corps et le Double," in *Mélusine* 11 (1912), 263–66; and in the same volume, see "Le Double psychique," 385–91.

4. H. Jung-Stilling, *Theorie der Geisterstunde,* in *Sämtliche Schriften,* vol. 6 (Stuttgart, 1837), 413 ff.

5. *Le Grand Livre du Mystérieux,* Reader's Digest Selection (Paris/Montreal/ Brussels/Zurich, 1985), 175 f. See especially T. Wereide's "Doppelgängererscheinungen in Norwegen," in *Neue Wissenschaft: Zeitschrift der Parapsychologie* 6, no. 10 (1946).

Chapter 1: The Ecstatic Journey

1. All works by Peter Dinzelbacher would have to be cited here; among others are *Vision und Visionsliteratur im Mittelalter,* Monographien z. Geschichte des Mittelalters 23 (Stuttgart, 1981); "Jenseitsvisionen–Jenseitsreisen," in V. Mertens and U. Müller's *Epische Stoffe des Mittelalters* (Stuttgart, 1984), 61–80; "Mittelalterliche Vision und moderne Sterbeforschung," in J. Kühnel, *et alii, Psychologie in der Mediävistik* (Göppingen, 1985), 9–49. Many texts with German translations can be found in his anthology *Mittelalterliche Visionsliteratur* (Darmstadt, 1989).

2. J. le Goff, *la Naissance du Purgatoire* (Paris, 1981), 154.

3. The Venerable Bede, *Historia ecclesiastica,* ed. C. Plummer (Oxford, 1896).

4. *Dialogi* IV, 37, ed. and trans. by A. de Vogüe and P. Antin, vol. 3 (Paris, 1980).

5. *Historia Francorum* VII, 1.

6. *Visio Alberici,* ed. M. Inguanez, *Miscellanea Cassinense* 11 (1932), 81–103.

7. *Autobiographie*, ed. and trans. by E.-R. Labande (Paris, 1981).

8. *Visio Tnugdali*, ed. A. Wagner (Erlangen, 1882). On the circulation of the text: N. F. Palmer, *The German and Dutch Translations of the Visio Tnugdali and their Circulation in the Late Middle Ages*, MTV 76 (Munich, 1981).

9. L. Gougaud, *Dévotions et Pratiques ascétiques du Moyen Age* (Paris, 1925). P Dinzelbacher, "Körperliche und seelische Vordebingungen religiöser Träume und Visionen," in T. Gregory, *Il Sogno nel Medioevo* (Rome, 1985), 57–86.

10. H. Farmer, "The Visio of Orm," in *Analecta Bollandiana* 75 (1957), 72–82.

11. Reported by Wulfstan de York in his forty-third homily, in ed. S. Napier, *Sammlung englischer Denkmäler* 4 (Berlin, 1883).

12. I used the visions mentioned above in the notes, those gathered by J. Klapper in *Exempla aus Handschriften des Mittelalters, Sammlung mittellat*, text 2 (Heidelberg, 1911), as well as in P. Dinzelbacher's anthology (1989).

13. Reported by Hariulf de Oudenburgh, ed. Migne, *Pat. lat* 174, col. 1287 ff.

14. *Visio Thurkilli*, ed. P. G. Schmidt (Leipzig, 1978).

15. *Godeschalcus und Visio Godeschalci*, ed. and trans. E. Assmann (Neumünster, 1979).

16. *Legenda aurea*, chapter 158. Readers may profit by reading the chapter that Leander Petzold devotes to "l'Ambassade venue de l'autre monde: Psychologie et Histoire d'un récit de Miracle," in his work *Märchen, Mythos, Sage. Beiträge zur Literatur und Volksdichtung* (Marbourg, 1989), 101–44. Another aspect of this question is taken up by Felix Karlinger in his excellent little book, hardly known in France, *Zauberschlaf und Entrückung, Zur Problematik der Jenseitszeit in der Volkserzählung* (Vienna, 1986).

17. *Vorauer Novelle und Reuner Relation*, photographic reproduction of the manuscripts by H. Gröchenig in *Litterae* 81 (Göppingen, 1981).

18. Guibert of Nogent, *De vita sua*, I, 24.

19. Ibid., II, 5.

20. G. Jónsson, *Byskupa Sögur*, II (Reykjavik, 1948), 243 ff.

21. Cited by Calmet, *Dissertation sur les Revenants en corps . . .* (Paris, 1751), new ed. (Paris, 1986), 237.

22. *Vision und Visionsliteratur im Mittelalter*, 48 f.

23. Ibid., 48 f.

24. King James Bible, Ecclesiastes 5:7.

25. J. Le Goff, "Le Christianisme et les Rêves" (IIe–VIIIe siècles), in *L'Imaginaire médiéval* (Paris, 1985), 265–316; here, 294.

Chapter 2: Pagan Ecstatics

1. *Fóstbroeðra saga*, chap. 23, ed. B. K. Thorolfsson and G. Jónsson, IF 6 (Reykjavik, 1943).

2. *Vigá-Glúms saga*, chapter 21.

3. *Havarðar saga isfirdings*, chapter 21.

4. *Fóstbroeðra saga*, chapter 20.

5. On the *gandr:* R. Boyer, *Le Monde du Double, la magie chez les anciens Scandinaves* (Paris, 1986), 124–26, *passsim;* P. Buchholz, *Schamanistische Züge in der altisländischen Überlieferung*, dissertation, Munster, 1968.

6. *Brennu-Njáls saga*, chapter 62.

7. Cited according to R. Boyer, *Le Monde du Double, la magie chez les anciens Scandinaves*, 41

8. *Hauks páttr hábrókar*, in *Flateyarbók*, vol. II, ed. S. Nordal (Akranes, 1944), 67 f.

9. The text is easily accessible in J. Renaud's beautiful translation, *La Saga des Féroïens* (Paris, 1983).

10. *Historia Norwegiae*, Latin text in P. Buchholz's *Schamanistische Züge in der altisländischen Überlieferung*, 24 f.

11. *Fóstbroeðra saga*, chapter 23.

12. Cited by K. Kiesewetter, *Die Geheimwissenschaften* (Leipzig, 1895), 588.

13. Ibid., 589.

14. *Der Vielförmige Hinzelmann* (Leipzig, 1704), reproduced in facsimilie in Göttingen in 1965. Thanks go to Christoph Gerhardt (Trèves) for having had the kindness to loan me his copy.

15. K. Kiesewetter, *Die Geheimwissenschaften*, 590–92.

16. Ibid., 589.

Chapter 3: An Unusual Concept of the Soul

1. For this whole development, see R. Boyer, *Le Monde du Double, la magie chez les anciens Scandinaves*, 33–54; H. Beck, "Die Seelenwörter des Germanischen," in R. Bergmann et. al., *Althochdeutsch*, vol. 2 (Heidelberg, 1987), 985–99; H. Eggers, "Altgermanische Seelenvorstellungen im Lichte des Heliand," in H. E., *Kleine Schriften* (Tübingen, 1982), 1–35. Each work contains bibliographic information that allows further research. I will not be discussing the *önd/and*, "soul, breath," which is used in the Christian texts as an equivalent of *anima*.

2. *Laðdoela saga*, chapter 48 f.

3. See Ida Blum, *Die Schutzgeister in der altnordischen Literatur,* dissertation, Strasbourg, 1912, 20 f. The original text does not employ the substantive *fylgja,* but the verb: ". . . *fylgði pér einn hvíta bjarnar húnn.*"

4. J. Th. Storacker, *Mennesket og arbeidet in den norske Folketro* (Ved Nils Lid, 1938), 74–76.

5. *Landnámabók, Sturlubók* 350, ed. J. Benediktsson, 2 vols, IF I 1–2 (Reykjavik, 1968).

6. V. Diószegi, "Die Überreste des Schamanismus in der Ungarischen Volkskultur," in *Acta Ethnographica Acad. Scientiarum Hungaricae* 7 (1958), 275–98; similarly, "Le Combat sous forme d'animal des Chamans," in *Acta Orientalia Acad. Scientiarum Hungaricae* 2 (1952), 315 f.

7. R. Boyer, *le Monde du Double, la magie chez les anciens Scandinaves,* 32.

8. *Dialogi,* ed. and trans. A. de Vogué and P. Antin, vol. III (Paris, 1980). (Sources chrétiennes 265).

9. See H. J. Klare, "Die Toten in der altnordischen Literatur," in *Acta Philologica Scandinavica* 8 (1933), 1–56; here, 9.

10. *Snorra Edda, Gylfaginning,* ed. A. Björnsson (Reykjavik, 1975), chapter 44. On page 33 in *Loki* (Paris, 1986), G. Dumézil follows another manuscript and places the passage in chapter 36. (On the ritual itself, see M. Bertolotti, "Le Ossa e la Pelle dei Buoi: Un Mito popolare tra Agiografica e Stregonaria," in *Quaderni Storici* 41 [1979], 470–99.)

11. Edited by Traube in Migne, *Pat. lat.* 3, col. 428–517.

12. Text in E. Faral, *La Légende arthurienne,* vol. 3. (Paris, 1969), 4–62; here, 25.

13. See C. Ginzburg, *Hexensabbat* (Berlin, 1989), 95 f.

14. See, for example, P. Gignoux, "Corps osseux et Âme osseuse: Essai sur le chamanisme dans l'Iran ancien," in *Journal asiatique* 267 (1979), 41–79.

15. Besides the previously cited studies by V. Diószegi and by C. Ginzburg, see M. Boskovic-Stulli, "Kresnik-Krsnik: Ein Wesen aus der kroatischen und slovenischen Volksüberlieferung," in *Fabula* 3 (1959–1960), 275–98; G. Ravis-Giordani, "Signes, Figures et Conduite de l'Entre-Vie-et-Mort: Mazzeri et Streie corses," in *Études corses* 12–13 (1979), 361 ff. For the Celtic world, see B. Benes, "Spuren von Schamanismus in der Sage Buile Suibhne," in *Zeitshcrift f. celtische Philologie* 28 (1961), 309–34.

16. See C. Lecouteux and Ph. Marcq, *les Esprits et les Morts* (Paris, 1980), 118 f.

17. Ibid., 117 f.

18. Raoul Glaber, *Les Cinq Livres de ses histoires,* ed. and trans. M. Prou (Paris, 1886).

19. Guibert de Nogent, *De Vita sua* I, 15.

20. Ed. G. Jónsson, *Islendinga Sögur,* vol. 7 (Reykjavik, 1947), 471–77.

21. On bees: H. Bächtold-Stäubli, *Handwörterbuch des deutchen Aberglaubens,* 10 vols. (Berlin/New York, 1987), vol. I, col. 1226–52.

22. For French translations, see P. Sébillot, *Le Folklore de France,* 4 vols. (Paris, 1968), vol. 2, 11; vol. 3, 315 and 332–34.

23. *Le Registre d'Inquisition de Jacques Fournier, évêque de Pamiers,* ed. J. Duvernoy, 3 vols. (Toulouse, 1965). See what E. Le Roy Ladurie took from this work in his *Montaillou, village occitan de 1294–1324* (Paris, 1975).

24. *Mantaillou, village occitan de 1294–1324,* 608.

25. *Le Registre d'Inquisition de Jacques Fournier, évêque de Pamiers,* 243.

26. *Mantaillou, village occitan de 1294–1324,* 589.

27. Ibid., 604 f.

28. Ibid., 608 f.

29. Ibid., 603.

Chapter 4: The Double and Fairies

1. Ed. J. Rychner, accompanied by the text of the *Ianuals lióð,* TLF 77 (Paris/Geneva, 1958).

2. For more ample information: C. Lecouteux, "Les Fées au Moyen Âge, quelques remarques," in *Mythologie française* 146 (1987), 26–31; and *Romanisch-germanische Kulturberührungen . . . ,* article cited.

3. On Melusinian legends, see C. Lecouteux, *Mélusine et le Chevalier au Cygne* (Paris, 1982).

4. *Der Ritter von Staufenberg,* ed. E. Grunewald, ATB 88 (Tübingen, 1979), 329 ff.

5. Lecouteux, *Mélusine et le Chevalier au Cygne,* 79–85.

6. L. Harf-Lancner, *Les Fées au Moyen Âge,* Nouvelle Bibliothèque du Moyen Âge 8 (Paris, 1984), 255. Other examples of the identity between fairies and animals can be found on 222 and the pages following it.

7. J. Renaud, *Archipels norrois: Orcades, Shetland et Hébrides dans le monde viking* GAG 477 (Göppingen, 1988), 253–94.

8. M. Eliade, *Le Chamanisme et les techniques archaïque de l'extase,* 73 f.

9. The texts touched upon here are summarized by C. Lecouteux, *Mélusine et le Chevalier au Cygne.*

10. Cited by A. J. Greimas, *Des Dieux et des Hommes: Études de Mythologie lituanienne* (Paris, 1985), 166.

11. Lecouteux, *Mélusine et le Chevalier au Cygne*, 143 ff.

12. Text and German translation by K. Muller-Lisowski, in *Zeitschrift f. celtische Philologie* 14.

13. Lecouteux, *Mélusine et le Chevalier au Cygne*, 173 ff.

Chapter 5: The Double and Witchcraft

1. See C. Ginzburg, *Hexensabbat: Entzifferung einer nächtlichen Geschichte* (Berlin, 1989).

2. Réginon de Prüm, *Libri duo de synodalibus causis et disciplinis ecclesiasticis* II, 364, ed. Migne, *Pat. lat.* 132, col. 352.

3. Burchard, *Decretum* X, vol. 1, ed. H. J. Schmitz, *Die Bussbücher* (Düsseldorf, 1898), new ed. (Graz, 1958).

4. Bernard Gui, *Manuel de l'Inquisiteur*, ed. and trans. G. Mollat, Classique de l'Histoire de France 8, vol. 2 (Paris, 1964), 22 (= *Practica* VI, 2).

5. See Claude Lecouteux, "Romanisch-germanische Kulturberührungen am Beispeil des Mahls der Feen," in *Mediävistik* 1 (1988), 87–99.

6. *Legenda aurea*, ed. Th. Graesse (Breslau, 1890), 449.

7. See C. Lecouteux, "Le Double, le Cauchemar, la Sorcière," quoted article.

8. Étienne de Bourbon, *Septem doni spiritus sancti*, no. 364, ed. partially by E. Lecoy de la Marche (Paris, 1940), 319–21.

9. See C. Lecouteux, "Fantômes et Revenants germaniques: Essai de presentation," 94-96.

10. Gautier Map, *De nugis curialium* II, 14, ed. Th. Wright (Oxford, 1850), or M. R. James, *Anecdota Oxoniensa* 14 (Oxford, 1914); trans. from the text: C. Lecouteux and P. Marcq, *Les Esprits et les Morts*, 37 f.

11. For all that follows, I take my information from the anthology by J. Hansen, *Zauberwahn, Inquisition und Hexenprozess im Mittelalter* (Munich/Leipzig, 1900); as well as *Quellen und Untersuchungen zur Geschichte des Hexenwahns und der Hexenverfolgung im Mittelalter* (Bonn, 1901); C. J. Baroja, *Les Sorcières et leur Monde* (Paris, 1972).

12. See A. Stöber, *Zur Geschichte des Volksaberglaubens im Anfange des 16. Jahrhunderts: Aus Dr. Johann Geilers von Kaisersberg "Emeis,"* (Bâle, 1856).

13. *Malleus maleficarum* II, 1, 3 (Lyon, 1669).

14. Texts in J. Hansen, *Quellen und Untersuchungen zur Geschichte des Hexenwahns und der Hexenverfolgung im Mittelalter*.

15. See C. Lecouteux, "Romanisch-germanische Kulturberührungen am Beispeil des Mahls der Feen."

16. Quoted by K. Kiesewetter, *Die Geheimwissenschaften* (Leipzig, 1895), 587 f.

17. Ibid., 572–76, with parallel texts by Jean Nidier (*Formicarius* II, 4), Nicolas Rémy (*Daemonolatria* I, 11), Jean Bodin (*Daemonomania*, chapter 12), Johann Georg Goedelmann (*Tractatus de magis etc.*, II, 4).

18. *Friðþjófs saga ins fraekna*, ed. L. Larsson, Sagabibl. 9 (Halle, 1901).

19. *Þorsteins saga vikingssonar*, ed. C. C. Rafn, in *Fornaldar Sögur Nordurlanda*, vol. 2 (Copenhagen, 1829–1830), 383–459.

20. *Kormak's Saga*, chapter 18, ed. E. O. Sveinsson, IF 8 (Reykjavik, 1939).

21. C. Ginzburg, *Les Batailles noctures: Sorcellerie at Rituels agraires en Frioul, XVIe–XVIIe siècle* (Lagrasse, 1980).

22. *Historia Langobardorum*, ed. G. Waiz in *Monumenta Germaniae Historica*, SS Rer. Germ. (Hanover, 1978).

23. H. Lixfeld, "Die Guntramsage . . . ," 87. A Lapland version may be found in A. Labba, *Anta: Les Mémoires d'un Lapon* (Paris, 1989), 551.

24. See, for example, J. Qvigstad, *Lappiske Eventyr og Sagn*, vol. 2, *Fra Troms og Finmark* (Oslo, 1928).

25. *Historia Langobardorum*, VI, 6.

26. C. Lecouteux, "Fantômes et Revenants germaniques: Essai de présentation," *Ét. Germ* 40 (1985), 141–60, here, 154.

27. See. R. Boyer, *Le Monde du Double*, 209, s.v. *fylgja*.

28. (Paris, 1988), 160 ff.

29. See V. Meyer-Matheis, *Die Vorstellung eines Alter Ego in Volkerzählungen*, dissertation, Fribourg/Br., 1974, 71.

30. See C. Lecouteux, "Vom Shrat zum Schrättel. Dämonisierungs-Mythologisierungs-Und Euphemisierungsprozess einer volkstümlichen Vorstellung," in *Euphorion* 78 (1985), 95–108.

31. T. Dömötör, *Volksglaube und Aberglaube der Ungarn* (Budapest, 1982), 93 ff.

32. F. Karlinger and E. Turczynski, *Rumänische Sagen und sagen aus Rumänien*, Europ. Sagen 11 (Berlin, 1982), 51 f.

33. A. Greimas, *Des Dieux et des Hommes: Études de Mythologie lituanienne*, 55.

34. V. Meyer-Matheis, *Die Vorstellung eines Alter Ego in Volkerzählungen*, 67 f.

35. Ibid., 70.

36. C. Lecouteux, *Les Nains et les Elfes au Moyen Âge*, 162.

37. Ed. Madeleine Jeay (Montreal/Paris, 1985), 143.

Chapter 6: Metamorphosis: The Double and Werewolves

1. R. Boyer, *Le Monde du Double,* 49. On werewolves, we may read: M. Jacoby, "Wargus, Vargr 'Verbrecher, Wolf,'" *Acta Univ. Upsaliensis* 12 (Uppsala, 1974) with bibliography; C. Lecouteux, "Voirloup et Loup-Garou, quelques Remarques," *Mythologie française* 143 (1986), 64–68; as well as "Les Voirloups de la forêt d'Othe," *Bulletin du Comité du Folklore champenois* 148 (1987), 18 f; and the works cited in the notes that follow.

2. Trans. by P. Grimal in *Romans, grecs, et latins,* Bibl. de la Pléiade 134 (Paris, 1963), 145–377.

3. *De Civitate Dei,* ed. B. Dombart and A. Kalb, trans. G. Combès (Bruges, 1960) (Bibliothèque Augustinienne). I number the sentences and keep the term *phantasticum.*

4. *De Civitate Dei* XVIII, 18, 2.

5. Ibid.; see also Laurence Harf-Lancner, "La Métamorphose illusoire: des théories chrétiennes de la métamorphose aux image médiévales du loup-garou," *Annales E.S.C.* 40 (1985), 208–26. See the critique of this article in C. Ginzberg, *Hexensabbat: Entzifferung einer nächtlichen Geschichte,* 177, note 7.

6. *De Civitate Dei,* XVIII, 18, 2.

7. See J. Le Goff, *La Naissance du Purgatoire,* 111 ff.

8. Cited by P. Ménard, "Les Histoires de Loup-Garou au Moyen Âge" in *Symposium in Honorem Prof. de Riquer* (Barcelona, 1986), 209–38, here, 216 f.

9. Burchard of Worms, *Decretum* XIX, 5, 151.

10. See M. Summers, *The Werewolf* (London, 1933), 206 f. The text is entitled *De hominibus qui se vertunt in lupos.* See also P. Ménard, "Les Histoires de Loup-Garou au Moyen Âge," 224 f.

11. Ibid., 205 f.

12. *Egils saga Skallagrímssonar,* ed. S. Nordal, IF 2 (Reykjavik, 1933); French trans. by R. Boyer in *Sagas islandaises,* Bibliothèque de la Pléiade 338 (Paris, 1987), 3–203.

13. *Harðar saga Grimkelssonar,* ed. S. Haft, Lund, 1960.

14. Cited by P. Ménard, "Les Histoires de Loup-Garou au Moyen Âge," 225.

15. *Melion,* ed. Prudence M. O'Hara Tobin in *Les Lais anonymes des XIIe et XIIIe siècles,* Geneva, 1976, 296–318.

16. Ed. J. Rychner in *Les Lais de Marie de France* (Paris, 1971), Classique Français du Moyen Age 93.

17. Trans. by P. Grimal in *Romans grecs et latins,* Bibl. de la Pléiade, 134 (Paris 1958).

18. J.-P. Vernant, *Mythe et pensée chez les grecs. Études de psychologie historique,* 253.

19. See Harf-Lancner, "La Métamorphose illusoire: des théories chrétiennes de la métamorphose aux images médiévales du loup-garou," a study from which I borrow the passage by Guillaume d'Auxerre. Harf's article leads nowhere and is only a basic review; belief in the Double is not addressed in it.

20. *Strengleikar eða Lioðabók,* ed. R. Keyser and C. R. Unger (Christiana, 1850).

21. *Þorstein páttr uxafóts,* ed. in Flateyarbók, vol. 1, 1944 ff, 274–90.

22. A. J. Greimas, *Des Dieux et des Hommes: Études de Mythologie lituanienne,* 121.

23. *Völsunga saga ok Ragnars saga Lodbrokar,* ed. M. Olsen (Copenhagen, 1906–1908); French trans. by R. Boyer in *La Saga de Sigurðr ou la Parole donnée,* Patrimoines/Scandinavie (Paris, 1989).

24. Text ed. by J. F. Dimock in *Giraldi Cambrensis Opera,* vol. V (London, 1867). See also P. Ménard, "Les Histoires de Loup-Garou au Moyen Âge," 215 f.

25. Ed. G. Perrie Williams, CFMA 38 (Paris, 1967).

26. *Merlin,* ed. A. Micha, TLF 281 (Paris/Geneva, 1980). On Merlin's transformation: 125, 135–38, 218 f.

27. See R. Boyer in *La Saga de Sigurðr ou la Parole donnée* (Paris, 1989), 246 f.

28. *The Mabinogion,* trans. G. and T. Jones, Everyman's Library 97 (London, 1966), 61 f, 71–73, 52. See also *Culhwch et Olwein,* 31.

Chapter 7: Autoscopy

1. See W. Krauss, *Das Doppelgängermotiv in der Romantik,* dissertation, Berlin, 1930, new edition (Nendein, 1967).

2. See Gerda Grober-Glück, "Zweites Gesicht und Wahsagekunst," in M. Zender, *Atlas der deutschen Volkskunde,* Neue Folge: Erläuterungen, vol. II (Marbourg, 1966), 1–95, especially 32–67 (birth dates of men gifted with second sight).

3. Trans. with rich commentary by R. Boyer, *Contributions du Centre d'études arctiques* 10 (Paris, 1973), 84 (= *Landnámabók, Sturlubók* 329).

4. Ibid., 65 (= *Sturlubók* 225).

5. Ed. R. Howlett, in *Chronicles of the Reigns of Stephen, Henry II and Richard I,* vol. 1 (London, 1884), 474 f. Complete translation of text: C. Lecouteux and P. Marcq, *Les Esprits et les Morts,* 195 f.

6. *Hrólfs saga kraka og Bjarkarímur,* ed. F. Jónsson (Copenhagen, 1904), chapter 33.

7. *Gunnlauga saga Ormstungu,* chapter 2.

8. *Vatnsdoela saga,* ed. E. O. Sveinsson, IF 8 (Reykjavik, 1939), chapter 42.

9. *Brennu-Njáls saga,* ed. E. O. Sveinsson, IF 12 (Reykjavik, 1954).

10. *Laxdoela saga,* ed. E. O. Sveinsson, IF 8 (Reykjavik), 1939.

11. *Helgakviða* Hiörvarðssonar, prose after strophe 34, ed. G. Neckel, in *Edda, Die Lieder des Codex Regius nebst verwandten Denkmälern* (Heidelberg, 1914).

12. *Svarfdoela saga,* ed. G. Jónsson, in *Islendinga Sögur,* vol. 8 (Reykjavik, 1945), 119–215.

13. *Vorlesungen über Metaphysik* (Erfurt, 1821), 230. See also 238 and 255–58.

14. References and other examples in H. J. Klare, "Die Toten in der altnordischen Literatur," 156.

15. *Dritte Fortsetzung von Erscheinungen der Geister* (Prenzlau/Leipzig, 1752), 472.

16. A. Jaffé, *Geistererscheinungen und Vorzeichen. Eine psychologische Deutung* (Zurich/Stuttgart, 1958).

17. Vera Myer-Matheis, *Die Vorstellung eines Alter Ego in Volkserzählunguen,* appendix, page 1.

18. Ibid., appendix, page 18.

19. Ibid., appendix, page 5.

Chapter 8: Shadow, Reflection, and Image

1. I am using the inquiries by F. Pradel, "Der Schatten im Volksglauben," *Mittheilungen der schlesischen Gesellschaft f. Volkskunde* 12 (1904), 1–36; J. von Negelein, "Bild, Spiegel und Schatten im Volksglauben," *Archiv f. Religionswissenschaft* 5, no. 1 (1902), 1–37; E. L. Rochholz, "Ohne Schatten, ohne Seele: Der Mythus vom Körperschatten und vom Schattengeist," *Germania* 5 (1860), 69–94.

2. *The Iliad* XXIII, 104; see also *The Odyssey* X, 495 and XI, 207.

3. See the substantial study by M. Halbwachs, "La Représentation de l'âme chez les Grecs, Le Double corporel et le Double spirituel," *Revue de métaphysique et de morale* 37 (1930), 493–534.

4. O. Rank, "Der Doppelgänger," 135.

5. Negelein, "Bild, Spiegel und Schatten im Volksglauben," 19.

6. Pradel, "Der Schatten im Volksglauben," 15.

7. Pradel, "Der Schatten im Volksglauben," 10; Rochholz, "Ohne Schatten, ohne Seele: Der Mythus vom Körperschatten und vom Schattengeist," 88.

8. Negelein, "Bild, Spiegel und Schatten im Volksglauben," 17, 22.

9. J. Grimm, *Deutsche Rechtsaltertümer* (Leipzig, 1899), 678.

10. See the studies cited in part 3, chapter 3, note 1 and K. Haberland, "Der Spiegel im Glauben und Brauch der Völker," *Zeitschrift f. Völkerpsychologie und Sprachwissenschaft* 13 (1882), 324–47.

11. E. T. A. Hoffmann, *The Tales of Hoffmann* (New York: Penguin USA, 1990).

12. Detailed summary, analysis, and parallels in O. Rank, "Der Doppelgänger."

13. R. Boyer, *Le Monde du Double, la magie chez les anciens Scandinaves.*

14. A. Abt, "Die Apologie des Apuleius von Madaura und die antike Zauberei, Giessen," *Religionsgeschichtliche Versuche und Vorarbeiten* 4, no.2 (1908).

15. *Le Marteau des sorcières*, trans. A. Danet (Paris, 1973).

16. J.-P. Vernant, *Mythe et pensée chez les grecs. Études de psychologie historique* (Paris, 1969), 252–53.

Appendix 1: The Soul and the Double

1. See Å. Hultkrantz, *Conceptions of the Soul Among North American Indians* (Stockholm, 1953); E. Rohde, *Psyché* (Paris, 1928); I. Paulson, *Die primitiven Seelenvorstellungen der nordeurasischen Völker* (Stockholm, 1958); E. Arbman, *Ecstasy or Religious Trance*, 3 vols. (Uppsala, 1963–1970).

2. J.-P. Vernant, *Mythe et pensée chez les grecs. Études de psychologie historique*, 73.

3. M. Eliade, *Le Chamanisme*, (Paris, 1968), 305 f.

4. Evelyne Lot-Falck, "Le Chamanisme en Sibéria," in *Asie du Sud-Est et Monde insulindien*, Bulletin du Centre de Documentation et de Recherche 41 (1973), 1 ff.

5. G. Laszló, *Steppenvölker und Germanen* (Herrsching/Ammersee, 1970); see especially the map on 44.

6. E. D. Phillips, "The Legend of Aristeas," *Artibus Asiae* 18 (1955), 161–77; E. Rohde, *Psyché*, 338.

7. M. Eliade, *Le Chamanisme*, 306.

8. E. Rohde, *Psyché*, 342.

9. Plato, *Republic* X, 614b, ff. See K. Ziegler and W. Sontheimer, *Der Kleine Pauly: Lexikon der Antike*, vol. 2 (Munich, 1979), col. 341 f.

10. M. Halbwachs, "La Représentation de l'Âme chez les Grecs: le Double corporel et le Double spirituel," in *Revue de Métaphysique et de Morale* 37 (1930), 493–534; here, 507 ff.

11. Ed. K. Stackmann, Teubneriana Library (Leipzig, 1983). The passages cited here are *De die natali* 3, 1–5.

12. P. Grimal, *Dictionnaire de la Mythologie grecque et romaine* (Paris, 1969), 44.

13. *De die natali* 3, 2: *eundem esse Genium et Larem multi veteres memoriae prodiderunt.*

14. I use the medieval text with the interlinear translation by Nokter: Nokter der Deutsche, *Martianus Capella, De nuptiis Philologiae et Mercurii*, ed. J. C. King, ATB 87 (Tübingen, 1979), 136 f (= *De nuptiis* II, 32).

15. See K. Ruh et. al., *Die deutsche Literatur des Mittelalters, verfasserlexikon*, vol. VI (Berlin/New York, 1987), col. 1212–36.

16. Notker. *Martianus Capella, De nuptiis Philologiae et Mercurii*, 137.

17. See I. Paulson, *Die primitiven Seelenvorstellungen der nordeurasischen Völker*.

18. C. Lecouteux, *Fantômes et Revenants au Moyen Âge*, 185.

19. See A. Vilkuna, "Über den finnischen Haltija."

20. See C. Lecouteux, "Ephialtes, Mara, Incubus: le Cauchemar chez les Peuples germaniques," *Ét. Des Dieux germ* 42 (1987), 1–24; as well as "le Double, le Cauchemar, la Sorcière," *Ét. germ* 43 (1988), 395–405.

21. See Erika Lindig, "Hausgeister," in *Artes populares* 14 (Frankfort/Berne/New York/Paris, 1987), 78, 80, pass.; Katharina M. Briggs, *The Anatomy of Puck* (London, 1958).

22. A. J. Greimas, *Des Dieux et des Hommes: Études de Mythologie lituanienne*, 87.

23. R. Boyer, *le Monde du Double, la magie chez les anciens Scandinaves*. 48–50; and *la Saga des gens du Val-au-Lac* (Paris, 1980), 25–28.

24. A. J. Greimas, *Des Dieux et des Hommes: Études de Mythologie lituanienne*, 119 f.

25. Ibid., 120.

Bibliography

The bibliography was updated for the 1996 edition. The reader may also refer to the notes to the Preface to the 1996 Edition.

Source Texts

Most of the Norse texts are easily accessible in R. Boyer's translations, *Saga islandaises*. Bibliothèque de la Pléiade 338. Paris, 1987. The lays in old French were collected and published by Prudence Mary O'Hara Tobin, *Lais anonymes des XIIIe et XIII siècles*. Public. Romane et Française 143. Genève, 1976.

Apuleus. In *Romans, grecs, et latins*. Trans. P. Grimal. Bibliothèque de la Pléiade 134. Paris, 1963.

Augustine, Saint. *La Cité de Dieu,* 4th edition. Ed. by B. Dombart, A. Kalb, and G. Combès. Bibliothèque Augustinienne. Bruges, 1960.

d'Arras, Jean. *Mélusine*. Ed. L. Stouff. Dijon, 1932. French trans. by Michèle Perret. *Mélusine*. Paris, 1979.

de Barri, Giraud. *Topographia hibernica*. Ed. J. F. Dimock. In *Giraldi Cambrensis Opera*, t. V. Londres, 1868.

de Bourbon, Etienne: A. Lecoy de la Marche, *Anecdotes historiques . . .* tirés fu recueil inédit d'Et. de B. Paris, 1877.

de Voragine, Jacques. *Legenda aurea*. Ed. Th. Graesse. Breslau, 1890.

de Worms, Burchard. *Decretorum libri XX.* Ed. Migne, *Pat. lat.* 140, COI. 538–1066.

Institoris, H., and J. Sprenger. *Malleus maleficarum*. 2 vols. Lyons, 1669. French trans. A. Danet, *Le Marteau des Sorcières*. Paris, 1973.

Map, Gautier. *De Nugis curialium*. Ed. G. Leibniz. In *Scriptores Rerum Brunsvicensium* 1, Hanover, 1707.

Mouskès, Philippe. *Chronique rimée.* 3 vols. Ed. De Reiffenberf. Bruxelles, 1836–1845.

Petronias. In *Romans, grecs, et latins.* Trans. P. Grimal. Bibliothèque de la Pleíade 134. Paris, 1963.

Philostratus. In *Romans, grecs, et latins.* Trans. P. Grimal. Bibliothèque de la Pleíade 134. Paris, 1963.

General

Aarne, A. and S. Thompson. *The Types of the Folktale.* FFC 184. Helsinki, 1961.

Aliver, B. "Conceptions of the Living Human Soul in the Norwegian Tradition." *Tenemos* 7 (1971), 7–33.

Bächtold-Stäubli, H. *Handwörterbuch des deutschen Aberglaubens.* 10 vols. Berlin, 1927–1942. New edition, Berlin/New York, 1987.

Baroja, C. J. *Les Sorcières et leur Monde.* Paris, 1972.

Bertolotti, M. "Le Ossa e la Pelle dei Buoi. Un mito popolare tra Agiografica e Stregoneria." *Quaderni Storici* 41 (1979), 470–79.

Boyer, R. *Le Monde du Double. La Magie chez les anciens Scandinaves.* Paris, 1986.

Buchholz, P. *SchamanistischeZüge in der altnordischen Überlie ferung.* Dissertation. Münster, 1968.

Calmet (Dom). *Les Aooaritions des Esprits et sur les Vampires.* Dissertation. Einsiedeln, 1749.

Chesnutt, M. "Nordic Variants of the Guntrum Legend." *Arv* 47 (1991), 153–65.

Closs, A. "Der Schamanismus bei den Indoeuropäern." *Innsbrucker Beiträge zur Kulturwissenschaft* 14 (1968), 289 ff.

Cross, T. P. *Motiv Index of Early Irish Literature.* Indiana Folklore Series 7. Bloomington, Indiana, 1952.

Dinzelbacher, P, *Vision und Visionsliteratur im Mittelalter.* Stuttgart, 1981.

———. "Mittelalterliche Vision und moderne Sterbeforschung." In *Psychologie in der Mediävistik.* GAG 431, 9–49. Göppingen, 1985.

Diószegi, V. "Le Combat sous Forme d'Animal des Chamans." *Acta Orientalia Acad. Scient. Hungaricae* 2 (1952), 315 f.

———. "Die Überreste des Schamanismus in der ungarischen Volkskultur." *Acta Ethnographica Acad. Scient. Hungaricae* 7 (1958), 97–134.

Dömötör, T. *Volksglaube und Aberglaube der Ungarn.* Budapest, 1982.

Eliade, M. *Le Chamanisme et les techniques archaïques de l'extase.* Paris, 1974.

Gaidoz, H. "L'Ame hors du corps et le Double." *Mélusine* 2 (1912), 263–66 and 385–91.

Gignoux, P. "Corps osseux et Ame osseuse. Essai sur le chamanisme dans l'Iran ancien." *Journal Asiatique* 267 (1979), 41–79.

Ginzburg, C. *Les Batailles nocturnes. Sorcellerie et Rituels agraires en Frioul.* Legrasse, 1980.

———. *Hexensabbat. Entzifferung einer nächtlichen Geschichte.* Berlin, 1989.

Grambo, R. "Traces of Shamanism in Norwegian Folktales and Popular Legends: Religious Beliefs Transmuted into Narrative Motifs." In *Fabula* 16 (1975), 40 ff.

———. "Fortrollet vilt. Varulv og mannbjøn." *Norsk Skogbruksmuseum Årbok* 1 (1958), 75–81.

Greimas, A. J. *Des Dieux et des Hommes. Etudes de Mytholgie lituanienne.* Paris, 1985.

Grimm, J. *Deutsche Mythologie.* 3 vols. Darmstadt, 1965.

Haberland, K. "Der Spiegel im Glauben und Brauch der Völker." *Zeitschrift f. Völkerpsychologie u. Sprachwissenschaft* 13 (1882), 324–47.

Halbwachs, M. "La Représentation de l'âme chez les Grecs. Le Double corporel et le Double spirituel." *Revue de Métaphysique et de morale* 37 (1930), 493–534.

Hansen, J. *Zauberwahn. Inquisition und Hexenprosess im Mittelalter.* Munich/Leipzig, 1900.

———. *Quellen und Untersuchungen zur Geschichte des Hexenwahns und der Hexenverfolgung im Mittelalter.* Bonn, 1901.

Höfler, O. *Kultische Geheimbünde der Germanen.* Frankfurt, 1934.

Jaffé, A. *Geistererscheinungen und Vorzeichen. Eine psychologische Deutung.* Stuttgart/Zurich, 1958.

Kiesewetter, K. *Die Geheimwissenschaften.* Leipzig, 1895.

Klaniczay, G. "Schamanistische Elemente im mitteleuropäischen Hexenwesen." In G. Klaniczay, *Heilige, Hexen, Vampire. Vom Nutzen des Übernatürlichen.* Berlin, 1991.

Lecouteux, C. *Fantômes et Revenants au Moyen Age.* Paris, 1986. New edition with a new preface, 1996.

———. *Les Nains et les Elfes au Moyen Age.* Paris, 1988.

———. "Mara, Ephialtes, Incubus: Le Cauchemar chez les Peuples germaniques." *Études Germaniques* 42 (1987), 1–24.

————. "Le Double, le Cauchemar, la Sorcière." *Études Germaniques* 43 (1988), 395–405.

Lecouteux, C. and P. Marcq. *Les Esprits et les Morts.* Paris, 1981.

————. *Pour un autre Moyen Age.* Paris, 1977.

Lexikon des Mittelalters. Zurich/Munich, 1977.

Lixfeld, H. "Die Guntramsage. AT 1645 A. Volkserzänlungen vom Alter Ego in Tiergestalt und ihre schamanistische Herkunft." *Fabula* 13 (1972), 66–107.

Meyer-Matheis, V. *Die Vorstellung eines Alter Ego in Volkserzänlungen.* Dissertation. Fribourg/Br., 1974.

Odstet, Ella *Varulven I svensk folktradition.* Skrifter utgiva genom Landsmåls och Folkeminnesarkivet, Ser. B: 1. Uppsala, 1943.

Paulson, I. *Die primitiven Seelenvorstellungen der nordeuraisischen Völker.* Stockholm, 1958.

Peuckert, W. E. "Der Zweite Leib." *Niederdeutsche Zeitschrift f. Volkskunde* 17 (1939), 174–97.

Pradel, F. "Der Schatten im Volksglauben." *Mittheilungen d. schlesischen Gesellschaft f. Volkskunde* 12 (1904), 1–36.

Rank, O. "Der Doppelgänger." *Imago 3,* no. 2 (1914), 97–164.

Ranke, K., ed. *Enzyklopädie des Märchens.* Berlin/New York, 1977. See also the art of W. Pape, col. 766–73.

Rohde, E, *Psyché.* Paris, 1928.

Senn, H. A. *Werewolf and Vampire in Romania.* Eastern European Monographs 99. New York, 1982.

Strömbäck, D. "The Concept of Soul in the Nordic Tradition." *Arv* 31 (1975), 5–22.

Stigsdotter, Margareta. "Maran och fölhamnan." In J. Stattin, *Folktro I Skåne.* Kristianstad, 1991.

Vernant, J. -P. *Mythe et Pensée chez les Grecs. Études de Psychologie historique.* Paris, 1969.

von Negelein, J. "Bild, Spiegel und Schatten im Volksglauben." *Archiv f. Religionswissenschaft* 5, no. 1 (1902), 1–37.

Weiser-Aall, Lily. "En studie om vardøger." *Norveg* 12 (1965), 73–112.

Ziegler, K., W. Sontheimer, H. Gärtner, eds. *Der Kleine Pauly. Lexikon der Antike.* 5 vols. Munich, 1979.

Index